The Tears of
Mount Sinjar

The Tears of
Mount Sinjar

Resisting brutal ISIS attacks on the Yazidi people ...

Homeira Soufi

Published in Australia by Silverbird Publishing.

Cover, design and typesetting by Luke Harris
Edited by Dr Euan Mitchell

ISBN:
978-0-6453834-9-2 (paperback)

A catalogue record for this
book is available from the
National Library of Australia

NATIONAL
LIBRARY
OF AUSTRALIA

ABOUT THE AUTHOR

I am Homeira Soufi, a Kurdish woman born and raised in a small mountainous village in Iran. As a little girl, I was known by others as the girl who wrote poems and was a good storyteller. On cold winter's nights, even my Granny would want me to tell them stories so she could enjoy the unexpected challenges and sometimes bizarre endings.

After I got my bachelor's degree in Persian literature from the literature Faculty of Urmia University, I married and migrated to Australia in 2014.

As a full-time mother, I made myself busy learning English at home. One day as I was talking to one of my friends, she asked, "How are you doing with all these Covid lockdowns? It's so stressful."

"Well, I'm doing fine," I said.

"I can see, but how?"

"I live in my world, all the adventures and stories," I smiled.

"You mean those stories that you used to tell us?"

"Yes."

"Can you tell me one? I have missed those. If you have time?"

And I told three of them, and then she asked me, "Why don't you try to write one?"

"But I don't like writing. It's hard and boring," I said.

She insisted, and I started to write one of my favourite ones called *The Tears of Mount Sinjar*; unaware that writing was going to be the most satisfying job I could have ever imagined doing; instead of people listening to me telling the stories, the joyful feeling of holding the reader's hands and walking them into the world that I see and live in, is inexpressible.

ACKNOWLEDGMENTS

I want to express my deepest thanks to my dear husband, who has been very supportive and thoughtful in this journey, and my beautiful kids, who have been very tolerant and patient with Mummy being busy writing most of the day every day.

To extend my deepest gratitude to my two dearest friends, Rhonda Taylor and Monireh Taheri, who kindly put their valuable time and interest into this story.

Also, to thank my three lovely sisters, Atifeh Soufi, Aliyah Soufi and Tuba Shekak, for their support. I am so glad to have them in my life.

Of course, this wonderful experience wouldn't have come to this precious ending that now we have in our hands without the help of experts in this regard; I am incredibly grateful to work with Dr Euan Mitchell and Luke Harris, as I can say with complete confidence that they are one of the best in their career.

Gate of Yezidi Temple
Image from A journey from London to Persepolis, 1865

INTRODUCTION

The Tears of Mount Sinjar is fiction inspired by real events. It is the story of Agrin, a young Kurdish Yezidi woman from the Sinjar region of northern Iraq, whose family and thousands of others were massacred in 2014 by ISIS (the Islamic State of Iraq and Syria). Yezidis are a minority ethnic people, numbering about one million, who believe in the Yezidi (or Yazidi) religion, one of the world's oldest belief systems. They believe in one God called Xwedê or Êzdan and their language is Kurdish-Kurmanji. Yezidis have endured centuries of persecution for their distinctive religious beliefs, initially by Arabs, later by Turks.

From August 2014, hundreds of Yezidi families were forced by ISIS to choose between death or conversion to Sunni Islam. Many fled to the Sinjar Mountains, but about 5,000 men and boys were mercilessly slaughtered and at least 10,000 women and children were enslaved and trafficked.

The Tears of Mount Sinjar is a novel built from first-hand accounts that transport the reader to the heart-breaking realities of the invasion that destroyed Agrin's family, among many. Her story brings to life the ways she and fellow Yezidis took revenge on ISIS before she sought asylum and freedom in Australia.

A small and picturesque village in between the hills, crossed by a winding dirt road, was the home of a kind and loving people who lived together in peace. There was a compact house with red flowers on its balcony near the edge of the village. One summer morning as the sun was rising, Agrin went to a window in the little house, pushed aside the curtains and opened the window to feel a cool breeze. It spread and wrapped the fragrance of flowers everywhere, joining the amusing sound of birds playing the music of life in her ears.

Agrin opened the door to the yard and went out with a jug full of water for her beautiful flowers. She looked at the flowers and touched the soft petals as she watered them. "Oh, the yard needs to be cleaned today," she said to herself, as she went down the steps. Agrin picked up the broom and began to sweep and spray the yard.

After she finished, Agrin stood up straight and looked around the yard. "That's what I call good tidying up; it smells so fresh now." She returned to the house and came out with a basket of laundry. She hung clothes on the clothesline until she heard the sound of crying coming from inside.

She hurried up the steps, entered the house and started talking to her daughter. "Good morning, Evin, my sweet girl. Don't cry now – Mummy is here. Did you sleep well, ha? Did you have some good dreams? I bet you did – you were laughing in your sleep last night."

The little girl stopped crying on hearing her mother's voice, and started clapping her tiny hands and feet. Droplets from tears were stuck in the lashes of her big black eyes. Her eight-month-old daughter's sweet laughter and cute noises melted Agrin's heart. She picked Evin up and hugged her. "Are you hungry? Do you want some milk?" she asked.

Evin was pulling her mother's clothes with her hand and bringing her head to her mother's breast. Agrin laughed. "Be patient, my baby girl! Are you really that hungry, sweetheart?"

Agrin sat by the small wooden cradle that she and her husband had decorated with beautiful colours and pearls, and began to breastfeed her daughter. Agrin knew well which sounds and games would make her daughter's sweet laughter rise and fill the house with joyous sounds. This time, Evin laughed with her mouth full of milk and it dribbled over her and her mother's clothes.

"Oh no! What was that? You cheeky, you spilt the milk all over us! Oh God, look at this mess. But, of course, most of it was your mother's fault, wasn't it? Your mother loves to see and hear your laughter so much that she doesn't let you have your milk in peace." Agrin began cleaning her baby's face. "Let's go and change these clothes and put on new clean ones. It's about time for your father to return from work and we don't want to be messy, do we?" She hugged Evin on the way to her room.

After changing Evin, Agrin sat her in a corner of the living room with some of her toys beside her. "Here, sweetie, you start playing, and I'll get back to work. We better not waste this beautiful morning weather. I have things to do before it gets hot." Agrin kissed her daughter, then went to do the housework.

She tidied the house, washed the dishes, and wiped the window panes.

Eventually, Agrin went to the yard with a bowl of seeds and water, opened a small shed, then started to talk to a hen. "Hello, good morning, my beautiful," she said, in her loving tone. "Did I wake you up? Let me put out some water and these yummy seeds for you." The hen got up and went to the water, where Agrin was excited to see some of the colourful chicks that had just hatched. She started counting them, "One, two, three, four. Four! How beautiful and cute. They are like you. Look at this one with black and red colouring. She is clearly yours … at least I hope so." Agrin patted her hen and said, "Congratulations, mummy, but you still have work for the rest of them to hatch. Come, buckle up and finish your job. It's a bit late, but not to worry, you still have one week to go." Agrin stood up. "Now I must go inside, my man is about to come home."

Agrin's husband, Delovan, was the village teacher, and they had decided to live in the village because of the distance and difficulty of navigating the local roads. The villagers had given them a small but comfortable house for their accommodation. The school year had now been over for some time. However, Agrin and Delovan were still staying in the village to help complete the school reconstruction and repair work so the school would be better prepared for the following year. Her husband loved children very much and he wanted them to have a pleasant and friendly environment in which to learn and grow. Delovan was working every day from early in the morning to late afternoon, and it was now time for him to return from the school.

Agrin spread a tablecloth, arranged the plates in order, then made a fresh and delicious drink of ayran from local yogurt and some fresh herbs. She took one of her beautiful flowers, placed it in a vase decorated with pieces of coloured broken glass, and put it in the middle of the tablecloth. She turned to her daughter and said, "Okay, now the table is ready, and the work is almost done, let me go and visit the hen and her chicks one more time before Baba comes home."

Agrin went to the yard, sat next to the shed, then began talking to the chickens about names for their chicks when her husband arrived.

From the gate, Delovan could see Agrin, but she did not notice him watching because she was busy playing with the chicks. Delovan stepped quietly towards her. When he got close enough, he bent down, held her waist and shouted, "What are you doing?"

Agrin jumped up, screaming, "Uhhh, my God! Delovan, you scared me! Why would you do that? You are so mean sometimes."

Delovan laughed and said, "Do you know how long I have been here, standing above you and listening? You didn't notice me at all! My sweet weirdo."

Agrin replied, "You could see I was busy."

Delovan nodded. "In the morning, when I saw the chicks were hatching, I said to myself, 'If Agrin wakes up and sees them, she won't leave these poor little cuties alone.'"

"Uh … all right, but that is not true. I'm not like that," Agrin said, with a smile.

"Oh yeah, well, tell me this, how many times have you come and visited them?"

Agrin laughed and said, "I don't know, maybe ten times, but look how cute they are!"

Delovan laughed and held Agrin's hand and said, "Yeah ... yeah ... you're right."

Agrin frowned. "Stop it, Delovan!"

"Okay, okay, sorry," he said. "Now let's go inside; I'm so tired."

As soon as Delovan entered the house, his little daughter Evin saw her father and started to shake her hands and feet, making noises and laughing. Delovan put his bag aside, took off his shoes and went over to Evin. "Hello, Baba's little princess, have you missed me? I missed you, too. What are you playing, sweetie, ha? Did you eat your food? Didn't you wait for Baba, ha ...? My cutie." He picked up Evin, hugged her, then carried her over to sit on his lap at the table. Delovan gave her a spoon and said, "Here, play with this, sweetheart."

He turned to Agrin and asked, "When did you wake up?"

"I saw you from the window, leaving ..."

"That early? So ... what did you do then?"

"As usual, busy with the housework," Agrin replied.

"Hmm, the aroma of your food is making me even hungrier. How long before it is ready?" Delovan said, pouring himself a glass of ayran.

"I'm coming — one second," Agrin said, as she prepared the salad. She put the salad in a bowl and put it on the table. While serving Delovan's food to him on a plate, she asked, "Delovan, if we stay here for another year, can you get us a cow or at least two goats? We have room to keep them."

"What made you think of this?" Delovan asked.

"Nothing really. The people of the village are kind to us, and our neighbours always help us, and bring us the things that we need, but, as I said, we have a place to take care of them. So why not? I like to make my yogurt and cottage cheese. I found a nice recipe to try out," Agrin said.

"My God, barely two years ago, you didn't know how to make even a simple omelette. Now look at you, becoming a perfect housewife!" Delovan said, smiling.

"Well, at that time, I was busy studying, going to school and, of course, enjoying your love with all that romance, which didn't leave any time for more in life," she said. "Now that we have decided I would stay home and take care of Evin myself until she goes to school, I have plenty of time to learn and experience all the things that I always wanted."

"You are unlike the others. My sister fights every day with her husband and says that it is difficult to take care of their cows and goats and asks to sell them, but you say buy them. Very well, now let me see what happens. If we stay here for the next year, we will buy something," Delovan said.

"Okay, thank you," Agrin said.

"After the schoolwork finishes, we must go back to the city — it might take another week or two. Your mother called me today complaining that she misses you and Evin; she hasn't seen her granddaughter for so long. And also my mother, she is missing us as well."

"They are right; I miss them, too," Agrin added.

After eating, Delovan, who was playing with Evin, called out to

Agrin in the kitchen, "When the weather cools down, I'll take you and Evin walking. I want to show you how the school is turning out; it's different now."

"Okay, that sounds great, I haven't seen it for a long time," Agrin said.

Later, Delovan was in the yard with Evin, waiting for Agrin to get ready for a walk.

After a while, Agrin emerged from the house and said to Delovan, "Finally, I'm ready, now let's go." As she came down the steps with her joyous smile, beautiful red dress, and her long wavy hair falling to her shoulders, Agrin secured all of Delovan's attention.

Delovan took her hand, and said, "Darling, you look beautiful in this dress; this colour makes you shine even more."

"Every time I wear it, you say something nice," Agrin replied, with a smile.

"Because I like it every time you wear it, I can't get enough of it," Delovan said. He kissed his beautiful wife on the forehead, then kissed little Evin's cheek as well. "Okay, we better go before it gets dark."

On the way, as she was enjoying the view, Agrin said, "Delovan, it would be great if we could stay here next year as well."

"I know; this village is lovely, isn't it?" Delovan replied.

"Yes, very much so. I mean, look around; it makes you feel alive. You see yourself as part of these mountains. Oh, it's such a powerful feeling." Agrin took a deep breath and continued, "The villagers are also nice and friendly, like our neighbours. Although we haven't been here for long, I am very attached to them and see them as my family."

"Yes, darling, me too. I have already put in my request to stay, so let's see what my boss decides."

As they were busy talking, one of Delovan's students and his father came along. The father said, "Hello, Delovan, hello, Mrs Agrin. How are you?"

Delovan smiled and said, "Hello, brother Ferman, we are all good. Thank you for asking." Delovan looked at his student, put his hand on his shoulder and said, "Hello, Jiyar, how are you, son? I see you are helping your father."

"Yes, teacher," Jiyar answered, with a smile.

"Well done, my son!" Delovan said.

Ferman said to Delovan, "My brother, we were just passing our school and noticed all the work is coming to an end. You rebuilt it so well that it looks perfect. Jiyar says that you studied engineering."

"Yes, my brother, I did, and in the case of school, yes, you are right, the reconstruction work is going very well and is almost finished," Delovan said.

"Everyone says that next year you must stay here, too. We don't want you to leave," Ferman said.

"God willing, I have made the same request to the office to permit me to stay here next year," Delovan said.

Ferman looked at his son Jiyar and put his arm around his shoulder, saying, "Well, Delovan, can you tell me, was my son a good student last year?"

"Yes, very good. Jiyar is a smart and polite child. I remember that he wrote in one of his exercise books that he wants to study engineering in the future, and his dream is to build strong and comfortable houses for his parents and the people of his village."

Ferman was happy to receive this compliment, and said, "I can see that he always has big dreams and talks about them all the time. In my duty as a father, I will do my best so he can have whatever he needs to have a brighter future like you." Ferman turned to Agrin. "Mrs Agrin, my dear sister, I will also ask my wife and my daughters to come and visit you, to see if you need anything or would like to be helped out."

Agrin thanked him and replied, "I will be happy to see them."

Then they said goodbye to each other.

Even when Jiyar was some distance away, he was still playing peekaboo with his hands, which made Evin laugh. Agrin took Evin's hand and said, "My daughter says 'bye' to Jiyar."

Agrin, Delovan and Evin continued on their way to the school. When they arrived, the school was so different and full of cheerful colours. Everywhere was clean and tidy and ready for the children.

"Wow! How much it has changed! Seeing this makes me wish to go back to my childhood again and be a student here," said Agrin, checking out the classrooms. She took a good look everywhere, saying, "School looks ready, so why did you say you still need two more weeks to finish the work?"

"It's because of the schoolyard. I want to make some changes and also make it safer for students to play," Delovan said.

"Good idea," Agrin said.

As they walked back home, it began to get dark. When they reached the gate, they saw a bowl of yogurt, some local butter, and a bucket of fresh milk on the steps.

"Mrs Gulê must have brought these; she told me about them the other day," said Agrin, while carrying them inside.

"Okay, then put those things in the fridge and let's go over and thank them," said Delovan.

"Okay, let me get the cake that I baked for us and take it for them as a thank-you, as well," said Agrin.

They went to Mrs Gulê's house. When they arrived in the yard of their house, Delovan went to Kheder, Gulê's husband, who was washing his hands and face, and said, "Hello, Uncle Kheder, how are you?"

Kheder straightened his back and looked up. When he saw Delovan, he walked forward with open arms. "Oh, look who has shown up, our favourite teacher with his beautiful family. Welcome, my son, how good to see you. How are you, my dear daughter, Agrin?"

"Thank you, Uncle Kheder," Agrin said.

"Gulê, come out and look who is here. We have guests," Kheder said, calling his wife.

Gulê came out in a hurry, happy to see their guests and went to greet them.

"Auntie, we cannot thank you enough. You are taking care of us all the time," Delovan said.

"You are most welcome," Gulê said. "As I have said before, you and Agrin are like my children."

"Thank you very much again," Delovan said.

"The house with a baby should always have fresh food. As you are far from your mother, I take her place and watch out for Agrin." Gulê laughed while holding little Evin's hand.

Agrin hugged Gulê and thanked her.

They all went to sit under a big tree in the corner of their yard, where Gulê had spread out a large, old rug with a few red and green small pillows. She had watered and swept the yard, and everything was beautiful and looked tidy.

Delovan gave Evin to Agrin, then went to sit next to Kheder and started talking. A few minutes later, Gulê came out with a tray of tea and cake, then sat next to Agrin. Two of Gulê's young grandchildren came and sat next to Agrin and played with Evin. One of them said, "Aunt Agrin, I also have a dummy like Evin does."

Agrin laughed. "Very good! Now tell me, how old are you?"

"Nazdar is almost six years," Gulê said. "A big girl who still has her dummy."

"But I don't use it like Evin! I give it to my dolly. She's still a baby and needs it," Nazdar said, in her defence.

Agrin laughed and said lovingly, "Well, that is a good idea. Now go and get your doll. I want to see her, and make sure you bring her dummy as well, in case she cries."

Kheder turned to Delovan and said, "I heard that this new group has captured some cities and villages." He sighed and continued, "Delovan, my son, it's not good with this news and these recent events that are happening every day. So far, we have experienced more than seventy wars and riots that have befallen our people and put us in disastrous situations. I am almost seventy years old. I have a lot of experience, I've heard many stories from my father and elders about our painful history, and the situation we face these days is the same as they warned us in their stories."

"Yes, Uncle, you are right. We have had many wars and horrific experiences in the history of our people. Still, now the countries of the world, such as the United States and Europe, and many other large organisations, are in a world that strives for humanitarianism and security and have legislated for these. If there is a war, it will not be like before. Soon they will help us. We are not people of aggression. They are serious about women and children. I mean, in this time, the world is a much better and safer place now than during those horrible wars."

"I do not know, my son; you know better. I only understand that our people have suffered enough. God forbid, we don't have another war. Our people finally have a peaceful life and are starting to have dreams and hopes for their future."

After a short pause of sadness, Kheder began to change the subject and told Delovan, "Son, the villagers are thrilled with you; you encourage young people to study. I even heard that you asked the children to teach their mother to read and write as well, and you have a lot of good books and read them to the men who can't read. You should know that we are so pleased and proud of what you are doing – learning is the ultimate reward."

"That is right, Uncle, and for our women and young girls it is even more important," Delovan said. "I did a lot of research and study on the culture of other countries at university. I realised that any civilisation that has knowledgeable and free women is better and more robust than other countries and, indeed, more peaceful. As a teacher, I also want to enable my people to gain knowledge and awareness."

"In our time, children were not sent to school, and there wasn't school anywhere close to us!" Kheder said. "People were afraid to send their children to school. Among my children, only boys learned to read and write, but girls, like my daughters and their mother, do not know anything. But these days, it is so different, and I'm so fortunate to see people choosing to be educated. Like Nazgol, who is sitting next to Agrin and playing with your daughter, she is now eight years old and is going to school with her brother and her sister. Nazdar will also go next year."

"Nazgol is a brilliant girl. She loves to learn about the stars and the universe. And I can't wait for Nazdar to start next year," Delovan said, smiling at the girls.

"Still, many people and village elders don't like children to go to school," Kheder said. "The same as Mrs Gulê, who is listening, always saying that girls shouldn't go to school, they should stay home and learn the art of housekeeping and learn how to raise children!"

"Is it true, my beautiful Aunt? Are you thinking that way?" Delovan said, frowning but with a smile on his face.

"Honestly, I did. I believed that way, as I learned from my mother," Gulê said. "But since I met Agrin and saw her talking and behaving like a homemaker and seeing how she treats children, I see a big difference. Now I regret it, and say to myself, 'I wish I knew this stuff, too, so that I could raise my children better.'"

Agrin held her hand and said, "Don't say that, Auntie, you have done an amazing job, and I have learned so much from you."

"Well, Uncle Kheder, Auntie, it's time for us to go home," Delovan said, standing up. "It's getting late and tomorrow we all have a lot to do. Thank you for having us and all your kindness; we appreciate it."

They all said goodbye, then Delovan and his family left.

On the way home, Delovan said, "Agrin, let me carry Evin. It's dark, be careful not to wake her up."

"Oh, yeah, right. Here …" Agrin said, passing Evin to Delovan, as she was thinking about Kheder's words of war.

When they arrived home, Agrin took Evin from Delovan's arms

and waited for him to open the door. They went inside and Delovan started changing his clothes, while Agrin put Evin in her cradle.

When Evin woke up again, Agrin went to her and said, "Sweetheart, what happened? Why did you wake up?" Agrin hugged Evin. "Now that you've slept well, you want to stay up all night and be naughty, ha?"

But when she saw that Evin was not feeling well and starting to cry, Agrin said, "Or not? Let me check if my little princess needs to be changed." Agrin changed Evin into new sleeping clothes, hugged her and said, "Now, let Mummy feed you, then be a good girl and go to sleep. Mummy and Baba need to have a rest too, okay?"

Delovan was sitting next to Agrin and Evin while doing some of his school's paperwork. Watching his wife and daughter playing and laughing, and hearing Agrin's words to Evin, warmed his heart. He looked at Agrin and said, "You know what?"

"No, what?" Agrin replied.

"You two are my whole life, my everything," Delovan said, putting his hand on his heart.

Agrin didn't say anything in response, but the beautiful smile across her face was the best reaction of all to Delovan's loving remarks.

After Agrin finished breastfeeding, she hugged her daughter and began to sing the lullaby she had composed to express her feelings:

Laylayê lay layê
Laylayê lay layê
Laylayê sor gulê narînê
Laylayê Çav reşê şêrînê ...

And she kept singing the same part.

Delovan, who was listening, asked in surprise, "Agrin! Why don't you sing the whole song? I'm listening, too."

"I don't want to."

Delovan, who had realised before that something was worrying Agrin, put his work aside, then went to Agrin, ran his hand through her hair and asked, "Are you worried about Uncle Kheder's words? Nothing bad is going to happen; these discussions and conversations about war are everywhere. I promise you that, even if something happens, I will protect my family with my life – and you know that."

"I know," Agrin said, "but what if something happens to you? I'm so worried, I can't overcome this thought."

"Nothing will happen. You are over-reacting, darling, and even if anything happens, you will take my place and take care of yourself and our precious daughter. You will make sure that she will have the best life that we have dreamed for her, as we made a deal the day she was born."

"Me? What can I do? Didn't you hear Uncle Kheder saying how cruel the wars can get?"

Delovan whispered in a serious tone, "I have always told you, if you see yourself as helpless, you are weak. So please, see yourself as powerful as you can be. This world doesn't show any mercy over weakness."

Agrin listened while playing with Evin's hair.

"Hey ... darling, look at me," Delovan said. "Unless I die, I will never let anything happen to you and Evin. I mean, look at these muscles I have built up." Delovan flexed his biceps and laughed. "How dare you still be afraid of anything while standing next to me!"

Agrin held his arm and smiled.

He continued, "Now, please, enough with these negative thoughts, I want you to be strong for me, too. I want you to be happy. Seeing your smile is the best thing that you can give me, and, let me be honest, my pride hurts when I see my wife feels insecure next to me. I don't like it, and I don't want to see you like this again."

Agrin looked at Delovan, and said, "Uh ... you are right. I'm sorry, I'll stop. These feelings don't make any sense. We are in a safe place, and our people are away from any argument."

"That's more like it, my sweetheart. Now let's sing the lullaby and put Evin to sleep before she loses it. Otherwise, she will keep us awake all night. You know our cheeky girl." Delovan started singing and Agrin followed him:

Laylayê lay layê
Laylayê lay layê
Laylayê sor gulê narînê
Laylayê Çav reşê şêrînê
Bênve dayê, xew şêrîne
Bênve lavê, xema nebine
Bilbil bnaline ser dara di lurine
Dema ahêngê axa me dixwîne
Ez ew Bilbila li ser daranim
Az derman derdê evîndaranim
Lankey hjinem ser demen êvara
Ahiya dekšinem ser bexte yara
Bexteke pêr berinê, yarê çav be xwîn
Bel belê Nalê nalinê, dobarê eš jûn delorinê

Laylayê laylayê
Laylayê laylayê
Laylayê sor gulê narînê
Laylayê Çav reşê şêrînê
Bênve dayê, xew şêrîne
Bênve lavê, xema nebine.

(Lay lay, my beautiful red flower, lay lay, my sweet baby, close your beautiful black eyes to sleep, as always you have sweet dreams, go to sleep, hope you never have any pain. Listen, a nightingale is sitting on the branch of a tree singing; she sings with tears when telling our land's story. I am that nightingale, who is sitting on the branch of a tree, singing so deep in sympathy, that my voice is becoming like a treatment for a lover's broken heart, as I'm rocking the cradles in the evening, I sing all about their story as I sigh deep in my heart, they have a heart-breaking story with their eyes full of tears of blood, listen to the nightingale singing in pain. La la, go to sleep my beautiful red flower, la la, my sweet baby, close your beautiful black eyes, go to sleep and dream, dreaming is sweet, I hope, like your sweet dreams, you never see pain.)

Agrin placed her sleeping little Evin in her cradle, wrapping a cord around her so that she wouldn't fall to the ground. She threw a beautiful green net over the cradle, the sides of which she had woven with sparkling pearls to catch the light and to protect Evin from flies and mosquitoes. Then Agrin went and put on her sleeping clothes.

Delovan said, "Until I finish my work, can you make me a glass of warm milk, please?"

"Okay, I will prepare it for you now." Agrin went to the kitchen, boiled the milk, then poured it into a glass. With a small bowl of honey, she put the glass of milk on a tray and took it to Delovan. She sat next to him and waited until his work was finished.

"I love the smell of fresh milk," Delovan said. "Why didn't you make a glass for yourself?"

"No, I do not want any," Agrin said.

He added a spoonful of honey to the milk and stirred, drank some, then said, "Yummy, come and try a little, it's so tasty."

"Ah, stop making that face," Agrin said. "How good it can be? It's just milk." She smiled.

"Your loss," Delovan said, then drank some more.

"You make it sound so yummy. Now I want some." Agrin laughed and went to grab the glass from Delovan.

"No, no, that's not going to work this time," Delovan said, pulling the glass away. "I'll give it to you … I'm not risking it like my drink the other night."

They started talking about their life together and their plans. They had so many sweet dreams they wanted to reach as a family. Talking about these dreams made Delovan and Agrin even more excited about their future.

Finally, Agrin said, "Look at the time. It's midnight and you have to go to work tomorrow!"

"Oh, my God, it's past twelve," Delovan said. "Also, I have to get some tools ready before the workers come. I'll leave early; I won't wake you." Delovan lay down in bed with Agrin, kissed her cheek, then whispered into her ear, "Why are you talking so much, woman? Look … you finished off the night."

"What! I don't understand you!" Agrin said, smiling. "You want me to talk and then you say I'm a chatterbox when I speak to you."

"Oh, my God … look at her, she is still talking," Delovan said, laughing.

"Well, that is how I am, like it or not," Agrin said, frowning. "It's your problem, so get used to it for the rest of your life, mister …"

"Crazy girl, look at her frowning face," Delovan said. "Come here now, you need a hug." Delovan hugged his wife as he kissed her good night.

2

The following day, the sunlight shone through the window on Agrin's face and woke her. Delovan had left early in the morning and Evin was still asleep. Agrin put on her clothes and closed the door so that her daughter wouldn't wake. She picked up a bowl of seeds and went to the yard. First, she went to check on the hen and her chicks and gave her seeds and some water, then she opened the gate for the rest of the chickens in the shed and sprinkled the seeds on the ground, putting some water next to them. "Ju, ju, ju," she called to them. The chickens came and started eating. "Very well, now let me see if you have laid any eggs today." She went inside and came out. "Oh, my God, five eggs!" Agrin said. "Thank you. I'll take them with your permission."

She went back into the shed again and started gathering the eggs, when a terrifying, loud explosion shook the ground. It was so intense that it poured dirt and dust from the corner of the roof over Agrin's head.

She rushed out, looked around, saw nothing, then ran to the alley where dust and smoke were rising from several houses on the other side. There was screaming and shouting all over the village. Little Evin was crying, so she hurried home.

Agrin had not yet reached the steps when a bomb exploded at the rear of the house and threw her back. She got to her feet, then saw through the dust that her house had collapsed. Agrin ran up what remained of the steps and found that a wall had fallen on Evin's cradle.

Agrin screamed in terror for her daughter. Dirt and bricks were all over the cradle and she started pulling them away. "Evin, cry! Please cry! Come on ... come on ..." She said to herself, "Agrin, hurry up!" She saw the corner of the cradle and with all her might she pulled it out. "Evin ... please, Mummy needs to hear your voice. Start crying, baby!"

Agrin's hands trembled so much, she could barely control them, as she pushed the dirt off the cradle. She hurried as she unwrapped Evin, then hugged her as she wiped the dust from her face. Agrin shouted with a trembling voice, "Evin? Evin? Breathe for Mummy! Cry, I'm begging you! Evin, breathe!"

Agrin noticed the hand she had put under Evin's head was warm and sticky. As she pulled her hand away, she realised the stickiness she felt was blood from a large cut in Evin's head. She stared in disbelief at her daughter and the blood on her hands. Fear and panic overtook her. "My God, my daughter, help!" she shouted. "Please, someone, help me! Delovan ... where are you? Please, someone, help me save my daughter!"

Agrin put her ear to Evin's heart but heard nothing. She checked her pulse but felt nothing. Her baby was gone! Blood dripped from the corner of her chin onto Evin's face. Agrin heard screams outside. She hugged Evin to her body and decided to try finding someone to help her.

Agrin took only a few steps before dizziness overcame her, and she felt her hands become weak and cold. With her daughter in her arms, Agrin lost consciousness and fell on the floor.

A few hours later, Agrin opened her eyes, not knowing how long she had been unconscious. Evin was still in her arms. She turned her head towards her daughter's face. "Evin, my beautiful daughter, why aren't you opening your eyes for Mummy?" Agrin was struggling to hold her head up as she looked around, mumbling under her breath, "Delovan, where are you? Please come back." She put her head under Evin's neck and cried.

Suddenly, Agrin heard the voices of several men coming from outside the house. At first, she thought she could hear Delovan, but the closer the voices came, she realised that they were speaking in Arabic.

One voice said, "The house is destroyed, brother, I do not think anyone is inside. We should not waste time in here."

Another said, "No, we follow the commander's order. Go inside and make sure."

Agrin heard their footsteps coming up the steps. She hugged Evin to her body and remained motionless.

A man stood over Agrin's head. "Brothers, come, there is a woman here. She doesn't move, I think she is dead."

"Check and see if she is alive," another man said, coming up the steps.

The first man put his hand on Agrin's shoulder to turn her over.

Agrin became so scared that she somehow resisted being turned over.

"She is still alive!" the man shouted.

The other men came and stood over Agrin's head. "Turn her over so I can see her face!" commanded one of them.

The first man pulled back Agrin's arm to see her face, but she gathered herself and sat back up, glaring at them. There were three dangerous-looking men standing above her head. Agrin cried and lifted her daughter to them. "Help me. My daughter is injured, she doesn't move."

"Wow! Look at God's creation," one of the men said, with a greedy look. "Her black eyes are mesmerising. She is, no doubt, one of the most beautiful women I have ever seen."

"Come on now, hurry, check if her baby is still alive – which doesn't look likely," a third man ordered.

Agrin, who understood their language well, was scared and held Evin tightly in her arms. One of the men walked over and put his hand on Evin's neck. "No, brother, the baby is dead."

"Take the baby away from her."

"Yes, brother," the man said, then grabbed Evin, trying to pull her out of Agrin's arms.

Agrin resisted fiercely. "No, don't touch her! Who are you? Get lost!" But when she saw that her strength didn't match his, and that he was about to take the baby out of her arms, she began to beg. "Please, for the love of God, please do not take her. Let her stay. Why are you taking my child from me? She is wounded, maybe she is still alive. You don't know, please ..."

However, the indifferent man pulled the baby out of her mother's arms, leaving only her daughter's dummy, which had been ripped from the red dress of Evin, in Agrin's hand.

The man threw Evin to the corner of the room and shouted at Agrin, "Shut up!" He grabbed Agrin's arm to lift her.

But Agrin was full of anger when she saw him throwing her

daughter and shouted even louder, "Do not touch me! Go away, you disgusting ..." She grabbed a piece of broken brick by her side, then bashed it into his face until he fell down.

The other two men grabbed Agrin's hands, shoved her to one side and then slapped her across the face a few times.

The man who had been bashed by Agrin stood up. He wiped his bloody face with his hand, then rushed at her. He pulled out his dagger and yelled, "Worthless woman, I will take your worthless life now!"

"Zubair, hold your hand," another man said. "This is one of the spoils of war. You can't kill her. She belongs to God and God's fighters. Overcome your anger, God forbid, you are a Mujahid."

Zubair stopped his attack on Agrin. Staring at her, he put his dagger back into his belt, then spat on the ground. He turned around and said, "May God forgive me." He wiped more blood from his face with his handkerchief. "Let's go now."

They dragged Agrin out with them.

"Leave me alone," she cried. "Where are you taking me? I won't leave my daughter alone."

When they reached the alley, Agrin called out to the neighbours and asked for help, but there was no one around. On the way, she saw several bodies lying on the ground. The village was in ruins. The few remaining doors were hanging open and all the windows were broken.

The men were taking Agrin to the centre of the village. On the way, they saw a man who had fallen onto his back and was trying to get up. One of the three men pointed his weapon at him and said, "Zubair, go to him, but be careful."

Agrin recognised him. He was Jiyar's father, Ferman. He had been shot in his chest and his white shirt was bloody. "Brother Ferman," Agrin called out in horror. She tried to free herself from the men's hands and shouted, "He is bleeding, help him, please!"

"He can't walk," Zubair said, holding Ferman by the shoulder. "Should we carry him?"

"Finish him," one of them ordered.

Zubair pulled out his dagger and, without delay, grabbed Ferman by the hair and cut his throat.

Seeing this, Agrin lost all strength in her legs and fell to the ground, shouting, "Nooo, what did you do? Why did you kill him? God help us! Who are these people?"

Zubair held his bloody dagger up to Agrin and shouted, "Shut up, stop screaming." He took her from the other two men, threw her over his shoulder, then started walking.

They reached the centre of the village and they took Agrin to where the other women were gathered in a circle and being guarded.

Gulê, seeing Agrin, went to her, hugged her and cried, "My daughter Agrin, what have they done to you? Where is your daughter?"

"She was killed. They wouldn't let me bring her body with me." Agrin showed Gulê the red dummy. "This is all I have left of Evin." Agrin pointed at her chief tormentor. "That man killed Ferman, Auntie. Who are these people? Why are they doing this?"

"I don't know, I don't know, my daughter, they came to the village and have been killing and capturing us all day, and they don't say anything," Gulê said, hitting herself on her lap.

Agrin raised her head and saw everywhere there were men in military uniforms, with long beards and armed with weapons.

Some had covered their faces with black handkerchiefs and held black flags. The men of the village had been herded together, and some were digging in the ground. Agrin looked for Delovan among them, but did not find him. In one corner, the little boys had been lined up, and were looking at each other's faces. Some soldiers were checking the boys' faces and underarms, sending several among the men and others to sit on the ground.

"Auntie, I don't see Delovan! Has he escaped?" Agrin said.

"No, mother, they got him too," Gulê said.

"Where is he? Why can't I see him?"

Gulê, along with two other women who were sitting next to her, cried and pointed him out. "Delovan is there, my daughter," said one of the women. "They took him and held him next to that car."

Agrin looked to the side and saw that Delovan was actually looking at her, all his clothes bloody, and his hands were tied tightly. Agrin wanted to go to him and started calling him.

"Hush, for God's sake – don't," Gulê said, covering Agrin's mouth.

"Sit down, Agrin, and do nothing," Gulê said. "If you call him, they'll find out who you are, then God knows what will happen to you."

"What? Why?" Agrin said.

"Do you see those bodies there?" Gulê asked. "Delovan killed them and wounded three others. That red-bearded man with a bloody face is their commander. Delovan attacked him with a knife. He was lucky, otherwise Delovan would have killed him as well. It's been several hours now that they have been beating Delovan and asking people to expose his family and look for Delovan's wife, sister and brother. But no one has said anything." Gulê whispered in Agrin's ears, "Now, be silent. If they find out that you are Delovan's wife, then to torment him, God knows what they will do to you in front of his eyes."

Delovan nodded his head and motioned for Agrin to sit down and do nothing.

Agrin, with tears in her eyes, showed Evin's dummy to him.

Delovan seeing Evin's dummy in Agrin's bloody hands, closed his eyes. Tears began falling from his eyes down to his chin. He stared at Agrin. Seeing his wife's bloody face and her frightened and tearful eyes added to his grief and anger. He wanted to reach out for her, but he knew they would stop him before he could reach her. He knew if he showed any weakness, Agrin would suffer more, so he held his emotions, raised his head again, stood firm, and looked at Agrin, who was being held in Gulê's arms and staring back at him.

The commander went to the pit that the men of the village had been digging and said, "Enough! Take the shovels from them and sit them all in one line around the pit."

The soldiers took all the men to the sides of the pit and aimed their weapons at them. One of the soldiers went to get Delovan.

"No! Let him stay; he is mine!" the commander shouted. Then he bellowed to the men of the village, "Now you are all captives of ISIS, and you should know that our jihad is only for God, and, in this world, you have nothing but torment and disbelief. You should believe in the religion of God so that you may rise with those who believe in the forever world, and God shall forgive you from burning in hell." The commander recited a sentence in Arabic, then asked the villagers to repeat a testimony after him.

"Why should we change our beliefs?" a village elder yelled back. "We believe in God; we want nothing but peace. If you didn't attack

27

us, we would have welcomed you as friends. Why is your God asking for our blood? We haven't done anything wrong."

"You are non-believers, you see the devil as God," one of the ISIS soldiers shouted.

"That is a lie," the elder insisted. "We believe in God, and you all know it. We are not afraid of you, you are a pack of thieves and liars."

"Under the name of God," called another villager, "explain your wild ways of life." The man was holding his terrified teenage son in his arms.

"You don't deserve to go to heaven, you should burn in hell as an infidel forever," the commander said, shooting at the man and his son until his automatic gun emptied of bullets. "Now, that was the last warning to all of you, so repeat after me ..." He realised no one was going to obey him, so he shouted, "Bring me those kids."

Some soldiers placed the young boys in front of him.

The commander continued, "I will shoot them if you disobey."

The men started to testify. The teenagers and children – in imitation of their grandfathers, fathers, uncles and cousins – testified as well. The soldiers lined up the men and stood with guns pointed at their heads. Their wives, mothers and children stared at them, holding their breath. No one could believe the scene in front of them.

The commander ordered his soldiers to shoot, and they all fired their guns.

The screams of the women rose, but the screams full of pain and the wailing of Delovan could be heard louder than anyone.

The commander laughed and walked over to where Delovan was kneeling. "Certainly, some of those men were your brothers or fathers and relatives, weren't they?"

Delovan got to his feet and, with all his might, hit the commander on the chest with his head. The commander was thrown back. "I dare you to unlock my hands!" Delovan yelled. "I will kill you with my bare hands, you bastard!"

Agrin was crawling on the ground to watch. The women had hold of her and asked her to control herself. Two men held Delovan and pushed him back to his knees.

The commander shook the dust off himself, then put his hand on Delovan's chest, and said, "You are a strong and brave man; you don't have fear inside. If you were on our side, you would have conquered many lands for God." He motioned for two of his men to take Delovan away.

The soldiers lifted him and carried him to the edge of the pit.

Gulê hugged Agrin tightly. Agrin looked at Delovan.

Delovan raised his eyes as he was pushed to his knees at the side of the pit. He looked across to his love.

The commander stood over Delovan's head and told him to repeat his testimony.

Delovan kept silent.

"Come on, hurry up, say it," the commander said.

But Delovan ignored him, and focused on Agrin because he didn't care about the commander's threats.

The commander pulled out his dagger and pulled Delovan's hair back, "If you do not utter your testimony, I will cut off your head and cut your body into pieces and throw each piece in a place where no mercy is allowed for the infidels. But if you tell me your testimony and believe in the only God that rules us all, you have my word that I will kill you with one bullet and you will die with no pain."

Delovan was willing to be torn to pieces, but not to give in to their meaningless games. He knew what would happen to him in front of his wife, and he did not want his wife to suffer the pain of watching the torture of her love, so he agreed to testify. While he was immersed in Agrin's eyes, the commander wrapped his dagger, then after Delovan finished his testimony, he took his gun out and pulled the trigger on Delovan's head.

Time stood still in the aching hearts of the two beautiful lovers. Agrin could not believe her eyes. The scene around her slowed, and she could see nothing, hear nothing, sense nothing, except Delovan – hearing Delovan's breathing and the gurgling of his throat. Red drops of blood flowed from his head and rested for a few seconds on his chin, then rolled over his chest. Agrin was holding her breath. All her attention was on her darling's beautiful eyes that were spilling love over and over and over again; desperate for a miracle to happen, hoping for a chance to fall into his arms one more time. The sound of a bullet shook Agrin and she closed her eyes, trembling. After a second, she opened her eyes and, with tears flowing, saw Delovan, her whole world, fallen on the ground. She could never believe that a mighty, powerful mountain could fall, too.

The women shouted and moaned. Agrin laid her head on the ground and wept and wept with grief over the death of her man and her baby girl – wishing again for a miracle, but this time not a miracle for life but her death. The women shouted so loud that the ISIS soldiers began holding their ears and soon became angry and frightened.

Two armed men approached to silence them, but the grieving women and girls started throwing stones and debris at them.

One of the women, shouting and gesturing with both hands, called, "Where are you, God? Why aren't you helping us? How can you witness our suffering and do nothing? Our men, our brothers, our sons, our young people shed their blood innocently. Oh God, why do you not hear us? How can you see and ..."

Two men went forward to silence the woman and started hitting her and others with their rifles. One woman attacked a soldier, grabbing his beard and dipping her fingers into his eyes, shouting, "I'll kill you, I'm not afraid of you. Go to hell!"

The soldier pushed her away from him and struck the poor woman in the face and neck with a dagger. The wounded and bloody woman fell to the ground. The soldier sat on the ground and covered his bloody eyes with both hands, screaming, "My eyes, I can't see!" He wiped his face, which was scratched and bloodied from the woman's attack.

His friends went to him and put him in the car and took him away.

The women lifted the half-dead body of the poor woman he had stabbed and took her into their midst. Agrin held the woman's head on her knee and tried to stop her bleeding, but, as the woman stared into Agrin's eyes, she died after a few seconds.

The commander fired several shots into the air. In the brief silence that followed, he declared his name as Ayoub Rashid. Then he took aim at the young boys, who clung to each other in fear and were crying. Turning to the women, he shouted, "Be quiet or I will shoot each one of them in front of your eyes."

The women fell silent in fear.

The commander selected some middle-aged women from among

the captives and told them to get up. He took them to one side and, pointing to a car, ordered some of his men to get in the vehicle with the women. He spoke to the driver for a few seconds and then let them drive away.

Agrin was sitting among the remaining women – the dead woman's head was still on her knees. Agrin was holding her hand, while staring at the commander and his bloody fingers, remembering the moment that he shot Delovan repeatedly. Delovan had fallen into the pit after being shot, and Agrin could now only see part of his clothes and legs.

After a while, Agrin raised her head and saw the car was coming back. She watched the car driving towards the pit, with two men standing on the back of the vehicle with guns drawn. They jumped down and removed the bodies they had collected in the village. The commander had sent them to collect the dead bodies from the village.

Agrin saw Evin's body was with one of the village women. Seeing Evin's small dusty hand, with a green pearl bracelet on her tiny forearm, her petite body and face, Agrin cried loudly. She lifted the head of the dead woman from her knee and placed her down. Agrin stood up, longing for her baby. She called her name with all her might and ran towards her.

Agrin had only taken a few steps when the commander saw her and ordered a soldier to hold her. A man grabbed her right arm and sat her down.

Gulê shouted, "For the love of God, sit down!"

The man holding Agrin by the hair prevented her from walking towards her daughter. Agrin kept looking at her husband and daughter, crying painfully.

The woman who was holding Evin was filled with tears when she saw Agrin. She knew well how desperate Agrin was to hug her baby for one last time. She wanted to take the child to Agrin but knew they would never let her. She saw Agrin's regretful and mothering looks, and knew what she so desperately wanted, so she straightened Evin's head with her hand, kissed her tiny hand and placed it on her chest. The woman brought her head close to Evin's head and hugged her lovingly. She rocked the baby girl the way a mother would while she soothes her baby with a lullaby.

Seeing her, Agrin put her two empty hands on her chest and hugged herself and started rocking with the woman.

The leader of the vehicle barked, "Hurry up and throw the bodies into the pit!"

A man with a gun slapped the woman on the shoulder and said, "What are you procrastinating about? Be quick, throw the baby in the pit — hurry."

The woman went to the pit without delay.

Agrin, who had moved a little closer to the pit, saw that the woman, without attracting attention, had placed Evin in Delovan's arms, put his shoulder over Evin's body and placed Evin's face under Delovan's neck and moved on to the other corpses.

Agrin could not tear her gaze away from her husband's bloody brown hair and wounded shoulders, his tied hands, her daughter's innocent dusty face and her bloody curly hair, her little feet with a few colourful necklaces that she had made for her. Finally, Agrin's loved ones were covered under the rain of dirt falling from the attacker's shovels and beliefs.

3

grin's obvious grief for her daughter attracted the commander's attention. After finishing his work, the commander came down to her and instructed the man who had hold of Agrin's hair, "Release her hair and lift her." He stood in front of Agrin and touched her hair, looking into her eyes, touching his beard, laughing. "Take her to the rest of the prisoners, but be gentle with her; she looks so fragile."

Gulê hugged Agrin. "Where did this torment come from?" Gulê asked. "Until yesterday, you were happy, your husband and daughter were beside you, and today they have buried both of them in front of your eyes. Why didn't they kill us all? I can't take all this pain."

After an hour, the soldiers lined up all the women in single file. Agrin stood in line next to Gulê, holding her hand while focusing all her attention on the commander, Ayoub Rashid. She followed him with her eyes, but whenever the commander looked back at her, Agrin looked down and would hide behind Gulê.

Later that evening, a white car and a bus stopped a few metres away from the women. Soldiers ran to open the door of the car. "Ahh, man, come on … don't just stand there," a man said from inside the car. "Help me get out."

"Yes sir." The soldier bent and took the man's arms. As he got out of the vehicle, the whole left side of the car rocked.

Ayoub Rashid rushed towards him. "Oh, brother Abu Muslim, my very, very big brother. Welcome, welcome, how have you been?"

"Oh, thank you, brother. Today was hot, and it was a long, uncomfortable journey. Let me sit and catch my breath," Abu Muslim said. He sat on a chair that was brought for him, then continued, "Your name will appear in books, Commander Ayoub Rashid. I am jealous of you fighting for God on the front line. I can see you in heaven among those who are named in the Holy Book."

"Oh, may God bless you, brother. Now I see you have your notebooks ready, and we're late this time!" Ayoub Rashid said.

"Yes, yes, I had to stop to take my medication. Now hold my glasses and let's get into business. Tell me, commander, how many people have we captured?"

"Forty-seven women as well as twenty boys who are all under nine."

"Well done," said Abu Muslim. He turned to the women who had been standing there for a long time, then pulled out a pen to write in his notebooks. "Say your full name and repeat your testimony after me," he ordered.

Most of the women were reluctant to follow Abu Muslim's orders, so the soldiers resorted to beating them in order to make them answer. Some still refused to respond, not caring if they were killed.

But the other women, who were their mothers and sisters, could not bear their pain through all the beatings, so they threw themselves at the attackers' feet, crying and begging, "Stop hitting them, for God's sake. Let us talk to them and convince them to answer you."

When it was Agrin's turn, she was pushed forward.

"Tell me your name," Abu Muslim demanded.

"Agrin Sheref."

Abu Muslim repeated her name as he wrote it down, then asked, "How old are you?"

"Twenty-nine," Agrin replied.

"Undo your hair," Abu Muslim ordered.

Agrin paused and looked at the commander standing firm next to Abu Muslim, who was staring at her. She reluctantly undid her hair.

"Very good, very good," Abu Muslim said. "Now repeat your testimony after me."

Agrin focused on the commander to make sure that she got his full attention. Without any further resistance, she said her testimony in a calm but grief-filled voice.

"Take her with the others," Abu Muslim commanded.

After all the women had been registered, Abu Muslim turned to Ayoub Rashid and said, "Choose one of these beautiful women for yourself as a reward. Especially now that some of your martyrs have been killed, and your face has been wounded, you have the right to receive a good reward, Ayoub Rashid."

Ayoub Rashid, who had been waiting for this chance, rushed to Agrin and grabbed her arm. "I choose this one."

"Okay. Now, do you want her only for tonight or more?"

The commander took Agrin's chin and lifted it, then said with a sneer, "No, I want her as booty, write this one under my name."

One of the men said, "Commander, why don't you choose a new and virginal girl? When we found this one, she had a baby with her."

Abu Muslim, while looking Agrin over, said, "Ayoub Rashid

knows what to choose. Brother, any time that you get tired of her and want to sell her, remember I'm her first buyer."

They all started laughing.

Agrin was disgusted and angry when she heard their insulting words, but she didn't react and kept quiet.

Abu Muslim looked at the other women and, pointing to them, separated thirteen, including several girls aged from ten to twelve. Gulê was one of those who stayed with Agrin.

The soldiers examined the women one by one and, if any had gold or jewellery, they removed it from their necks and hands, then forced them onto their bus.

The soldiers gathered the horrified little boys, registered them and put them in the car and took them away as well. They took Agrin and the rest of the women into a room in one of the few houses still standing and locked them inside.

The young women and girls in the locked room started screaming for their sisters, mothers and daughters, who had been separated from them and taken away by bus.

Agrin looked around the door, the walls and through the windows, but they had emptied the room.

"Isn't she the wife of Delovan, our village's teacher?" asked one young woman.

"Yes, my daughter, the poor woman is," Gulê said.

"What is she doing? She seems to be looking for something."

Gulê looked at Agrin and walked over to her anxiously. "My daughter, what are you doing? Are you looking for something? Come and sit next to me. Come, dear, and cry – don't hold this pain inside yourself. Crying out is the help we can get now, my daughter."

"I'm looking for something, Auntie," Agrin said, pulling away and continuing to search.

"What is it?" asked Gulê, taking hold of Agrin's arm. "What are you looking for?"

"I do not know, Auntie, but please let me look," Agrin said, taking her arm out of Gulê's hand.

"Has she lost her mind?" one woman wondered out loud. "Has she gone crazy?"

"She has the right to go crazy," another woman said. "A few hours ago, her husband was killed by that disgusting man, and now the murderer of her love wants to take her as a reward." The woman spat on the ground in disgust.

Gulê became more upset and worried and asked Agrin to sit down.

The sound of the door opening made everyone hold each other and run to the corner of the room in fear. An armed man stood by the door, while two others, one carrying water and the other with a bag of dates, entered the room.

The man standing next to the door shouted, "Each one of you, come forward and take a glass of water and some dates. If you resist, you will get harsh punishment."

Everyone took turns drinking water and picking some dates. When it was Agrin's turn, she took a glass of water, drank it and went to pick a date.

The man with the water grabbed Agrin tight and said, "This one is so beautiful, this one is for me." He tried to touch her neck.

The armed guard shouted, "This woman is for the commander!"

"Okay, but after the commander is finished with her, I shall have my turn."

"I'm telling you the commander took her as booty for himself," the guard barked. "As long as he does not sell her or give her as a gift, no one is allowed to approach her, so go back to your work, otherwise I will report you."

The man let go of Agrin after hearing these words.

His friend said to him with a laugh, "Come on, man, be patient and wait. In a few hours, the commander and the rest of the Mujahideen will return from the operation. Then you will receive your satisfaction as well." He looked around the women and laughed, saying, "There are enough women for all the Mujahideen."

After distributing the food and water, the soldiers left and closed the door again.

"My dear daughter, come and sit down with me," Gulê said to Agrin. "God is great. He will help us."

Agrin sighed and whispered in distress, "God? Help? Uh ... who wants help? Help to do what? It's too late to help; I don't need help any more. Only if God can turn back the time."

"Don't say that, my daughter, don't lose your hope and beliefs. God will help us; he watches us," Gulê said.

Agrin looked at Gulê with tears in her eyes, shook her head and sighed, "Okay, Auntie, okay, I won't." Agrin hung her head between her knees and sighed again in despair.

One of the women, who had a wounded face and tired eyes, which had turned red from crying so much, went and sat next to Agrin and whispered, "Hey, Agrin, I do not want you to kill yourself, but ..." She paused for a second and then continued, "I don't know what to say — look here ..." She took out a small piece of broken glass and put it into Agrin's hands. The woman held Agrin's hands and said,

"You might need this piece of glass more than I do."

Agrin took the glass and thanked her. The woman got up and went to sit down on the other side of the room. Agrin looked at the piece of glass in her hand and started dragging it across the cement floor to sharpen it more.

Gulê noticed Agrin was doing something and went over to her. When Gulê saw the glass in Agrin's hand, she said, "Give me the glass. Do you want to kill yourself? You can't do that. Give it to me, Agrin."

"Stop, Auntie, stop it. Let go of my hand," Agrin said. "I will not kill myself; death is the last thing I want right now, I promise you."

"What do you want to do, then?" Gulê asked.

"I'll kill him," Agrin said.

"You can't my daughter, there's no chance," Gulê said, holding her hands.

"I'll make the chance. I won't let him live while my Delovan is under tons of cold dirt."

Gulê went silent, understanding what Agrin was saying. After a few moments, Gulê said, "But, my daughter, taking revenge on them could take your life. Didn't you see how horrible they are? It's dangerous."

"Dangerous? Dangerous to do what? To lose what, Auntie? To kill my baby, huh? To kill my husband? Why should I be afraid if I have nothing left for them to take away?" Agrin's tears were now dripping on the piece of glass.

"You will put your life in danger. They have no mercy. You can't succeed. That monster will kill you," Gulê insisted.

Agrin said firmly, "I'm dead already, Auntie, and they've forgotten to bury me."

"Okay, my daughter, okay, I'm begging you to act wisely." Gulê sat beside her.

Hours later there were noises outside the room. Agrin and other women went to the window and saw the lights of cars arriving. Agrin hid the piece of glass in her clothes. Fear and panic overtook everyone again. "What will happen now?" a woman cried. "What do they want to do with us?"

A little girl grabbed Agrin's dress. "Mrs Agrin, Mrs Agrin, I'm so scared."

Agrin turned to her and said, "Don't cry, darling, everything will be fine. Where is your mother?"

"They took her away on the bus with my sister," she replied.

"Shush, sweetie, please don't cry," Agrin said. "You can stay with me until your mother comes back, okay?"

The girl threw herself into Agrin's arms. "Please, Mrs Agrin, don't let them take you away as well."

"I will stay, darling. I promise I will take care of you until your mother comes back. Okay now, stop crying." Agrin realised that at any time, the soldiers might separate them, and she wouldn't be able to do anything. This would be a broken promise and would hurt her and make the little girl more frightened.

Agrin wiped the girl's tears and kissed her face, and said, "Listen to what I tell you. They may separate us. If they take you away, do not cry so much that you bother them and make them mad enough to hurt you. Listen to them, be careful. Look for a sneaky way out or a good place to hide and, if you find one, go there and stay there until help comes, okay? If not, find a friend or wherever you go make a friend. They will take care of you. Promise me you'll take care of yourself, okay?"

"Okay, Mrs Agrin," the girl said, hugging Agrin tightly.

"Well, don't cry now, tell me your name."

"My name is Melek Serbest."

"What a beautiful name! So, you are an angel, aren't you? That is what your name tells me! Tell me more, were you one of Delovan's students?"

"Yes, I loved him so much; he was the best teacher," said the girl. "I always brought flowers for him. When these evil people came, I was with my father at school with Mr Delovan. He took my friend and me into the classroom and closed the door and went to fight them with my dad. I was looking out the window and saw them capture him and kill my dad. I miss him, and I miss my father very much."

Agrin now recognised her. Sometimes Delovan would come home with a small bouquet in his hand and say that one of his students had made it for him. Once, he bought a small doll from the market to thank her for her kindness. Agrin's eyes filled with tears, she hugged Melek tight and said, "Uh, God, my daughter, I miss him so much, too. You should know that Delovan always brought home your flowers, and I would put them in the vase next to Delovan's work table. You made lovely bouquets."

grin heard the sound of the door opening. "Okay, sweetheart," she said, holding Melek's face in her hand and looking into her eyes, "stay with Aunt Gulê, and remember what I said: make a friend wherever you go, okay?" Agrin hugged and kissed the little girl, then turned to Gulê. "Auntie, please find a way to keep her with you." Agrin placed Melek into Gulê's arms.

The door opened to reveal two men with guns, one on either side of the door, and the commander between them in his military uniform with his hand on his weapon. The commander entered and looked for Agrin. He grabbed her arm and pulled her out from among the women.

"Where are you taking her?" Gulê asked. "Please leave her alone."

A few other women began to cry and beg.

"Shut up, and back off," the guard shouted, and aimed his gun at them.

Agrin was taken out of the house and walked a few paces away. She was halted in front of the next house and waited until two men came out from inside the house. The door was left ajar and one soldier went to fetch their commander.

When the commander approached, the soldier standing outside

the door said, "Commander Ayoub Rashid, the house and the food has been prepared for you."

"Very well, you can leave now," the commander said, then turned to Agrin. "Come on, go inside." He grabbed her by one arm and pushed her inside.

He washed his face, washed the blood off his dagger, dried it and put it back inside his belt. "Wash your face and clean the blood from your neck." The commander finished drying his hands, then handed over the towel to Agrin. She took the towel from his hand, held it underwater, and started cleaning her face and neck. "Untie your hair again," the commander said, leaning over her head and running his hand through Agrin's hair as he started smelling it. "You smell nice; follow me."

Ayoub Rashid led Agrin to another room. He pointed to a corner and said, "Go and sit there." He sat himself at the table that had been set for him, then began to eat.

The commander's phone started ringing. "Hello, brother, yes, congratulations on the victory of this operation to you as well, brother. May God help us with bigger victories that we have ahead. I'll see you in war or may God bless us as Shahid in heaven, brother." He hung up his phone.

After he finished eating, the commander grabbed his belt and took Agrin to another room. The bedroom was dark with little light coming from the hall. He threw his belt on the floor and pulled the curtains. "Come closer now," he said, and touched Agrin's hair. He admired her beauty while looking into her eyes. He reached out to take her dress off.

"No, stop, don't touch me!" Agrin said, pushing him back.

"If you want to disobey, let me warn you, I hate seeing a woman defy her master."

"Please, I can't do it. I'm begging you to let me go."

"So, this is how you want to be treated," he said, grabbing Agrin's breast and tearing her dress down.

"No-no ... please, I m sorry, I got scared. Please let me take off my dress. I'll do it myself ... please," Agrin pleaded, holding his hands.

The commander released his hands and relaxed a little, stepping back. He undid his uniform and threw it to the ground beside his war belt, allowing himself to enjoy the scene of the beauty he now owned.

Agrin's hands were shaking. She took a step back, with tears stuck in the corners of her eyes, looking at the man whom it was impossible for her to defeat. She reached for the strap of her dress and undid it. She lifted the dress over her head and, not sure what to do next, threw it on the ground at her feet.

"Will you look at that flawless body and that hair! It's no doubt that God knows how to reward his Mujahideen," the commander said, with pleasure. He could not bear it any longer and went to Agrin.

Agrin started pushing him back and resisting, but the commander shrugged. He grabbed Agrin and threw her to the ground. Agrin crawled backwards, but he grabbed her legs and stopped her by sitting on her legs. He tore off Agrin's singlet, then fell on her body to end one of his best days in the war with joyful reward from his God.

Agrin had no strength left to resist him. Despite Agrin's cries, the commander was overwhelmed with joy and could not see or hear anything else. He turned his head towards Agrin's breasts.

But Agrin reached out for the piece of sharp glass still hidden in her dress on the floor. Using all her strength and the hatred she was feeling, Agrin plunged the sharp piece of glass into the commander's left eye. With a howling cry, he tried to push her away.

Agrin shouted as well and stabbed the glass harder into his eye.

Commander Ayoub Rashid screamed, "Aaaghhh … get away from me!" He tried to push Agrin away as he cradled his eye with his hands and crawled backwards.

Agrin rushed for the dagger in his belt and plunged the blade with all her might into the commander's heart.

He pulled back, looking at her. Blood oozed from the corner of his lips, then after a few seconds, the commander fell to the ground.

Agrin let go of the dagger and sat back on her knees, staring at the glass in his eye, the wound on his face that Delovan had stabbed with his knife, and his other open shocked eye. She stared at the dagger she had stuck in his heart.

After a few moments, the trembling of her hands subsided, her breathing calmed down, and she picked up her clothes, still looking at him. She put on her clothes and tied the front of her torn dress across her chest tightly. She touched her wedding ring, which she had hidden in her dress next to the piece of glass. She took it out and put it back on her finger, and tied up her hair. She looked inside his belt and found a gun, two grenades and Delovan's small handmade knife. She fastened the belt around her waist and went to leave the room.

Agrin stood at the door for a moment and looked back at the commander's body and his hands; at the same time she was re-living the memory of the moment the bullet had hit Delovan's head. The bloody face of Delovan was etched into her eyes. She returned to the commander's body, bent down and pulled the dagger out of his heart, then put it in her belt and left the room.

Agrin turned off the hallway lamp, then walked into the other rooms of the house, looking out the windows. One of the windows led to the backyard, which was secluded and dark. She went to the kitchen, opened the refrigerator, took some food, filled the water bottle with water and put it inside the belt.

She climbed out of the window and hid in the dark. She ran to the mountain along the road so that she wouldn't get lost. When she was far enough away, she stopped and took a deep breath and drank some water. The village lights were still visible in the distance. She stood and looked at the village for some time, then, sighing deeply, kept walking.

After a few hours traipsing across the darkened countryside, Agrin became confused and stopped. She didn't know where to go next and her legs were tired and weak. She sat next to a rock and drank more water, touching her cut head gently. Her blood had dried, but it was still so painful and kept making her dizzy. Walking any further wasn't possible because she couldn't see the way ahead, so she sat for a few minutes to rest. However, her body and soul were more tired than she realised, and her eyes grew heavy and, gradually, sleep overcame her.

5

Agrin opened her eyes to the rising sun. She had slept for longer than she had wanted and quickly got to her feet. She looked everywhere to make sure no one was around and that it was safe for her to leave.

By about noon, Agrin was facing a high mountain behind some smaller hills. She walked to the highest hill to get a better view of her surroundings. When she reached the top of the mountain, she heard the cracks of gunshots and a few bullets whizzed by her. Without looking back, she ran and hid behind a rock. She looked back and saw that three men were running towards her.

Agrin was terrified and started running for the other side of the mountain, but saw the other side of the hill was downhill, and there was a long distance to the other peak. There were a few small hills between her and her attackers, which offered no protection from their bullets. She turned back to the mountain and was looking for a place to hide among the rocks when she heard the voice of one of them.

"She should be nearby. Come on, hurry up!"

Agrin hid herself underneath a large rock. She could hear them running to the other side of the mountain.

Another man panted, "I can't see her; she's not on this side."

"Yasir, don't just stand there – run down the mountain! She might lie down somewhere. We have to find her, there is no way I am going to leave till we get her, so keep looking."

"Why are you so desperate to have her, Zubair?" a third voice asked. "We shouldn't have come this far – they ordered us not to. She is a dangerous woman. She killed Ayoub Rashid, for God's sake. Even we were scared to look into his bloodied eyes. She's already wounded your face with a piece of brick. Now she has his weapon. You know if we get killed by her, we might never go to heaven."

"Oh, shut up, Abu Ubaideh," Zubair hissed. "She is a woman. Just a woman, okay? Now go and look around the mountain again. And remember, don't kill her; I want her alive."

From her hiding spot, Agrin could hear feet running in different directions.

After a while, the voices returned. "I couldn't find her," Yasir's voice spluttered, as he caught his breath. "There is no sign of her down there."

"She must've hidden here somewhere," Zubair said.

Zubair's voice was so close that Agrin realised he must be standing on top of the large rock she was hiding under. Fortunately, she'd had enough time to push aside the soft soil underneath the rock, burrow further under, and then pull the soil back over herself. Agrin had also taken two grenades from the commander's belt. She now had one beside her face and the other she held with a finger ready to pull the pin. The grenades were her guarantors.

"Well, I'm going after Abu Ubaideh," Zubair's said. "You keep looking as well, but be careful."

"Okay, let me catch my breath, then," Yasir said. He went to sit down just a few metres below the rock under which Agrin was hiding. She was able to watch him take a thermos from his belt and drink.

Agrin took out the pin from the grenade in her hand and held its lever in place. She stretched her hand out from her burrow, exposing her forearm, then waited for Yasir to make a noise so that he would not hear the grenade being thrown.

A moment later, he stretched his legs and lay down.

Agrin tossed the grenade downhill towards him. It rolled close to Yasir, but a small, dry bush stopped the grenade from reaching him. She clawed more soil back for cover and braced herself.

Yasir noticed the noise behind him, stood up and looked around. But the grenade's blast did not give him any further opportunity to find Agrin. Shrapnel bloodied his body as he slumped to ground.

Fragments from the explosion landed in front of Agrin, but she remained under the rock, silent and still. She could hear the other men running back towards her hiding spot. The other two men came into view below the rock with their weapons drawn.

Zubair used his rifle to prod Yasir's blood-soaked and blackened body. "Ah, stupid man!" Zubair cried. "I told him to be careful. Come on, we have to find that witch."

"Zubair, don't be crazy. Let's go back," Abu Ubaideh protested, as he looked around. "I do not want to be killed by a woman."

"No way, I have to find her. I'll never let a woman play with me like this and get away with our blood on her hands. Now stop being an embarrassment and search."

Zubair disappeared first down the mountain. Agrin could hear him calling out, "Where are you, witch? Show yourself!"

Agrin remained motionless and silent. Moments later, she heard two gunshots, followed by an agonising scream. The sound of running came closer. She heard Zubair cursing Abu Ubaideh. It wasn't long before Zubair re-appeared below Agrin's hiding place.

Zubair was looking around in fear, then began shooting at almost every rock near Agrin. No doubt he had now guessed she might be hiding among them. "Hey, come out, show yourself!" he shouted. "I should have thrown you away like your stupid baby! Come on, are you scared? You worthless creature ..."

Agrin heard Zubair's footsteps as he clambered back on top of her rock. He had stopped hurling insults, but she could hear his heavy breathing. She closed her eyes and held her breath for as long as she could. The sounds of his footsteps faded away.

Agrin opened her eyes and let out a sigh of relief.

Suddenly, a hand somehow grabbed one of her legs. "Aha ...! Got you, you witch! You might get help from the devil, but I have help from God. Come out ..." Zubair began dragging Agrin out.

The second grenade fell from Agrin's hand before she could pull its pin. She tried to grab it but couldn't reach. She started screaming and kicked Zubair's hands with her other foot and clung to the rocks. She tried to pull out her dagger, but the blade was stuck. She reached for a stone and hit Zubair on the chest. "Let me go! Get lost!"

Zubair dropped her leg and reached for his weapon.

Agrin was able to draw her dagger.

Zubair aimed his gun at her and yelled, "Don't move! Drop the dagger! I will never be killed by a worthless woman."

Agrin stayed on her knees, saying nothing.

"I don't want to kill you," Zubair said, "not until after I tear that dress off you and hear you screaming in pain to add to my joy."

Agrin was looking at him, clenching the dagger in her hand. "But I won't take that risk."

"No doubt your dead body will serve me with the same joy," Zubair said, waving the muzzle of his gun in her face. "Now, you tell me where to aim and shoot you so that nothing detracts from your beauty, huh? The middle of your eyes? Or perhaps your heart." He pointed his rifle at her head and Agrin closed her eyes.

The sound of gunfire shocked Agrin. She opened her eyes to see Zubair crumple to his knees and his weapon fall to the ground. He was puzzled as to who had shot him and where the bullet had come from. He touched his bloody chest, looking at his bloody hand and then looked backed at Agrin.

Agrin took the opportunity to grasp the dagger even tighter, then launch herself at Zubair and plunged the blade into his heart, twisting it as hard as she could. Zubair fell to the ground. Agrin pulled her dagger out and wiped the blood on the grass.

Agrin stood up as she put the dagger back in her belt. She saw a man running towards her with his gun aimed at her.

He shouted, "Don't move! Stay still, until I get close or I will shoot you."

Agrin held her hands up, realising the man was speaking Kurdish. She called back, "Help me, please ..."

When the man reached Agrin, he quickly checked Zubair's body to make sure he was dead, then turned back to her. "Are you okay? What are you doing here alone? Did they hurt you?"

"They came after me. They attacked our village, killed all the men. They have captured so many women and kids. I ran away to find help. Come on, we have to hurry, our village is not far."

"We can't," the man said, as he turned back to Zubair to search for any valuable weapons on his body.

Agrin was shocked. "But they are ripping them apart and killing them. We have to hurry."

"I know!" the man yelled.

"You know? Why didn't you come to help us? Why didn't anyone come for us?"

The man did not answer at first. He unbuckled the belt from Zubair's body. He put the belt on the ground and began going through it. "Hurry up, help me. We need to collect useful things. We must go before they come."

Agrin was confused and asked, "Where? Aren't you coming to help my village?"

The man stood for a moment, then said to Agrin, "Look, they have attacked everywhere; they attacked our village as well. I can do nothing right now. They might be on their way here right now, if they have heard us. So hurry up, help me out!"

"Who are these people? Why do they attack us? Why has nobody stopped them?"

"I do not know, woman," he said. "Now enough crying and start helping me, this is not the time. Come on – now!"

Agrin started to help him choose everything they might need.

"We are going to those mountains," he said, pointing into the distance. "That hill is safer. But you can see from here that the road is open and therefore dangerous, so you have to be careful and concentrate. Anytime I ask you to lie on the the ground, you do it right away, okay?"

"Okay," Agrin said.

"Good, let's go. I'm running out of time."

They walked down to the roadside. He said, "Wait here, let me check the road." Once he was sure he could hear no cars or other worrying sounds, they started walking again.

They hadn't gone more than a few metres when they heard the sound of a car coming towards them along the road. "Lay down," the man whispered. "Don't move, so the dust doesn't rise, or they will notice."

Agrin lay motionless next to him.

Three cars crossed the road a short distance apart. They waited until they could no longer hear the cars.

Agrin wanted to get up, but the man put his hand on Agrin's back and pushed her to the ground. "Wait, don't rush."

Soon, they could hear the sound of several more cars approaching.

They waited in silence on the ground for what seemed like ages after the cars had driven by. Finally, the man took his hand off Agrin's back and said, "Let's go now."

6

Agrin and the mysterious man reached the foot of the mountain. "Okay, it's getting dark," he said, "and we are close, but there is still around half an hour left to travel."

Agrin nodded, glad to catch her breath.

He strode over to some rocks and pushed them aside, before using his feet to clear away some soil and expose a circular door. He lifted the door to reveal a deep hole. He turned to Agrin. "I dug this hole. It's the only safe place around here that you can hide. My village is right behind this mountain. I have to go there. You hide in this hole until I return."

"What? I'll not go in there," Agrin said. "I'll come to the village with you." She stepped back from the hole.

"No, it's dangerous. This morning the village was full of enemy soldiers; they may still be there."

"Then why are you going? At least wait until it's dark, then go."

"I can't wait that long," he said. "You are wasting time – get in there, please."

"No, I'm not going in there," Agrin said firmly. "I will hide some-where around here."

The man grabbed her arm and pushed Agrin down the hole.

"Get in there. If they catch me, the first thing they will do is search around here." He stood over the hole, waiting to see if she would stay put.

Agrin was terrified and wanted to leap out of the hole.

"Stay … don't make me …" he growled, as he pushed down on Agrin's shoulder. "I'd rather kill you than have you in their hands."

Reluctantly, Agrin sat down.

"Here, have this gun," he said, handing Agrin a pistol. He released the safety switch on the gun. "Look … like this, it will shoot." Then he put the safety switch back on. Then he pointed at Agrin's belt. "You have your dagger and grenade. Have this water as well," he said, handing her a small canteen. "I will be back soon."

After these gestures, Agrin, was reassured that the man did not intend to hurt her. She had to trust him and wait in the hole, like he said.

"Listen to me. If, by any chance, I don't return, you wait until it's dark. Then go up this mountain. You'll find a large dry tree with some bushes around its base. Pull the biggest dry bush aside, and you'll see there is a door behind, which you can enter, okay?"

"Why? What is in there?" Agrin asked.

The man paused for a second, then continued, "Promise me that you will do that, please."

"Okay, I promise," Agrin said.

The man put the lid back and covered it with dirt. He made sure that it was covered well before he stood up and asked, "What is your name?"

"Agrin."

He tapped on one side of the lid. "Agrin, when you want to come out, push this side of the door up. I haven't put the rock on this side, okay?"

"Okay."

"My name is Mevan," he said. "I will be back soon."

Agrin heard his footsteps running away.

She gathered herself together with thoughts of her little daughter and her husband, remembering their laughter. The happy moments were so clear that she almost believed they were there with her. But out of nowhere, the bitter moments of their deaths and their lifeless bodies came rushing back to her, darkening all the lights inside her. The stone cold-hearted world had taken the soul of her life and left her a dead, meaningless life with cruel memories.

"Ahhh, what if I open my eyes and see everything has been nothing but a nightmare?" she asked aloud, as she hugged herself in pain, wishing for sleep in her husband's arms, and to wake to the sound of her daughter laughing, playing, with sunlight on her face. The more she dug in, the more the bitterness of the truth tormented her as she realised that she would never see those days again. She felt her love for her family and others who were gone … including those far away – like her parents. Disturbing thoughts were running through her mind one after another, making her breathing heavy, scratchy and scared.

"Maybe they have attacked the city," she muttered to herself. "I wonder whether they have captured or killed them – my mother, my father, my brothers … something must have happened to them, otherwise, they would have come for me. What about Delovan's parents? His sisters, his brother? What if they are all dead? Oh, no, no … please, no …" She held her head and cried, taking Evin's dummy from her clothes and kissing it, putting it on her cheek, and sobbing.

A while later, Agrin heard footsteps coming towards her hole. She became as silent as she could. She grew more and more alarmed as the sound of footsteps came closer and closer, then stopped at the top of the hole. Agrin held her pistol ready for action.

"Agrin, it's me, Mevan. Don't be afraid." He pushed the dirt and stones aside and pulled up the door to help her out.

Agrin couldn't see Mevan clearly in the dark, but could make out that he was carrying a small bucket in his hand. She did not know how long she had been in the hole.

"Come on, hurry, let's get you up the hill," said Mevan.

Together they ran up the hill as quietly as they could. When they reached the withered trunk of a large tree, Mevan put the bucket and a bag on the ground. At the base of the tree were thorn bushes. Mevan pushed the biggest bush to one side to reveal a small door across a hollow in the base of the tree's trunk. Inside was a narrow tunnel that appeared to go deep into the ground.

Mevan turned to Agrin and said, "Go inside."

Agrin paused for a moment.

"Hurry," he said.

Very carefully, Agrin eased her way in. Mevan followed her with all the things he had collected. He pulled the door, to which he had tied the dry bush, to re-seal the entrance, then fastened the door from the inside with a rope.

Agrin crawled on her hands and knees to reach the end of the tunnel, which opened into a small room dimly lit by a small lamp connected to a battery. There was a powerful odour that made her feel sick. She heard the faint cry of a child. She looked around but saw nothing.

Mevan came up next to her and Agrin moved aside. Mevan pulled a baby from under a blanket and hugged him. "Breathe, my son, I brought you milk," he said, in a trembling voice. He put the baby on his knees and opened the bucket, poured it into the baby's bottle and gave it to the baby. He said, "Eat, my son. Drink some milk, sweetheart."

Agrin, who was astonished and confused, looked at Mevan. Without saying a word, she walked backwards, step by step, until she reached the wall and sat down on the ground. She was looking at Mevan, who was trying to feed the baby.

No matter how hard Mevan tried, his son would not take the bottle of milk. Instead, the baby would push away the bottle and continue to cry.

"Why don't you eat? Drink some milk," Mevan said.

The baby still refused to drink the milk and kept crying.

Mevan stood up as best he could in the small room, then put the bottle in the baby's mouth while rocking him in his arms. He looked at Agrin and his eyes pleaded for her to help, but Agrin looked away in tears.

"Can you calm him down?" Mevan asked softly. "Agid, my son is not more than three months. He hasn't eaten for a long time and I don't know how to feed him."

Agrin shook her head. "No." Her hands were shaking and she was weeping.

Mevan moved over to the other side of the room, trying to calm the baby by walking and rocking him. He felt disappointed and helpless. He shifted to where a blanket was on the ground, which he pulled aside to reveal the body of a young woman.

Agrin didn't know what was going on. Who was that woman and how did she die? She sat on her knees to see better.

Mevan removed the woman's beautiful hair from her face and laid Agid on her chest. "Come on, my son, you are with your mother now. Have some milk in her arms, please. I don't want to lose you as well, baby." Mevan tried to feed him, but again it didn't work. He placed the baby on the mother's chest, turned away, and held his head with his hands.

When Agrin saw the baby holding his head up and looking for his mother's breasts, she felt drops of milk seep through her torn clothes. She sat next to the woman's head, looking at her face and bloody hands. She picked up the baby and laid him on her lap. She opened her clothes and took Evin's dummy out from between her breasts. Agrin held it out to the baby in an attempt to attract him to drink from her own breast.

Finally, the baby grabbed Agrin's breast with his little hands and started drinking. She remembered her daughter as soon as she felt the baby's little hand on her breasts and his tiny sharp nails in her skin. She started touching the baby's hair, rubbing her finger on his soft, cold cheeks.

When Mevan heard drinking, he raised his head and turned to Agrin. "Did he accept the bottle?" He went to look, but once he saw that Agrin was breastfeeding, Mevan stepped back and sat down in silence.

He wondered what terrible thing must have happened to Agrin, but did not allow himself to question her. He knew he should not dare to ask for the answer from a mother feeding his son in tears without her own baby. His baby was in her arms drinking, and he was grateful for the luck that his son had. Mevan picked up a small blanket in the corner and put it over Agrin's shoulders to make her comfortable and warm. "I cannot ever thank you enough," he said gently.

Agrin wiped her tears and nodded.

After the baby was full, Agrin tied her clothes back together again, then laid the baby over her shoulders and tapped his back slowly until he burped. Then she laid the baby on the blanket and started taking off his clothes to check if she needed to change him.

Agrin saw a beautiful handmade pearl necklace placed on the baby's tummy.

Mevan noticed and shifted forward.

Agrin saw Mevan's eyes fill with tears and put the necklace in his hands.

"Thank you, Agrin," he said, as he put the necklace in his pocket. "Let me get you my son's bag." He passed her a blue bag. "Here, it is all his stuff. I'm not sure if it's all he needs."

She looked through the bag. "There is enough." She cleaned the baby, put some clean clothes on him, then picked him up and hugged him and started to rock him.

Mevan watched until his son closed his eyes after all the hardships his little body had been through.

"Agrin, the top of your shoulder is injured," Mevan said, "and I can see a piece of stone still in it."

Agrin looked at her shoulder. She realised it was hurting, but had ignored the pain, not knowing how bad it was. "I don't remember when this happened," Agrin said, as she tried to cover it.

"I think it's from when that bastard dragged you out and across the ground today," Mevan said. "I saw that happen, but it took me some time to shoot him without putting you at risk."

"Thank you," Agrin said humbly.

"I do have some stuff here," Mevan said. "Let me take care of it before it gets worse; it's starting to bleed again." He grabbed his small backpack, sat next to Agrin, and continued, "Let me make a place to put Agid down." Mevan did this quickly, then, from his bag, he took some supplies and cleaned the area around Agrin's wound.

Agrin was quiet but so uncomfortable and scared.

He could see this and said, "Don't worry, I know how to take care of it. Now I can see the stone. It's not that deep; I will try to pull it out. If the pain is too much, let me know and I'll stop."

"Okay," Agrin said, nodding her head.

"Okay, here we go." Mevan began extracting the piece of stone. "The stone is almost out … one more a second … here, it's out." Mevan put the piece of stone on the ground in front of Agrin. He staunched the bleeding and patched the wound well with one of Agid's small fabrics. "It's finished now," Mevan said, as he cleaned the blood off his hands.

"Thank you," Agrin said.

"Are you okay?" he asked.

"Yes."

Mevan moved back to the slumped figure of his wife, looking at her with sadness. He took a small shovel and an axe, then dug in a few places until he found an almost soft spot. He started digging, then after he had dug enough, he went back to sit next to his wife and looked at her tearfully.

"I'm so sorry," Agrin said.

Mevan could only nod his head in reply.

Agrin picked up the baby and went to the other side of the cave, so that Mevan could have his time to mourn.

Mevan sat next to his wife, looking at her, touching her beautiful blonde hair. He started taking off her dress and put it aside.

Agrin could not take her eyes off the poor wounded dead woman, her injured and bruised body, her bloodied hands. Mevan picked up a handkerchief, then opened a small water container and filled a bowl with water. He soaked it and wiped his wife's beautiful face, with his own face distorted by a broken heart and tears. He put the handkerchief in the water again, cleaned her chest and shoulders, all the while he seemed to be imagining how much pain she had gone through. He washed her hands with the water. He picked up the sheet and spread it on the ground, hugged his wife and laid her on the sheet. He arranged her hair and divided it into two parts, placing it over her chest. He kissed her hands and crossed them, wrapping the sheets around her, covering her body but leaving her face exposed. He hugged her and carried her to the grave.

Near the grave, Mevan's legs weakened as he looked into his wife's face and couldn't put her in the grave. He sat back on the grave and hugged his wife again, put his head under her neck, then broke down in painful and angry tears.

Agrin cried as she watched him suffering from the pain — she knew how it burned inside.

After a while, Mevan put his wife in the grave and covered her beautiful face. She seemed to have finally fallen into a deep sleep after enduring such terrible hardships. As he poured fists full of dirt onto his love in the grave, Mevan's flickering eyes seemed to be recalling the story that had befallen him and his family.

7

That day he had been in another town for business and, as soon as he heard the news of the attack, he jumped in his car and drove towards home. On the way, people tried to stop him by shouting: "Don't go – they are everywhere!", "They'll kill you!" and "They have captured half the city and are killing everyone!" Thinking about all this news, Mevan knew he wouldn't get anywhere by car. If he took a risk and drove, his chances of success were slim. He changed his plan and, instead, began to make his way to his village by running through the mountains.

After a long time running up and down the mountains, Mevan became exhausted. But every time he thought of his wife, son, and family, he wondered what they were doing now and would be re-energised to run at full speed.

After nightfall, he reached his village. He saw the cars and armed troops. As he was unarmed, Mevan ran back to a hiding place he had made for other reasons on a nearby mountain. He picked up some of the weapons he had hidden there. He strapped his gun over his back, grabbed his knife and placed it in his waistband, then rushed out of his hiding place, running down to his village.

Mevan hid behind one of the houses, which was a little further away from the others. After checking to make sure no one was around, he climbed to the roof and lay on its edge, looking at the roads and his surroundings.

He saw a number of the attackers getting into cars and leaving the village. There was no sign of the villagers or women and children. He waited for a while, and almost all of the attackers left the village. But a few of their cars remained.

Mevan jumped down from the roof, then started sprinting to his parent's house along darkened pathways behind the lights of houses. He passed behind the home of one of his neighbours and stopped when he heard the voices of several men.

Mevan hid in the darkness and could hear the cries and screams of women. He looked round the wall of the house and saw two men forcing two women inside. One of the women resisted and slapped a man, punching him on the chest, shouting, "Let me go — you're disgusting! I won't go in!"

"Shut up, you worthless creature," the man growled. "You are in our service now — our slaves. If you disobey me one more time, I will cut your head off." He slapped the woman and threw her into the house, following her in. The other man pushed the second woman inside and shut the door behind them.

Mevan was filled with rage. "I will tear you to pieces, you disgusting worms," he mumbled, as he crept towards the front of the house. He was about to go into the yard, when he heard the voices of several other men coming towards him. He slipped back into the dark to hide.

Another six men bundled another three women into the yard of the house next door. Three of them went inside with the women, while the others stayed in the yard.

When Mevan heard those women screaming for help, he wanted to break into the house and fight their attackers, not caring what would happen afterwards. But he stopped himself and worked hard to overcome his emotions. He knew that he really had no chance of saving those women. He knew he had better act logically, but he was so full of hatred that tears flowed from his eyes. He took a few breaths, took a step back towards his house. But he was so angry, as he thought of those women, that he couldn't move forward. He had to stand for a few seconds to regain his composure.

Mevan became more and more worried about his family and started running to his house. He reached his father's house and looked in through the windows. No one was inside. He went to a corner at the back of the house to enter his yard. From there, he could see a light was on inside the house.

Mevan hid and waited. A short time later, he saw a man coming out of the house, rearranging his clothes. The man shouted over his shoulder, "Abu Tale, I will go to the others when you have finished, and if no one else comes for her, bring the woman back with you, okay?" He slung his weapon behind him and started walking away.

Mevan aimed his gun at the man's head, put his finger on the trigger, and was about to shoot, when he heard his son crying and his wife screaming from inside. He removed his finger from the trigger, to remove the temptation to shoot, and remained motionless until the man walked away. Mevan walked around the house and stood outside a window. He could see his son crying alone on the floor in the hallway.

Mevan heard his wife scream, and he rushed behind the house, opened the kitchen window and climbed in. He grabbed a large knife from the dish basket and walked through the passage to his bedroom. The door was half-open, and he stood behind the door and looked in from the side.

The scene in front of his eyes made Mevan furious. He lunged at the aggressor and stabbed him in the neck with all his might. This single blow was enough to kill the man. Mevan kicked his dead body off the bed, then threw him against the wall. He pounced on the body, stabbing it until he was out of breath. All that remained on the floor was a bloody piece of pulverised meat.

Mevan turned back to his wife and untied her hands while he caught his breath.

"Where have you been, Mevan, where have …?" his wife cried, tears pouring down her cheeks.

"Shush, don't cry, Henan," he said, as he helped her up. "It's over, I'm here now."

"We lost everything, Mevan, everything," Henan cried.

"Shhh, calm down, I said." He went to the hall, turned off the light, and looked out the window to ensure no one was coming. "Hurry up, now," he whispered as he picked up Agid and went back to Henan.

Henan couldn't walk. Mevan took a sheet and wrapped it around his wife. With Agid in his arms, Mevan found his son's bag and stuffed in some essential items as well as clothes for Henan. He went over to the man's body, then picked up his gun and other valuable items.

Mevan went back to Henan and took her by the hand. "Let's go — we can climb out the kitchen window." They went into the kitchen. "You'll have to calm Agid," Mevan whispered, "or they'll hear us. We can't leave the house while he is crying."

Henan whispered back, "I'll breastfeed him." The baby calmed as Henan breastfed him.

Mevan climbed out of the window and looked around everywhere. When he saw no one, he helped Henan and Agid through the window, then closed it.

"Where are we going?" Henan asked

"To our hiding place."

"Okay." Henan followed him.

They hadn't walked far before Henan stopped. Mevan turned around and asked, "What's happened? Why have you stopped?"

"I can't go on," Henan replied.

"Okay, you sit here," Mevan said. "I will get Agid up there, and I'll come back for you." He took his son and ran up the mountain.

After a short time, Mevan came back and sat down in front of Henan. "Okay, now, sweetheart," he said, panting as he bent down, "come on my back and hold me tight." Henan climbed onto Mevan's back and held on tight, as they trudged up the mountain.

At the base of the large tree, he put her down and helped her enter the hiding place where Agid was already tucked away. Mevan returned to the entrance of the tunnel and looked about to ensure no one had seen them. He brushed the dirt around the base of the tree to hide their footprints, then pulled the dry bush and door back into position.

Henan sat in the small room at the end of the tunnel. She was hugging her son and crying as she breastfed him.

Mevan threw the bag to the ground, then, with all his might, he let out a shout fuelled by the intensity of his anger and rage. He threw his weapon around, which scared Agid, who stopped holding his mother's breast and cried. Henan was also frightened at seeing

Mevan behave this way. She didn't dare look at his eyes.

Mevan felt destroyed. But when he saw his son was crying and realised he had frightened his wife, Mevan suppressed his anger and became quiet. He sat on the ground and lowered his head.

A long time passed without any words or looks between them. Mevan finally turned to his wife, sitting with all her pain and staring at Agid sleeping in her arms.

He went and sat beside her, then gently took Agid from her arms and put him in a corner on a small blanket. He returned to Henan and gently tried to pull back the sheet wrapped around her to check her injuries.

Henan held the sheet tighter and begged him, "Please don't do that. I don't want you to see me, I'm begging you."

But Mevan didn't listen and pulled the sheet away and saw her whole body was black and red due to a beating and rape. Her mouth was bloody and the corner of one eye was swollen. There were bruises and red marks from handcuffs and rope on her weak, thin wrists. When Mevan saw what had been done to his wife, his breath quickened with rage and tears streamed down his cheeks, his hands tightening into fists.

Henan was frightened and worried as she looked at her husband, because she didn't know whether he was going to beat or kill her, or if he would hug her with sadness and a broken heart. She had never seen him like this.

While Henan's aching and wounded hands were shaking with fear and cold, Mevan picked up the sheet again and wrapped it around her.

When Mevan realised how afraid Henan was, he came to his

senses and looked into his wife's eyes, wiping away her tears. "Let me help you put on your clothes," he said calmly.

"No, you go to Agid, I can dress myself," Henan said.

Mevan didn't say anything and went to pick up her dress.

"Please, Mevan, let me dress myself, I'm begging you," Henan said, trying to pull the dress out of Mevan's hands.

Mevan was in tears. "Henan, please stop it. Why are you covering yourself from me? You are tormenting me more by doing this. Stop it and let go of the dress, now."

"Okay," Henan said, pulling her hands back.

"No, no, don't cry please, don't be afraid," Mevan said, as he wiped her tears. "I didn't mean to raise my voice." He went and grabbed a handkerchief, then washed it out. He sat next to Henan, cleaned her face and hands, then sat behind her to gather his wife's beautiful hair and braid it as he did for her every morning.

Mevan then sat in front of his wife and took off his jacket. He handed it to her, saying, "Come, wear this. It's cold."

Henan put on the jacket, then Mevan made a comfortable place and carried her there. "Thank you," she said quietly.

"Here, drink some water," Mevan said, offering her a cup.

"No, I am not thirsty."

"Please drink some anyway," Mevan said. "You need it; your lips are dry."

"Okay, I will, but you have some first."

"Take it, Henan, don't argue with me, please. Come and have a sip."

But Henan refused again and didn't take the cup, as tears poured down her face.

Mevan took a sip, then said, "Come, take it now, please."

Henan nodded and drank the water.

Mevan put some food next to her and said, "You have some food and rest; I'll go back to the village, after the others."

"No, don't go," Henan said anxiously. 'It's too dangerous there."

Mevan ignored her protest and asked, "Do you know where the men were taken, or in whose house they have been kept? If I go and find a way to free them first, then together we can take care of the enemy easily."

Henan didn't say anything.

As he was preparing himself to leave, Mevan pleaded with her, "Henan, tell me everything you saw. Whatever comes to your mind could help me to find the men."

"There are no men left in the village," she sobbed, "they killed them all."

"What? What did you say?" Mevan exclaimed. "For God's sake, please stop crying and tell me what the hell happened."

"After they bombed the village, people came out of their houses to escape, but soldiers surrounded the village and captured everyone. The elders tried to talk to them and told them that we had never harmed anyone. They told the soldiers to take everything in the village, to take everything we own, but not to kill anyone. But the soldiers didn't listen; they killed all the men, even little boys." Henan pulled the sheet back over her head, crying.

Mevan was shocked. He fell on his knees and stayed speechless.

After a long silence, Agid began to cry and Henan took the sheet off her head. She picked up her son and started feeding him, looking at Mevan.

"Do you need anything, Henan?" Mevan asked.

Henan looked down at Agid.

"Come on, tell me – what?" Mevan said. "Do you want some water? Or food?"

"No."

"Then, what is it?"

"I want you to kill me," Henan said.

"Kill you?" Mevan cried, falling to his knees next to her. "Why? What are you saying?"

"I'm in a lot of pain," she replied. "I can't take it, I don't want to live or even breathe. I hate myself, I feel disgusting about myself, I want to peel my skin off so that I won't feel it any more."

"No-no, don't talk like this, Henan. Stop scratching your skin." He took her hands and held them in his.

"I will never be the same Henan again, Mevan. I am devastated. I can't even look into your eyes I'm so ashamed. If you still love me, then don't let me suffer. Pleeease, Mevan."

"Henaaaaaan – don't! Enough." Mevan let her hands go and turned his face away.

"Please, It will take you a second to end my suffering, then take Agid out of here. Without me, you can do something for him – save him."

"How can you ask me that? How can you even think to give up on us like this? I don't want to look at you right now." Mevan couldn't look at her as tears fell from his eyes.

"You are a selfish man. How can you see me like this and do nothing about it? I'm ugly, disgusting, I can't live this shameful life. I have already died inside. I'm finished, burned out. I'm begging you, Mevan!"

He tried to ignore her.

"Mevan, Mevan ... I'm talking to you. Look at me." She reached for his gun in his waistband.

"No, stop, stooop, Henan," he cried, as he swatted her hand away. "Come to your senses, woman. I hate to see you this weak. Stop this madness and be silent for a moment." Mevan moved back next to her. He took a deep breath and looked back at his wife. He reached for his gun and knife, then put them well away from her. "Give me Agid, please."

Henan reluctantly handed him their baby.

Mevan placed Agid on the blanket next to Henan, then held her face in his hands. "Listen, sweetheart, if there's any shame and humiliation, it's on me, not you. I'm the one who failed and couldn't take care of you — my family. I swear to God I'm not mad at you. If you do start hating me, I understand, and I want to hear that. I deserve it, but don't beat yourself." He wiped his wife's tears as he continued, "None of this is your fault. It's all mine, and it's hurting me more seeing you afraid of me, pulling yourself away from me."

Henan was looking into her husband's eyes and listening tearfully.

"Here, hold Agid, feed him," Mevan said, as he took a blanket and put it over Henan's legs. He sat next to her and held her in his arms.

Henan put her head on Mevan's chest and sighed deeply.

"Don't cry now, sweetheart. I promise you, I'll get us out of here and make things right. Trust me and leave everything to me." Mevan touched her cheeks and kissed her head.

After a while, Mevan saw Henan had calmed down. He reached for Agid's bag and put it under Henan's head. "Darling, you try to sleep as well, while Agid is sleeping, and I will be sitting here next to you. I need to think of a way to get us out of here safely."

"Okay," Henan said.

Henan felt intense pain all over her body. She looked down and saw that she was bleeding. She pulled up the blanket to cover herself. She didn't want Mevan to know. She put her head back on the bag next to Agid's head and tried to rest, but every time she closed her eyes, all she saw was their bloody hands, their hateful faces, their greedy gazes, their sweaty, strong smells ... then her husband's face, his wide eyes seeing her in the hands of the man raping her. Over and over again. It became so real and painful to her that she had to open her eyes, wanting to never close them again and see those horrible images. She tried to distract herself by gazing at her son and tapping her fingers lightly on his shoulders.

A few hours passed. Mevan went over to Henan, who was still deep in thought. He sat down next to her and put his hand on her forehead.

Henan raised her head a little and said, "What happened?"

"It's not good suffering in silence," he said. "Your body is so cold and your face is so pale, you must be bleeding."

Henan sat up and looked at her feet. There was blood seeping through the bottom of the blanket. "Don't worry, I'm fine." She pulled the blanket tighter to conceal more blood on her clothes.

"I can't wait here like this," Mevan said. "It is still dark. I'll sneak into the village. Maybe I can find something that can help me to carry you and the baby. Or maybe even find a phone."

"Where is yours?"

"I don't know," Mevan said. "I must have lost it on the way. I can't find it anywhere." He grabbed his belt and fastened it around his waist. He put two guns in it and one at his back. He took down the backpack that he had hung on the wall and strapped it on, ready to leave. "Do not come out of here. There is enough water and food for days. I might be a long time, but I will be back. We will get out of here and I'll take you to the hospital. Okay, darling?"

"Okay," she murmured, "but please be careful."

"I will, darling, don't worry." As he was about to exit through the tunnel, Mevan looked back and saw an expression in Henan's face so strange and profound that it broke his heart and weakened his knees as he went to move forward.

He dropped his gun and bag and turned back to her. He held his wife's face in his hands and wiped the warm tears on her cheek with his finger. "You and Agid are safe here. No one will find you, I promise. And when I get you out of here safely, we will go to the hospital, okay?"

She nodded. "Okay."

"Good. Now, you rest and have some food and water and take care of yourself and the baby."

Henan put her hand on her husband's cheek and ran her fingers through his soft hair. She slid her hand down over his heart and fixed him with her eyes for a long moment before hugging him tightly. "Thank you for everything, Mevan," she whispered, and kissed him. "I love you so much."

"I love you too, sweetheart. Don't cry, please. Before you know it, I'll be back with help."

"I'm sure you will come back, and nothing will happen to you. Don't worry about us, we will be all right."

Mevan tucked the blanket around Henan and looked deeply into her eyes. He kissed her cheeks, then kissed his son's head. "Okay, goodbye for now." He crawled up the tunnel and carefully removed the little door. After making sure no one was around, he climbed out, then re-sealed the entrance and ran down the mountain.

Mevan was close to his village when he heard the voices of several men talking to each other. He hid and remained motionless.

"We looked everywhere and there is no sign of her. We're wasting our time," a man said.

"Yes, he is right, big brother. If she was around, we would hear her baby crying, anyways," said another man.

"I still can't believe that she was able to martyr a man like Abu Taleh."

"I know, right – the man was torn in pieces," said one of them.

"What *martyr*? Are you out of your mind? A slave woman killed him in the bed, that is not a martyr. I doubt he will even go to heaven."

"Be silent!" their leader yelled. "Instead of talking, keep looking for her. Go to the other side of the village and look there as well. I don't care how long it takes, that wild woman needs to be captured and her head must be chopped off. Did you not see how defiant the other women became after they saw the body of Abu Taleh? That woman must be punished in front of their eyes to be a lesson for them. Otherwise, they will follow in her footsteps."

"Yes, brother, they don't have any fear, and they are as dangerous as their men. Weren't you with us to hear the commander give a speech about them?"

"No, what did he say?"

"He said we are so lucky that these people didn't have weapons and haven't trained for war. Otherwise, I would doubt our victory."

"What? He said that! Oh no, no! That is nonsense! I myself could kill hundreds of them without any doubts."

"Yeah, yeah," another man said, "I bet Abu Taleh said the same thing before a woman called Henan turned into his nightmare."

"Hey, I've had enough with you, kid! Which side are you on? Huh ...? Do you feel pity for God's enemies? Those infidels? Come on and say it – spit it out!"

"Hey, hey, brother, calm down. He is fifteen years old – too young to understand the situation like you. We have to be kind and patient with each other."

"That is what I said," another man said. "They didn't fight with us because they were people of peace and they wanted peace, but we forced them to become believers, and so they did. After that, they were one of us, but we killed them, anyway. That wasn't the way that I have been taught."

"Shut up before I cut your head off right here! Who do you think you are, questioning our Holy Book and our leader's order? Repent now, as a real Mujahid never questions, they obey. You hear me? A real believer only follows."

"Yes, brother. He is right – it's the devil making you question. You better go and repent."

They kept talking as they walked away.

Mevan stayed where he was, listening and waiting until he was sure it was safe to move. When all had been quiet for a few minutes, he crept behind a line of houses to reach the roof of a house with one of the best views over the village.

Only moments after Mevan climbed onto the roof, a car arrived and parked in front of a nearby house, which belonged to one of Mevan's uncles. Three men came out of the house to greet the people in the car. A man and several young women and girls, who were not from his village, stepped out of the car. They were warmly greeted by the three men and taken inside the house.

Mevan could hear voices inside, congratulating each other. But it wasn't long before they started saying good night and talking about how tired everyone was.

Mevan climbed down from the roof. There wasn't much time left before the sun would rise. He had to return to Henan soon. He peered through a window of the house on which he had been perched. It was dark and quiet inside. He eased up the window, then stopped to make sure he could hear no more sounds. The place seemed empty, so he crawled through the window.

Clothes and pillows were lying all over the floor. Some of the windows on the other side of the house were broken. Mevan went to the kitchen and opened the refrigerator door. There were some pills and medicine inside, which he put in his backpack, before stuffing in as much food as he could. He shut the fridge and continued to look for something useful like a phone. He searched all over the house, room by room, under blankets and pillows and in cupboards and drawers, but there were no phones anywhere.

Mevan slipped out to the stable, hoping to find a wheelbarrow, but there wasn't one. Dawn was approaching and he had to head back to his hide-out. He filled his pockets with other bits and pieces that might come in handy, then disappeared into the darkness and fled to his mountain.

When he reached the hidden door, Mevan looked around, then squatted to open the entrance to his tunnel. He took off his backpack and placed it in the entrance, climbed in, then smoothed away the footprints in the dirt with his hands. He pulled the thorny bush and door back into place to remove any sign he had been there.

He could hear Agid crying. As quickly as he could, he crawled down the tunnel to the little room. Henan was lying on the floor. Mevan said to Henan in a bright voice, "I went to Uncle Kocher's house and brought you some painkillers and antibiotics from their refrigerator. Here, let me get you some water to swallow them. And when it gets dark again, we will leave. I'll carry you."

Henan did not respond.

"Henan … Henan, did you hear me?" Mevan asked, as he inched closer to her. Agid was in her arms, wrapped in his blanket. Mevan kneeled next to her and whispered, "Henan? Are you sleeping?" He gently picked up Agid, saying, "Hush, my boy, let your mother sleep a little longer … shush … don't cry, son."

As he started rocking his baby, Mevan saw blood on Agid's blanket. He looked over his son and asked, "Where does this blood come from? Are you injured? Henan, wake up! Agid's clothes are all bloody. Henan, come on – wake up, darling! There is something wrong with the baby." He began to shake Henan, but she was limp in his hands. He turned her over and removed the blanket she was under. Then he saw her bloody hand – she had sliced the veins in her wrist. Turning her onto his side, he saw that she had also sliced the veins of her other wrist.

She was gone …

Mevan was so shocked he did not move. He stayed kneeling,

staring at her face, not allowing himself to believe what he could see. His hands felt as cold as hers. One by one, his tears began to fall on Henan's pale face.

He found his voice, "No, no, no, Henan, wake up, please – open your eyes! Henan, get up, I'm begging you, darling, don't leave me." He didn't have to be strong any more; there was no one to be strong for. He put his head on her forehead and held her hands tightly.

Hours passed while he stayed on his knees, holding his love in his arms. "Henan, my beautiful, Henan, didn't I promise you I would take care of you? Oh, Henan, you shouldn't leave me alone. How could you? How can I live without you?" he cried, as he caressed her hair, shedding tears over his forever sleeping love.

Mevan became aware of Agid crying at his side. He let go of Henan and hugged his son, trying to calm him down. "Now, you tell me, huh, what do I do, Henan? What should I do with our baby? He is crying, he needs you." Mevan rocked Agid in his arms. "Henan, he is licking my hand, he is hungry, what in the hell am I supposed to do?" he yelled, then began crying along with his son.

After a little while, Mevan remembered there was a container of milk in his uncle's refrigerator. He put Agid down and went to the tunnel door. The sun was out, but he had no real option but to risk his life to save Agid's.

Mevan slipped back down the tunnel to hug his son again. He picked up Agid and placed him next to Henan's body. Mevan sat back on his heels, looking at his son. "Baba, sweetheart, stay here with your mother. I'll go to get some milk, okay? I will come back." With tears flowing from his eyes, Mevan looked at Henan and said to Agid, "Don't be like your mother, son. Don't leave me alone. Okay,

Baba?" He placed the crying baby in his mother's arms, then threw a blanket over both of them. Mevan crawled back to the tunnel's entrance. He looked out but wasn't sure what time of day it was – he had to be careful.

He closed the tunnel door behind him and ran down the mountain towards his village. As he approached, he could see dust rising from the centre of the village. He took cover wherever he could, until he was close enough to see what was going on.

There were more cars in the village than yesterday and a crowd had gathered in the centre. It wasn't clear if they were coming or going, but Mevan wasn't going to wait around to find out. There was a slim but real chance he could run through the mountains to another village. Perhaps they could help him. He was desperate enough to try.

Staying low, Mevan carefully backed away from his village. When he was sure no one had spotted him, he started running through the mountains towards the next village.

About halfway there, he heard what sounded like an explosion. Then the sounds of gunfire. He thought that it could be Kurdish forces clashing with the enemy. He ran towards the sounds and came across a woman called Agrin.

8

Back inside his hide-out, with Agrin watching on, Mevan had finished burying his wife, but was so engrossed in his memories of her that he sat in silence for a long time. He was struggling to believe he would not be able to see his love any more. Finally, he stood up and placed Henan's white scarf over her grave.

After a while, he picked up Henan's black dress, then gave it to Agrin saying, "Come, please wear this dress, yours is not useable any more."

"Thank you," Agrin said, as she took the dress.

"Please give me the baby."

Agrin silently handed him Agid.

Mevan hugged Agid. He went to the corner and sat down facing the wall.

Agrin waited for a few minutes, then she took off her clothes and put on Henan's dress. "I'm done," she said.

Mevan turned around, picked up some water and food, then put them next to Agrin, saying, "Come, have some water. You must be hungry as well."

Agrin drank some water. "Thank you," she said, and started eating." She saw that Mevan was not eating. "Why don't you eat

83

something, too?"

"I'm okay."

After eating a few bites, she said, "Here, have a little piece."

"I'm not hungry; it's for you and the baby."

But Agrin insisted.

"Okay, thank you," Mevan said, accepting the food. After eating a little, he asked, "Do you have a phone with you?"

"No, I don't. I looked for one in those men's clothes, but couldn't find any."

Mevan shook his head and said, "This is not good; we are wasting time. Let me check outside." He went to the door of the tunnel and lifted it a little and saw daylight. He closed the door again and crawled back to the room. "We can't go out now, it's too risky. Yesterday morning when I went to the village, it was full of enemy soldiers, maybe they are around here, too."

"Do you know who these people are and why they hate us this much?" Agrin asked, looking into his eyes in desperation, hoping for an answer.

"I don't know, but we will find out," he said, in a heavy tone filled with anger. "They have to be paid back."

They waited until dark. "It's the right time now," Mevan said, then prepared himself to leave. "I'll go to check if I can go inside the village to get some water and whatever else I can find. If not, I'll come back, and we will leave anyway."

"What if you get caught, they will kill you. What about your son?"

"I have to go," he replied. "We can't stay here much longer."

"What do we do if something happens to you? I can't take care of your son — I won't accept the responsibility."

"We have to get out of here, but we will need more water and food because I don't know what situation we will come across in the mountains. I have to try my luck." He kissed his son, then handed him back to Agrin and said, "Please take care of him until I come back."

"No, I refuse," Agrin said. "What if you get caught? They have no mercy. If you leave, I'll go too, not stay with your son."

Mevan placed the baby on the blanket. He raised his voice, saying, "Then leave him here until he dies, too. Stop arguing with me, woman. We are in this unwanted war, with people who have no mercy, not even for a three-month-old baby. They have no heart, Agrin, and our people are in their hands. So please …"

Reluctantly, Agrin picked up Agid.

Mevan paused for a moment. He didn't want to make her afraid. He looked at his crying son in Agrin's arms. The last heart-breaking scene of saying goodbye to his wife swam before his eyes. He refocused on Agrin, and said, "I promise I will come back for both of you. God forbid, if anything goes wrong, you will do the right thing. Promise me."

"Okay, I promise," Agrin said. "I'll wait here until you return, but please come back for your son."

"I will." He turned away and carefully left their hide-out.

When Mevan was halfway to his village, he was able to see in the distance the headlights of two cars leaving the village. He moved stealthily towards the village, but when he arrived it seemed empty.

He started walking through the village, but stopped when he heard a woman screaming. He crept towards the sound and, as he got closer, he saw several men laughing and talking. He hid in the darkness between two houses, then dared to steal a glance around the corner.

There were two cars parked in front of his uncle's large house. He crawled over to the house in front of his uncle's. He peered inside to make sure no one was there, then opened a window and slipped inside the house.

No lights were on, but Mevan could see reasonably well because light was streaming in from the front courtyard of his uncle's house. He went to the living-room window, which was facing the courtyard, then opened it a crack so he could better hear anything that might be said. He saw two figures come out of the house with a large sack.

"You go ahead, we will have our dinner and rest a little!" a man shouted.

Another man appeared in the doorway of the house, with a bag in his hand. "Hey, you forgot about these!"

One of the men walked back to the doorway and took the bag. "Hmph," he grunted, then tried to re-assert his authority. "Hassan, when you follow us later, remember to place your own bombs on the main road of the village. Do not waste them, okay? Also, make sure those women can't run away. Tomorrow we must hand them over to the person in charge of the spoils."

The two men walked off with their sack and bag into the night. Hassan, still standing in the doorway, waiting for them to leave, then went inside and closed the door.

Mevan guessed the men were carrying explosives, probably landmines. He crept to another window in the house so he could watch them. Suddenly, the sounds of screaming and crying rang out through the night. He quickly shifted to another window and could see a struggle going on in the doorway of his uncle's house.

A young girl shouted, "Leave me alone, go away, I'm not coming! Let go of my hand. You're disgusting – I hate you!"

Mevan, heartbroken, identified her. It was his own niece, Kany.

A giant man pulled her by the hands, and yelled, "You stupid little girl, let go of the door and come! Otherwise, I will break your hand. Let go, I say!"

"Break it – even kill me! I hate you, you smelly beast!"

Mevan cocked his gun and pointed it at the man's head, ready to shoot.

Hassan came back out to his doorway after hearing Kany's screaming. He called out to the giant man, "Why don't you take one of the other two slaves? One of the women begged me not to take this girl. She says the girl is injured and if she takes any more punishment, she will die." There was no immediate reply, so Hassan continued, "The woman is right – look at her wounded face and body – she was in Shoaib's hands an hour before. Go and take another one, Zahir, leave this one to rest."

"It's none of your business, Hassan, I want this wild one," Zahir snarled. "I don't care about her death." With that, he picked up Kany and carried her under his arms.

"Where are you taking her now?" Hassan asked.

"I'm going into that house over there to teach this little screamer some lessons," he said, laughing.

"Okay, whatever …" Hassan groaned and shook his head. "Finish soon – we have to help the others with the mines."

Mevan moved from his position and pulled out his dagger. He

found a suitable dark place to hide while Zahir was bringing Kany to the house that Mevan was in. He could hear their voices coming closer as they struggled towards the front door.

Kany begged, "Let me go, let me go!"

Mevan readied himself for the right opportunity to fight and free Kany.

The front door was kicked open. Zahir entered the hallway, slung Kany over his shoulder, then kicked the door shut. He snapped at her, "You should obey me and perform your duties, instead of struggling and making me angrier. I'm warning you, child." He dumped Kany on the floor, then started to chuckle as he undid his belt. "Be a good reward for this Mujahid of God. Didn't you become a Muslim of God? How can you not carry out the orders of your religion?"

"Go away and get lost!" Kany shouted. "The first thing you said was a lie. You promised that you would not kill us by believing in your faith, but you killed my whole family — my father. You, with your disgusting face, you beheaded my young brother with your hand." Kany inched backwards across the floor, trying to keep her distance from Zahir.

"Shut up, beware of God's anger," he cried. "He has no mercy on infidels. May God send you to hell by me tonight." Zahir bent down to catch her.

"What God — the one who created you?" Kany shouted. "I'll never be afraid of him, neither you nor death."

"Shut up, I said," he barked, as he made his move. "Hell is made for women like you." He grabbed Kany's arms and shoved her backwards across the floor.

Kany stood up and stepped back again, looking for something to throw at him. "Don't come any closer! Get lost!" She tried to grab a vase, but it was too heavy for her to lift.

Zahir stroked his long, red beard and started chuckling, shaking his head, saying, "You do not even have the power to lift a small vase. So now you will stand in front of me. You have been rude and keep disobeying me. Women are so stupid. If the others couldn't teach you right, then I will teach you a good lesson: to be a good slave for your whole pitiful life."

But as Zahir stepped into to take her, Kany grabbed a fistful of dirt from inside the vase and threw it at his face.

"Ughhh!" Zahir cried, as he frantically tried to brush the dirt from his eyes.

This gave Kany the chance to run away from him into the nearest room. She was shocked but relieved to discover Mevan hiding in the room.

He quickly motioned for her not to look at him and to continue screaming and shouting.

Kany nodded and hurled more insults at Zahir: "You're a disgusting man! You are stupid — a foolish man! I'm not afraid of you, you are a lying thief! God hates you!"

Hearing Kany's words, Zahir became enraged and followed her into the room, while brushing the dirt from his eyes. He growled, "You will regret every moment for the rest of your miserable life."

As soon as Zahir put his first step inside the room, Mevan sprang from his hiding spot and without hesitation thrust his dagger into the man's chest with all his might. Zahir fell to his knees.

Kany sat on the floor crying. She covered her face and sobbed,

"Kill him, Uncle, kill him! He was the one who killed my brother and beheaded your father – he killed them both."

On hearing these words, Mevan grabbed Zahir's collar, drew his sword and plunged it into the Mujahid's body several times.

The man fell to the ground in a bleeding, writhing, choking mess.

Mevan went to his niece, with her torn clothes and half-naked body, her bruised and shaky hands, her wounded forehead and frightened face staring at him in pain. He knelt beside her and said, "He is gone. Do not cry, it's over – I'm here now."

Kany wiped her tears and said, "Uncle Mevan, they are horrible, mean men." She held her arms out to him.

He embraced her. "I know, sweetheart, my poor little girl, I know these monsters." He waited while Kany sobbed some more. "Hush, my baby, hush … you are safe now. You can calm yourself and stop crying."

Kany nodded and started getting to her feet.

Mevan helped her stand up. He unbuttoned his coat, then put it over Kany's shoulders. He asked, "Do you know how many of them are in the village?"

"Four of them and three of us," she replied. "Shirin and Barin are inside the house."

"How many men are with them?"

"One of them is inside that house with the girls, two others went to the village."

"So, three left?" Mevan whispered.

"Yes, Uncle."

Mevan nodded and asked again, "Two women are definitely inside that house, you said?"

"Yes, they took the rest by bus. Your sister Narin and my sister and my mother. They took them all to the city," she said tearfully. "Henan was in the village with us, too. She killed one of them and ran away. They looked for her, but couldn't find her."

Mevan, on hearing Henan's name, frowned and said, "We have no time – they may come back for you at any moment." He locked the door and closed the curtains, then picked up Kany and carried her in his arms to the back window.

She could not climb out, so Mevan had to help her through, then carry her again.

They made it to another house where Mevan opened the window and helped Kany inside. Mevan quickly looked through the house to check no one was there. He crept back to Kany and crouched down next to her. "Now, you go hide somewhere safe," he whispered, "and, whatever happens, do not come out until I call you."

Mevan returned to the nearby house with Zahir's corpse and turned him over. He unwrapped his clothes, took his phone from his pocket, then turned it off and put it in his own pants pocket. He slipped back out the window and crept towards his uncle's house.

Mevan paused to check no one was in the street, then hunched over as he raced across to the brightly lit front yard of his uncle's house. He snuck up and crouched behind the half-open front door. At first he couldn't hear anything going on inside, but then suddenly Mevan could hear a man who sounded like he was on a phone call: "Yes, yes … we are going to put bombs in the whole village tonight, then go to the next village tomorrow."

Mevan glanced around the door, saw no one, then crept inside and quietly closed the door. A key was still in the door, so he locked it. He stepped as silently as he could along a corridor towards the room where the man was on the phone. Mevan looked around the door and saw it was Hassan who was busy talking on the phone, and that he wasn't holding any weapons.

Shirin and Barin were sitting in the corner of the room with their hands tied.

Mevan took his dagger in hand and waited for the right opportunity.

Hassan soon hung up the phone, walked over to the women, stood over them, and said, "How old are you two, ha? You barely look twenty to me. But, then again, you are probably twenty-something. Good guess, huh?"

The two women said nothing and avoided his eyes.

"Yeah, yeah, don't answer me. Rest until the others return in an hour or two. Your main job will start again. And you know what that is? Come on … it's easy – serving men and birthing kids." He laughed.

Mevan launched himself from behind the door and stabbed Hassan. Blood spurted from Hassan's arm, but this didn't stop Hassan pushing Mevan back and knocking the dagger out of his hand. It gave Hassan the chance to reach for a nearby gun.

Just as Hassan gripped the gun, Mevan was able to strike him with his elbow and the gun fell from Hassan's hand. But Hassan hit back and they continued to fight.

Mevan knocked Hassan down and grabbed his neck with his hands. He squeezed hard, trying to strangle Hassan. But Hassan punched Mevan in the face and neck, then shoved him aside.

Shirin suddenly pounded Hassan with her tied fists. This

surprised Hassan and allowed Barin to reach for Mevan's dagger on the ground. Even with her tied hands, Barin was able to plunge the dagger into Hassan's side.

Hassan immediately stopped fighting and began to breathe heavily.

Mevan let go of Hassan as Shirin picked up Hassan's gun from the floor. She aimed it at Hassan's head. Mevan held up a hand and said, "Do not shoot – they will hear us!"

Mevan pulled his dagger from Hassan's side and plunged it into his heart. Hassan died on the spot.

Mevan extracted his dagger, wiped it clean, then cut the rope around the women's wrists. "We must hurry," he said to them, "those other two might come any time."

Barin said, "Your niece Kany is here as well."

"I know, she is safe. Hurry up, we have to go."

The young women nodded.

On their way out of the house, Mevan picked up a few of the weapons that were lying around and Hassan's phone. He led the women to the house where Kany was hiding and opened the window. He whispered, "Go inside and call Kany. She is in there."

The two women entered the house. Mevan handed a gun to Shirin and quickly showed her how to use it, saying, "Use this when necessary, okay? I have to go."

"Okay," Shirin replied, "but where are you going?"

"I'm going to hide on one of the rooftops and wait for those two men to come back."

"Can't we leave?" Barin asked. "We can head to the mountains before they come back. We want to get as far away as we can."

"What if something terrible happens to you?" Shirin asked. "There is two of them, fully armed."

When Kany heard their voices, she came to the window and said, "Uncle Mevan, please let's go to the mountains – we will be safe there. What if they kill you, too?"

"Please trust your uncle, Kany," Mevan replied. "Maybe they are on their way back now and as soon as they find out that their friend has been killed, they will inform the others. We cannot take that risk. Now go inside and hide. Whatever happens, do not come out after me. If things go bad for me, you can still escape behind the houses and lead Shirin and Barin to my hiding place. Okay, my daughter?"

"Yes, Uncle Mevan, I will," Kany said, "but please be careful."

Mevan closed the window and crept back to the house where Hassan's body was locked inside. He climbed up on the roof, which had a good view of the yard and the road.

After waiting a while, Mevan heard footsteps. A few moments later, he saw the other two men at the crossroad in the middle of the village. The sound of their voices carried clearly to him.

One said, "Let's plant a few mines here, from this side of the road across to the other."

"Yeah, that's a good idea. Let's get it done fast," the other man said. "This is the last lot, okay? I'm starving."

"Okay, okay," the first man said, as he opened the bag he was carrying.

Mevan aimed his gun at the head of the first one, put his finger on the trigger, held his breath and squeezed.

The bullet hit the man right in the head and he fell to the ground.

His companion, who did not know where the shot had come from, hurried to hide himself. But Mevan didn't let him go far and shot the man in the leg, making him scream out in pain. The man did his best to limp towards a wall for cover, but the next bullet hit him in the chest. The man dropped to his knees, then fell face-forward onto the ground.

Mevan climbed down from the roof and walked towards the two bodies. He turned the second man over and stood over his head.

He was still alive. He stared back at Mevan, breathing hard.

As soon as Mevan saw his face, he recognised him as the one who had came out of his house. The painful image of this thug's smiling face had burned into Mevan's memory as the man was walking away from his home. Without saying a word, Mevan looked into his eyes, pulled out his pistol and shot the man in the head.

Mevan turned out the dead man's clothes, picked up his phone and everything useful that he could find, then put it all in the bag with the mines. He untied their belongings and belts from their waists, grabbed the other dead man's phone, then put them all in the bag.

He returned to the house where the young women were waiting and opened the window. "It's all okay now — you can come out."

As they came towards him, Mevan said, "Barin, go find some clothes or pants for Kany. Take whatever we might need like food. Don't forget water … and salt … and also any medicine and food you might find."

After a quick search, they all came back to Mevan. Shirin wrapped some food in a bundle and tied it on her back. Barin had found a pair of men's Kurdish pants, which she helped Kany put on. Then they were ready to leave.

Kany went to the window. Mevan helped her through, then picked her up and hugged her. Mevan then helped Shirin and Barin climb out the window with all their supplies.

They ventured out into the street in front of the house, still looking around cautiously. Mevan said to them, "Hurry up, follow me, we have to go up into the hills."

They all started walking, but Kany soon stopped. Mevan turned to her and asked, "What's wrong? Are you okay?"

"No, my legs are cramping," Kany replied tearfully. "I can't walk."

Mevan's shoulders slumped. He thought for a moment, then said, "Okay, you stay here and hide, then I'll come back for you, okay?"

Kany nodded. "Okay."

Mevan helped her over to a yard where there was a wall for Kany to hide behind.

It wasn't long before Mevan, Shirin and Barin arrived at the tunnel. Mevan opened the door and called out, "Agrin, Agrin, I'm back! Can you hear me? Please answer!"

"Yes!" Agrin called back.

Mevan sent the girls down the tunnel, then covered up the entrance.

He sprinted back down the mountain towards his village, hoping not to lose his footing in the dark. When he arrived back in the village, Mevan couldn't quite remember which wall he had left Kany behind. He called out, "Kany? Where are you? Kany!"

"Here, I'm on this side, Uncle," Kany called back.

Mevan went to her and found her crying in the dark. He lowered his voice and asked, "Are you okay?"

"I don't like the darkness," she said. "Why did you leave me alone?"

"You are right, my daughter. I should have taken you first. It will never happen again, I promise you." With that, Mevan put Kany on his back and raced up the hill with as much energy as he had left.

"Don't cry, my daughter," Mevan panted, as they approached the hide-out. "Here, we have arrived."

They entered the tunnel and locked themselves in.

Shirin and Barin helped Kany into the little room and sat her down. Agrin was standing to one side, holding Agid.

"My daughter, let me get you some water," Mevan said.

"Thank you," Kany said. She looked over at Agid in the arms of a woman she did not recognise. "Uncle, did you find Henan?"

"Yes."

"Then, where is she?"

Mevan paused for a moment, then whispered, "She is dead."

"What? Dead? How? Did they kill her? How did you save Agid?"

"Now is not the time, Kany," he said. "I will tell you later."

Kany started crying and Agrin noticed her bleeding, so she walked over and put her hand on Kany's shoulder, then said sympathetically, "Please don't cry. Do you want to hold Agid?"

"Yes, I missed him so much."

Agrin handed Agid to Kany. She kissed Agid's tiny hands.

Agrin asked, "Kany, all of your clothes are bloody. Have you been injured?"

"No, it's … it's because …" Kany was ashamed and couldn't say any more.

"Okay, I get it, sweetheart," Agrin said, "but you have to do something about it, or it might get worse."

"I know, but I don't know what to do. I bled all over my uncle's clothes as well. I'm so embarrassed and terrified, I wish my mother was here."

"My name is Agrin, darling, and I will help you."

They hugged each other.

Agrin went over to the bag that had been brought back from the village. She took out some painkillers and antibiotics, then said, "Shirin ... please get me some water."

While Shirin went about pouring a cup of water, Agrin started taking off Kany's clothes. Kany's body was bruised and injured. Agrin felt so sorry for the girl and horrified at what she saw, but managed to control her emotions and tears, so she wouldn't scare poor Kany any more. "Okay, darling, it's all good now," whispered Agrin. "I will clean and dry you, then you can use one of Agid's nappies to make sure you stay clean."

After they had finished and Kany had swallowed some antibiotics, Mevan brought them some food and placed it on the ground next to Kany. "Come, have some food, and there is water as well. There is no telephone reception here, but I'm going out to see if I can call someone and get any news or some help."

"Be careful, Uncle," Shirin said.

"I will." He kissed Agid, then handed him to Agrin. He took his weapons and left.

"Aunt Agrin, you are not from our village, are you?" Kany asked.

"No, I'm not."

"Do you know what happened to Henan and how Uncle found Agid?" Kany asked.

"No, I do not know. After he saved my life, he brought me here. His wife was dead, her body was there."

"Where is she now?" Barin asked.

Agrin pointed to Henan's grave, and said, "That is her grave. I asked Mevan what happened to her, but he didn't answer."

"Poor Henan, they must have killed her," Shirin said, sighing. "I do not know how Mevan found them. He must have been devastated. They took my son – he was eight years old. I did everything I could to stop them, but they took him with the other little boys. God knows where he is now. I saw his face behind the bus window shouting my name to save him. He was so scared. He was terrified when he saw his father and all those men beheaded in front of his eyes. If it weren't for him, I would have killed myself the second after they killed my husband and my family ... But because of my son, I have to stay alive until I get him back. I have to get him back ..."

"Don't cry, my poor sister," Barin said, as she hugged Shirin. "You will find him. I promise you that this is not how it ends. We will find our family, and this enemy will have to pay for what they did."

"Yes, Shirin, she is right," Kany said. "They killed our family and kidnapped them. Uncle Mevan told me, too. He promised that we will find them."

"Why do they do this to us? What was all that hate about?" Shirin asked, looking at Agid and sighing. "At night, whoever came, took one of the girls by force. One of the soldiers came to Henan, who had her baby in her arms, and grabbed her by the arm to take her. But whatever he did, whether he hit her or grabbed her hair, she did not give up and go with him. She was holding onto the side of the door with all her might, until he gave up on her and went to Agid and pulled the child out of her arms. Agid was crying as the man held him like a bag and said, 'I'll take your baby, if you don't come.

And you will never see your son again.' Then the man left with Agid, and poor Henan ran after him, begging."

Tears flowed from Kany's eyes while Shirin told this story, remembering the horrors she had seen and been through.

Shirin took a deep breath, then continued, "But next morning, the sounds of shooting came from outside. We saw them dragging that man's body past us and we were overjoyed because we knew Henan had killed him. We shouted her name out loud – that's how they should pay."

"That night I also heard them saying that one woman from the upper village did a similar thing," Barin said. "She killed one of their important commanders by stabbing him in the eye with broken glass and running away."

Just then, the women heard a noise behind them. "Uncle Mevan!" Kany exclaimed. "You are back so soon."

Shirin went to him and asked, "So what happened? Have you got any news?"

Barin added, "Is there anyone to help us?"

9

"Uncle, why aren't you saying anything? How long have you been back?" Kany asked, worrying that he had heard them talking about Henan. "We didn't even hear your footsteps approaching above."

Mevan was panting lightly and looked concerned. "Well ... this time I got a chance to speak on one of the captured phones with one of my friends. He said that these enemies are everywhere and we have to go to the mountains — that is our only chance. Many of our people have taken refuge at Mount Sinjar. If we move there now, we will be far enough away from danger. Our warriors are all around the mountain, trying to pave the way for people to reach safety. If you have a phone, then turn it off so that it does not run out of charge. Let's pack up, now."

Everyone simply nodded and started packing up. It was clear this plan was their best chance of survival.

"Uncle Mevan, Agid won't stop crying and I can't calm him down," Kany said, as she rocked him.

"Agrin, can you take care of Agid for me? I will do the work. Please," Mevan said.

Agrin handed the bag with supplies from the village to Mevan.

She picked up Agid's bag, went to the corner of the room, and started feeding him.

"Uncle Mevan, we are ready," Barin said. "While Agrin feeds the baby, we will take what we need up to the tunnel's exit."

Mevan replied, "Yes, my daughter, do that." He handed the bag and the rest of the things to the young women.

"Agrin let me take Agid out," Mevan said, "and then I'll help Kany."

"He hasn't finished yet," Agrin said.

"Okay, don't rush, I'll wait," Mevan said, and sat down by his wife's grave.

"Uncle, I wish she was still alive," Kany said. "What happened to her?"

Mevan hugged her and wiped her tears, then said, heartbroken, "Don't cry, my daughter. She has gone now. She broke her promise and left me alone in the middle of nowhere."

"I miss her so much," Kany said.

"I do miss her, too," Mevan said.

Agrin's eyes filled with tears while overhearing their pain about Henan. When Agid was full, he fell asleep on Agrin's arm. She went and sat next to Mevan and Kany, then said, "May her beautiful soul rest in peace. I'm so sorry, Mevan." She then stood up and left with Agid.

A few minutes later, Kany and Mevan came out of the tunnel as well. Mevan closed the door and made sure no one would be able to find the grave of his love. He said, "She deserves to rest as peacefully and as far away from the troubles as the big mountain that has her buried in its heart."

Mevan carried Kany on his back and said to the girls, who were waiting for him to lead, "We don't know where our enemies are located now and what we will come across on our way. Try to be as quiet as you can and follow in my footsteps. Before the sun comes up, we have to go as far as we can."

It was almost dawn when they decided to rest. They had come a long way, and everyone was exhausted.

"Let's sit down and drink some water, but no more time than that. We have to get to the top of that hill," Mevan said, pointing towards a hill, which was difficult to see in the dark. "Otherwise, it will be easy for us to be seen by enemies."

"Yes, Uncle," Barin said, "and when the sun comes up, it will also be too hot and hard to climb, and we do not have enough water."

"There is not much left, but we can get there," Mevan said. "Then we will rest, okay?" He went to check on Agrin, who had fallen behind, and asked, "Can you continue? You are behind."

"Yes, I am breastfeeding him on the way."

"Okay, then this time, we will walk slower, so you can catch up," Mevan said.

After a few minutes of rest, Mevan carried Kany on his back and asked Shirin, "Can you take that small sheet and tie Kany onto my back? I'm not sure if she can hold on to me. I'm scared she will fall off my back on the way."

"Okay," Shirin said, and tied the sheet around her. "It's done, Uncle," she said.

"That is better, thank you," Mevan said. "Are you comfortable, Kany?"

"Yes, Uncle," answered Kany, in a weak voice.

"Okay, then, let's get going," said Mevan.

It was late morning when they reached the place Mevan had pointed out. "Let's hide under that rock," Mevan said. "We will rest there."

Mevan opened the sheet and, with the help of Barin and Shirin, put Kany down.

"Uncle, your neck is burnt very badly on both sides," Barin said.

"It's not that important, my daughter," Mevan said. "You go and check on Kany and give her something to eat."

Mevan took the baby's bag and put it next to Agrin. He sat next to them holding Agid's hands, then said, "Agrin, how is my son? Is he okay? He cried a lot on the way; it made me worried. Was there any problem with him? You should tell us if we need to stop for the baby when he needs to be taken care of."

"No, he is fine," she said, as she began changing Agid's nappy. "Somehow he dropped his dummy on the way, and he couldn't sleep without it. But after I gave him my daughter's dummy, he went to sleep."

"Thank you for taking care of him. I promise I will find your daughter and bring her back to you. I'll help you to find your husband and family."

"You can't," Agrin said, then paused for a moment. "They are dead. My daughter and my husband were killed, and all I have left of them is this ring and this little red dummy, which was left in my hand when they pulled her body from my arms and threw her on the ground, then dragged me away." Her tears started falling on Agid's cheeks.

Mevan hugged her and wiped her tears. "Barin, my daughter," Mevan said, in a deep voice, "please bring some water for Agrin."

"Don't cry, Uncle, please," Kany said. "I don't want to see you cry."

"These tears are from anger, sweetheart, which is burning inside my heart …" After a few seconds, Mevan composed himself and dried his tears. "For now, the important thing is to take you all to a safe place. I'll go and look around and check if I am able to phone someone." He turned to Agrin and said, "They will pay for this, I promise you," then left.

Barin picked up a bottle of water and went to comfort Agrin. "My poor sister, how old was your baby?"

"Eight months," Agrin said.

"Auntie, I'm so sorry for what happened to you," Kany cried.

"Thank you, my daughter," Agrin said. "Agid is crying; I better look after him. At least this poor little boy won't suffer more than this." She picked up Agid, sat next to Kany, then said, "And you, Kany, you have to rest here. Put your head on my lap and try to sleep a little."

After a while, Mevan came back and said to the women, "There was nothing around. I couldn't get to call anyone, there is no reception around here."

"So what are we going to do now?" Barin asked.

"We will rest for around an hour. We still have a couple of hours before it gets too hot, then we can rest somewhere until it cools down a little."

After an hour of rest, Mevan said, "Okay, girls, we better start walking." He lifted Kany onto his back.

"Where are you taking us?" Shirin asked.

"To wherever is safer for you," Mevan said.

Shirin said, "My son is in their hands. Our families have all been killed or taken captive. I do not want to run away to a safe place. The thing I want now is to fight for my son, to fight them back. The further I go from my son, the more it hurts me and makes my legs less able to leave."

"We are not running away, Shirin," Mevan said. "We have to get to our warriors and our Kurdish forces and see what the situation is. Doing anything else is going to get us killed."

"I'm not afraid of dying. If it causes their death, I'm willing to die," Shirin said, with hatred in her voice.

"Your death doesn't help your people, only our enemies," Mevan said. "It is a joy for them, but a loss for our people – nothing else. The friend who I was able to phone earlier told me that thousands of people from the city also went to the mountains. But also that the enemies have surrounded most of the hills, and fighting can erupt at any time. The right thing to do is to take you all to a safe place now. At any moment, they could be found around here and attack us. Now listen to me and walk, please ..."

Barin supported Mevan's words, saying, "He is right, you can't do anything. We don't know anything about them. You don't even know where your son is."

Shirin looked back with regret and said, "Okay, Uncle Mevan, whatever you say. I'll do that, but for God's sake, as you promised Agrin, promise me that you will help me bring my son back."

"I promise you, my daughter, Shirin, I will do everything to get our children and women back. Now let's move."

They picked up their belongings and continued their journey. Mevan tried several times along the way to phone family and friends, but, if a call went through, no one would answer. They reached the top of another hill and sat in the shade of a rock. They were all exhausted and sleepy.

"It's almost afternoon now and the weather is becoming too hot," Mevan said. "We'd better stay here and rest." He put Kany down with the help of Shirin and Barin. "I'm going to look around now, to make sure there is no danger. You try to have a good rest." He picked up his gun and left.

Agrin handed Agid to Barin and went to Kany, who looked sick and pale. Agrin touched her face. "Let me see how your injuries are and change you again. There are still a few of Agid's nappies left."

Kany lowered her head in embarrassment at the thought of taking off her pants. "That's okay, Auntie, let it be like this."

"No, sweetie, you have to let me," Agrin insisted. "If it gets infected, it will hurt more. So don't be shy, my daughter."

"Aunt Agrin, it burns so much, and my leg cramps are so bad." Kany overcame her shyness and started crying.

Agrin and Shirin helped Kany take her clothes off. They were both shocked when they saw her whole body had become worse.

Shirin realised that Kany had seen the shock on her face, and she was now scared. Shirin rearranged her face and said, "Don't worry, Kany, it's getting better, isn't it, Agrin?"

Agrin said sympathetically, "Yes, and if I clean it and put on some of Agid's cream, you will be much better."

The pain was way more than what a young girl could handle. She started crying and calling out to her mother, "Mummy, oh God, it hurts so bad! Please stop! It burns, please stop!"

Agrin started asking questions to take her mind off the pain. "Tell me, Kany, how old are you?"

"In another two months, I will be thirteen."

"Oh, that is great, so in two months, we will have a birthday party for you. What do you say, Shirin?"

"Yes, of course," Shirin said, as she held Kany's head and hands. "Now, what do you want us to give you as a gift, Kany? Come on, tell us, what would you like?"

Kany, despite her pain, began to enjoy their talk. With a small smile on her beautiful, crying face, she replied, "Maybe a dress."

"A dress! What colour?" Agrin asked.

"I like red and green," Kany said.

"Okay, Shirin," Agrin said, "a beautiful dress for Kany's birthday in two months – don't forget it!"

Meanwhile, Mevan was searching the mountain, but there was no one around. He tried several times to make a phone call, but the phone belonged to one of the enemies he had slain, and he didn't have many numbers of his family and friends memorised. He started to ring one of his brothers, but then remembered Henan saying that he had been killed. Heartbroken, Mevan hung up the phone.

He still couldn't believe that his brothers, father and beautiful mother were all dead. He called his sister's phone several times. "Narin, it's me, Mevan, answer the phone. Please." But no one answered. He texted a message to her.

After much effort but with no news, he returned to the women in despair.

The closer Mevan got, the more he was disturbed by the sound of Kany's moans. As he drew closer, he saw that Agrin and Shirin were taking care of her. He stopped and then sat on a rock.

Seeing Mevan, Barin picked up Agid and walked over to sit next to him. She asked, "What happened, Uncle? Any news?"

"No, I got nothing," Mevan said. He focused his eyes on Kany. "She has suffered a lot in their hands, hasn't she?"

Barin said sadly, "Those men were heartless. They took Kany and some girls younger than her because they screamed and suffered more. They called us infidels and slaves." She sighed and looked at Kany, then continued, "Her whole body is injured. She is timid around you and doesn't show or say anything. But even a grown woman couldn't take the pain that she is in."

Mevan nodded his head in sadness and went silent for a few seconds. He then asked, "What about you? Your mother, your sister — what happened to them? Your father?"

"They are worse off than I am," Barin said.

"What about your father? Barin ... my daughter — what happened? Did they kill him as well?"

Tears started running from Barin's eyes. "Yes, they beheaded him," she sobbed. "We saw him smile one last time, a second before their dagger cut his neck. He was looking at us until his last moment ..."

"Come, come here, sweetheart, don't cry," Mevan said, as he hugged Barin. "I'm so sorry. Your father was an amazing man. He and I were good friends."

"He loved you like his brother," Barin said.

"So was he to me," Mevan sighed.

"I lost everyone," Barin said. "I don't know what to do or where to go. I'm terrified, Uncle Mevan."

"Don't cry, sweetheart, you have me," Mevan said. "I'll take care of you like my own daughter – like Kany. I won't let any harm come to you while I'm alive, okay?"

Barin hugged Mevan and started crying.

Mevan held her in his arms until she calmed down, then kissed her on the head. "Now, my darling daughter, give Agid to me and go help the others. When Kany is comfortable again, call me."

Agrin sorted out Kany's clothes and handed her some of the pills from the bag. "My daughter, you are all done, for now," Agrin said. "Hopefully, these pills will make your pain go away for a while so that you can rest a little bit."

"I'll call Uncle Mevan to come here," Barin said.

Mevan came and sat next to Kany and kissed her on the forehead. "Have some water and rest, my daughter."

"May I have the baby?" Agrin asked Mevan.

"Okay, but you need to rest as well," Mevan replied. "I can take care of him."

"But I want to feed him and put him to sleep," Agrin said.

"Okay, thank you," said Mevan.

When everyone was lying down, Agrin closed her eyes and rested with Agid in her arms.

Later that evening, Mevan said, "We better get going."

Everyone readied themselves, then followed Mevan. They continued their long trek, but they still hadn't had news from anyone else.

Suddenly, they heard the sound of a helicopter.

Mevan stopped and looked at the sky. As the sound came closer, he said, "Hurry, we have to hide somewhere. Quick – hurry up and take cover!"

"Uncle, do you think our enemies are in that helicopter? Are they looking for us?" Barin asked, as she looked at the sky.

"I don't know – maybe," Mevan replied. "We can't risk being seen till we know for sure."

They waited while the helicopter came closer, but it didn't hover over them, it kept flying into the distance.

When they came out from hiding, Mevan said, "We have to move fast to get to Mount Sinjar. The path from here is challenging to walk at night, so we need to try to get there before dark."

They continued on their way until it was dark and they could barely see the path. Still, they somehow kept trudging along, knowing it wouldn't be safe to stop yet.

All of a sudden, Mevan's foot slipped. He struggled to stop himself from falling and only just managed to keep his balance. "Sorry, Kany," Mevan said. "Are you okay? Did you get hurt?"

"No, I'm fine," Kany answered, in a weak voice.

"We better stop and stay here for the night," Mevan said to the women.

With the help of a faint glow from his phone, Mevan made a place for Kany to rest and put her down.

Agrin sat next to Kany. "Are you feeling any better?" Agrin asked. "How is your pain?"

"I don't know," Kany said, grabbing Agrin's hand and squeezing it. "I'm tired of this pain. I want to die."

"Okay, okay … calm down," Agrin said. "You are going to be all right, sweetie, I promise you. Let me clean and change you again."

Kany nodded. "Okay."

Mevan knew it was time to move away, and said, "I'll go look around, so that you will be comfortable."

After Agrin had taken care of Kany with a little help from Barin and Shirin, they called for Mevan to come back. When they were all gathered together, each of them drank a little water and ate some food.

As they were getting ready to sleep, Mevan's phone lit up. There was a message. Mevan gasped when he read the text. "It's from my sister."

"What? What does it say, Uncle?" Shirin asked. "Is she okay? Is it bad news?"

Mevan held out his phone to Shirin.

She read the message out: "I'm not allowed to speak to men. Is there a woman who can talk to me?"

"What are you waiting for?" Agrin said. "I'll call her. What's her name?"

"Her name is Narin," Mevan said. He called, but the phone kept ringing.

Agrin took the phone from Mevan and waited for someone to answer. "Hello ... hello ..." Agrin said.

A man's voice answered. "Come and speak ... a woman is talking but speak in Arabic, so that I can understand."

A woman's voice said, "Hello?"

"Hello!" Agrin replied in Kurdish. "Narin, are you okay? Where are you now?"

The man's voice came back on the phone. "No, no, no! I said to speak in Arabic – I do not understand your language. If you don't, I'll hang up the phone."

"No, please," Agrin said, as best she could in Arabic. "I do not know Arabic as much. Please let me talk to her – I just want to know if she is okay."

"Okay, but no more than that," he said.

"Narin, is that you?" Agrin said.

"No, they took her to Mosul with some other girls. Several women told her that if they took her to Mosul, they would take everything from her. So she gave me her phone. I had to turn it off, and I hid it until yesterday when I was sold to this man. He is letting me have it."

"Okay, so where are you now?" Agrin asked.

The woman burst into tears. "I don't know. Please help me."

The man took her phone, and Agrin heard him say in the background, "If you want to cry and lie, I will hang up the phone. Come on now, speak the truth. You are where you belong. Tell her to come here as well. Do you want her to burn in hell or serve the Mujahideen? May God forgive her, huh? Learn your lessons and do it correctly, you stupid woman."

Agrin was about to say something, then the man started talking into the phone again. "What's your name? Where are you now? Come here so that you can have your sister."

Mevan motioned to Agrin to ask where he wanted her to come, so Agrin said, "Okay, where should I come?"

"You come to this address and give my name and phone number. I will come out for you," the man said.

"Why don't you let her go?" Agrin said. "Don't you see how much she is scared? She wants to be with her family. She doesn't want to be there."

"How can I let her go? She is mine. I bought her, but I might exchange her for you, if you are as attractive as your voice. If not, as long as you're a virgin, I still would be happy to exchange her with you. What do you say?" The man laughed.

Mevan got angry at his disgusting words and tried to grab the phone, but Agrin held his hand and willed him to be patient. She continued to speak to the man, "Okay, I will think about it. Can you give the phone back to her, please? You said we can talk."

"You will never come. I'm not stupid, you are wasting my time. She is happy here and doesn't need you. Also, her religion doesn't allow her to talk to infidels."

"But I became a Muslim," Agrin said.

"You don't say?" the man replied.

"I'm telling you the truth. Please let me talk to her."

"Okay, if she obeys me and does her religious duties and you also state your testimony now, after me, so that I can believe you, I swear to God that I will not take her phone away, and I will let her call you. Sometimes."

Shirin became anxious and whispered to Agrin not to accept the offer or change her beliefs.

But Agrin ignored her and repeated the testimony as the man said it, then asked him to pass the phone back to the woman.

The man said, "You accepted the religion of God without delay, it does show that God wants you to be saved. You have to come here and become one of the Mujahideen's wives. May God soften your heart for the next steps, as well. Okay, I'll give her the phone now, but say your goodbyes, then I'll let you talk to her later."

The woman came back on the phone. "Why did you accept?"

Agrin replied calmly, "Because of you. Nothing is really changed when it is done by force. So, you are not guilty for changing beliefs, as you and I really know. We are born Yazidi, and we die Yazidi. So do not put your life in danger, just go along with them for now like

I did. God sees for Himself, so please act wisely. If they take you somewhere, please inform us. Now, tell me your name and your family, so we can tell them."

"My name is Siber Aziz. Okay, I'll do as you say, but I'm terrified. I have been sold to two men in the market so far. The first one was fierce and hated me a lot. Then this man — one of his wives is not mean, but the other one hits me all the time. I want to commit suicide, but one of the girls who tried to commit suicide got caught and they took her away. She was raped in the room with so many men at the same time. They burned some of the girls alive in a cage after they caught them running away. Since then, I've been too afraid to commit suicide. What if they get me before I can?"

"Do not commit suicide," Agrin said. "You must be strong and stay alive. Please, don't give up, we need you and your people need you. This is not how it ends. Look out for any opportunity that arises to escape. Try to stay connected, we will find your family and find a way to bring you back. I promise you, you will be saved. I escaped, too, so do not lose your hope, okay?"

Siber, who had calmed down hearing Agrin's words, said, "I hope so. What is your name?"

"I am Agrin Sheref."

Mevan whispered in Agrin's ear, "Tell her to send the name of all girls and women she knows, and the full names of the men she was or is with, and whatever else she thinks might be helpful."

Agrin repeated Mevan's message to her.

"Okay, I will write all their names and send them to you," Siber agreed.

The man's voice rose again in the background. "Enough — finish the talking. Hurry up and give me the phone." He hung up.

"What? What happened?" Mevan asked.

"That man grabbed the phone," Agrin said.

"Poor Siber, we have to do something for her," Shirin said.

Mevan took the phone back from Agrin, picked up his gun and disappeared into the dark.

"Where did Uncle go?" Kany asked.

"He needs some time alone, Kany," Agrin said. "He just found out something about his sister. I can see how he breaks inside, even though he tries not to show it."

"I pray to God to make him stronger than his pain," Shirin said.

"I am worried about my mother," Kany said, and began crying. "I miss her so very much. She could be in horrible pain right now! Or what if they have killed her or burned her?"

"I'm sure she is okay," Shirin said. "We will find her and bring her back. We need to get out of here and get to our forces. We will fight those heartless thieves and bring our families back."

"You are not alone," said Barin. "We are all here for you and will take care of you. Okay, sweetheart?"

Hearing these words, Kany soon calmed down and dried her tears. Then she dragged herself over to Agrin and said, "Aunt Agrin, can I put my head on your lap again? You feel like my mother."

"Sure, darling," Agrin replied. "Let me sit right, so you'll be comfortable."

"I can wait until you breastfeed Agid," Kany said.

"No, no, it's okay. Like last time, we will do all right."

"Last time I felt my mother here with me when I slept on your lap, Auntie. I even saw her in my dream." Kany put her head down to sleep on Agrin's lap.

They all lay back and tried to catch up on sleep.

A little while later, Mevan returned. Agrin was not quite asleep but said nothing. Mevan came over to her and made sure she, the baby and Kany were all comfortable. He checked Barin and put his bag under Shirin's head.

Barin opened her eyes. "Uncle Mevan."

"Yes, Baba."

"You came back," Barin said. "We were worried. How are you feeling?"

"I'll be fine. Here, my daughter, put your head on this bag not the rock." She lay back down, then Mevan moved to a clear spot, lay down on a rock and closed his eyes.

Very early in the morning, Mevan went over to Shirin and said, "Wake up, Shirin, we have to leave."

"Morning, Uncle," Shirin said.

"Morning, my daughter. Wake up the others. We must leave before the sun comes out."

Shirin got up and woke the others. Everyone helped each other get ready and they set off again.

After they had gone quite a way, the sound of gunfire rang out from far in the distance. They didn't know what was going on, but Mevan was sure it was a fight with their enemies.

After several attempts, he managed to phone someone again. He stood still and said into the phone, "Listen — help me. I have women and children with me. We are approaching the top of the mountains. I do not know if it is safe or not? Can you help? Tell me what's going on around here and which way should we head?"

The man on the other end replied, "Don't head to the roads and stay far away. They have closed the roads. They want to keep people inside the mountains so they suffer. But help is on its way. They are delivering food to the people by helicopter."

"I haven't seen anyone so far," Mevan said. "Where exactly are the people? We heard gunfire – where is it coming from?" .

"The ISIS are attacking people who are heading to the mountains. There are Kurdish forces fighting them to buy time for people to escape."

"Where are you now? Is there anyone to come and help us out?"

"How many people are with you?"

"Four people," Mevan replied. "Shervan's daughter Kany is with me, too. She is sick and can't walk. Also my son."

"Henan, Narin? Your mother? Are they with you, too?"

"No, only my son and Kany are here," Mevan said.

"How come? Where are they?"

"Now is not the time, Sarhad. I can't talk," Mevan said sadly.

"Okay, keep walking," Sarhad said. "From where you are now, you will reach some other people by the end of the day. I will try to get to you somehow."

"Okay, thanks, I'll talk to you later." Mevan hung up and said to Agrin, who was sitting next to him, "He is my friend. He says if we continue on our way, we will reach the others today. I know you all are so tired, but we have to go on. It's not safe here. They are going to keep attacking anyone they come across." Mevan passed some water to Kany.

By noon, the hot weather and dusty winds were making it too

hard for them to continue walking. Mevan turned and looked at their meandering, plodding steps. Mevan asked Kany on his back, "How are you doing, Baba? Are you okay? Kany? Baba, you okay back there?"

Kany did not answer.

Worried, Mevan asked again, "Kany, do you hear me?"

Shirin went to Kany and gently slapped her face a few times, but she didn't see any movement.

Mevan looked around and spotted a boulder that was shaded and sheltered from the wind. With the help of the women, Mevan eased Kany down from his back.

Agrin walked over and felt Kany's neck. "She is alive. Her pulse is weak but still there. Give me some water." She sprinkled some water on Kany's face and held the water to her lips. Calling her name a few times, Agrin managed to wake Kany and make her drink a few sips of water.

Mevan was relieved to see Kany was definitely still alive. He said to her, "You better stay here in the shade. I'll find some help. Our people are not far from us." Mevan started preparing to leave.

"I'm coming with you, too, Uncle Mevan," Barin said, standing next to him.

"No, if I go alone, I'll get there faster. You have to stay here to help Shirin and Agrin."

"Uncle, have some water and food for yourself," Shirin said.

"No need, we don't have much left. I'll be all right," Mevan replied.

"No, we won't let you leave," Agrin said. "You have to at least have some water."

"Uncle Mevan, your neck has gotten worse," Barin said.

Mevan ignored her warning — he was busy putting his gun on his belt and tying his shoes.

Agrin picked up a bottle of water with a few bits of bread and placed them in Mevan's belt. She pulled down the collar of his shirt to look at his neck. She went back to Agid's bag, took his cream out, put some on her finger and rubbed it on Mevan's neck, which was all red and burnt. "There, that's done," Agrin said. "Hopefully, this cream will help with the burning. If you cover it from the sun with a scarf, it won't burn as much."

Shirin took off her scarf and put it around Mevan's neck. "There, Uncle Mevan, now it's better."

"Thank you," Mevan said. He went to Kany, who was scared to see him leaving. "Hey, sweetheart, I see your eyes are full of tears again. Why Baba? I'll come back soon, okay, my daughter?"

"Okay, Uncle," Kany said. "I'm so sorry."

"You're sorry? Why?"

"Because of your neck," Kany said, and started crying.

"Don't say that, my daughter," Mevan said. "I'm okay. Don't cry, darling, this is nothing. It's already much better."

"Okay, Uncle, I love you so much," Kany said, hugging him.

"I'll come back soon, but if I am late, don't come after me and don't change your location. Otherwise, it will be hard to find you, and you might face our enemies. I cannot stress this enough. Okay?"

Kany nodded.

Mevan handed one of the captured phones to Agrin and said, "Keep this phone with you. I'll turn it off for now, but you check it from time to time. Siber may call again and we have to find out where she is. The first number in the call list is mine." He pulled his own phone from his pocket. "It's for this one, which I am taking with me."

"Okay," Agrin said.

He kissed Agid in Agrin's arms, said goodbye to everyone, then ran towards the mountain.

Agrin went to Kany and said, "You lost consciousness for a while back there. Let me look at your wound again to see how it is."

Shirin, who was still watching Mevan walking away, sighed and said, "May God take care of our uncle. He is the only one left for us."

"Don't worry, Shirin, everyone knows him," Barin assured her. "My father always said that he is 'the man of hard days'. He saved my father so many times — no man can defeat him."

"I know," Shirin said. "My brother always talked about him, too. Everyone knows how smart he is. He said that when Uncle Mevan started to make that hiding place to hide his gasoline and other business materials, everyone laughed. But then came the day he had prepared for and he saved all his things, and he also helped out other people of the village. He always cares about his people."

All of Barin's and Shirin's words made Agrin remember her family's words and description of Delovan, and tears welled in her eyes.

"Why are you crying, Agrin?" Barin asked. "Please say something."

Agrin, who was cleaning up Kany, replied quietly, "Your talking reminded me of my husband, Delovan. And for a few seconds, I was able to forget about my husband's and daughter's deaths. Sometimes I deliberately imagine that they are still alive and, one day soon, I'll be able to see them. Then the reality of their deaths hits me in the chest — the pain of missing them presses my heart so bad that it gets too hard for me to even breathe."

Kany threw herself in Agrin's arms and hugged her tightly. They sat down in silence.

The sound of the breeze rustling the dry leaves and bushes on the ground was like a peaceful lullaby. Soon they closed their tired eyes and fell asleep.

After a good rest, Shirin woke and looked in the direction that Mevan had gone. She turned to Agrin and said, "How many hours has it been since Mevan left? I say we should turn on the phone, to see if he has called or sent a message."

Agrin turned on the phone and said, "Yes, you are right. Many messages have come, and many calls have been made to this phone."

"Maybe it's Siber," Shirin said. "Read the message."

Agrin opened the messages and scrolled through them. "They all are for the owner of this phone. His family is trying to contact him."

"Family! What family? Did he have a family?" Barin cried. "Do you want me to believe that he had a mother or father or kids or wife? Huh? Then how could he kill our mum and dad and brother. How could he behead my sixteen-year-old brother? I will never believe he had sisters or daughters in his home and yet he raped us. I miss my family so much. I miss them, Agrin, and I can't ever see them again."

Agrin put down the phone and hugged her, saying, "I don't know how. I don't think I will ever understand them."

"What should we do with these messages?" Shirin asked, as she looked at the messages. I'd better turn the phone off again."

"But first, call Mevan," Agrin said. "See where he is."

Shirin called and waited. "He is not answering. Let me send him a message." She sent a short message to ask Mevan where he was, then handed the phone back to Agrin.

A few hours passed, with no reply from Mevan.

"Maybe we should go after him," Barin said.

"No, it's not safe," Shirin said. "He may come anytime soon."

"But if we head in his direction ..." Barin began to say.

"No, Barin," Agrin said. "He said to stay and we will."

"Okay, then," Barin said. "I will go up to that hill and watch."

"Okay," Agrin replied, "but be careful and don't go further than that."

"Okay," Barin said, and she ran towards the hill.

More than an hour later, Shirin said, "It's been a while. Why hasn't Barin come back yet?"

"Be patient," Agrin said.

"Wait, I think I see her," Shirin said, looking hard into the distance.

"Are you sure?" Agrin said.

"Yes, it's her, but ... my God, Agrin! There are three men running after her!"

"What? Let me see!" Agrin cried. "Come on, Shirin, don't just stand there."

"Do you think those men are ISIS?" Shirin asked.

"I don't know," Agrin replied. "It's too far away to see. But her running might not be a good sign." She readied herself to leave and fastened the war belt around her waist.

"Are we running away?" Kany asked.

"No," Agrin said, "we don't have time to take that chance. We will fight." Agrin pointed to their captured weapons. "Shirin, take one of those guns and hide between those rocks."

"Okay," Shirin said.

"Kany, you hold Agid and don't let him cry," Agrin said, handing Kany a weapon. "Take this gun, just in case. We won't let them get to you."

"What about the bag?" Shirin asked

"Leave it to me," Agrin said.

"Hey, Agrin, wait!" Shirin said. "Keep one grenade in your hand in case you are surrounded."

Agrin took the grenade and Shirin ran to hide. Agrin ran towards the men to put some space between them and Kany holding Agid.

A minute later they heard Barin shouting, "Agrin ... Shirin ... where are you? Come! Uncle Mevan is returning with help."

When Agrin heard Barin calling out that there was no danger, she took a deep breath and put down her gun.

"Hello ... where are you?" Barin shouted.

"Here, come help me out," Shirin said.

"What are you doing up there?" Barin asked, as she helped her. "Why are you armed?"

"Oh, for God's sake, Barin, you scared us to death," Shirin said.

"Why were you scared?" asked Barin, breathing heavily.

"We saw you running like hell," Shirin said. "We thought there were ISIS after you, you crazy girl."

Mevan came running up to them, with two men following. "Hello, Shirin. Where are the others?" he asked.

"They're hiding. We thought Barin was in danger and that was why she was running," Shirin said. "We didn't recognise you at a distance."

Kany came out with Agid and ran to Mevan and hugged him.

"Where is Agrin?" asked Mevan

"She hid behind those rocks," said Shirin.

Mevan turned to see Agrin coming down from the rocks with a bloody foot. He went to her. "Wait — let me help you down." He helped her down, then hugged her. "What happened to your foot?"

"I hurried up the cliff, and a piece of sharp stone went through my foot, but I pulled it out," Agrin said.

Barin said, "I'm so sorry we scared you. I was just so excited to tell you that I didn't think it through." She went over to check out Agrin's injury.

"Don't be sorry, my sister," Shirin said. "From now on, I will probably be scared of my own shadow, and I'll have to prepare for it. It's not your fault."

"Let me take a look at your foot and see how bad it is," Mevan said, as he sat down next to Agrin. "It's still bleeding."

Agrin lifted the hem of her pants. She was injured on the ankle, and it looked serious.

Mevan untied the scarf from around his neck. "I'll tie it with this and see if it stops the bleeding." He started wrapping it around Agrin's foot.

Shirin reached down to Agrin's ankle. "Let me take the pearl from your ankle so Mevan can tie it more easily."

"No, please do not open it," Agrin said, holding Shirin's hands. "Let it stay."

Mevan was surprised by her sharp reaction and said, "No need to take it off, Shirin, I'll roll it down. Don't worry, Agrin, let her hand go and relax." He lowered the pearl a little, then wrapped the scarf around the wound and tied it tightly. He helped her stand, then said, "Now, let's see if you can walk."

"Yeah, I can. Don't worry," Agrin replied.

"Okay, then, we have to go," Mevan said. "Where are our weapons? I can't see them."

"I hid them," Agrin replied. "They are behind that rock."

Mevan went to one of the men who had come with him and said, "Kazu, go and get the bag behind that rock but be careful, it is full of mines."

After making sure everything was ready to go, Mevan tied Kany onto his back again. Another man went to Agrin and said, "Give me your baby and let me carry him, sister Agrin. You are injured."

"Thank you, brother ..." Agrin said.

"Serbest, my sister," he said.

"Thank you, brother Serbest."

10

Serbest held Agid in his arms and hugged him. Kazu took the bag with the mines and the rest of the equipment, and they all headed deeper into the mountains.

Towards sunset, they reached the rest of the displaced people who were on the run. From the top of the hill where Agrin was standing, she looked out at the crowd of people. Some were sitting to rest and catch their breath, some kept walking to nowhere in particular as long as they remained in the mountains.

As Mevan and his group came closer, people went to help them.

"Come to this site, my son," said a woman. "Sit on this rock so I can help you with your daughter."

"Yes, thank you, Auntie," Mevan said.

The woman called out to a teenage boy, "Bring me the basket, my son."

Her son left, then soon returned with a few bottles of water and a small bag.

The woman said to Kany, "Come, my daughter, drink some water. What has happened to you?"

Kany replied in a low, angry voice full of hate, "I was, their prisoner."

"Oh, my poor girl, what have they done to you? Oh, sweetheart, thank God you are not with them any more." The woman hugged Kany.

"Thank you."

After a few moments, the woman turned her attention to the others. "There is enough water for all of you, but we don't have enough food. I saved it for children and those who need it."

A man standing next to the woman said, "The helicopter came yesterday and dropped us some food and water packages. Still, it wasn't enough. We are not sure if they can come again, and we don't know how long we will be stuck here."

"Hopefully, they will help us again," the woman said, while putting some dates on a piece of bread for Kany.

Kazu said, "You know, brother Mevan, ISIS fighters are around as well. They are coming and stealing our food and water and packages, but I heard that the whole world is united in a quest to help us."

The woman interrupted while she prepared more to eat. "My eldest son spoke on the phone with our relatives. They said they will send more food and help, and they are trying to open a safe road to get all of us out. Come, my daughter, this food is for you." The woman also offered bread and dates to Agrin.

"No, I'm not hungry," Agrin said. "Let it be for the children."

"Your baby is too young, my daughter. If you don't eat, you won't be able to breastfeed him," the woman insisted.

Kany said, "Yes, Aunt Agrin, last time you said that Agid is still hungry and you don't have any more milk. Please take this as well." She took half her food and handed it to Agrin.

Mevan became worried about Agid when he heard Kany's words.

He grabbed the food from the woman and gave it to Agrin. "Come, have it please, for my son."

Agrin took the food and thanked the woman and Kany.

Because of the love and affection shown by the woman and her family, Mevan's group stayed with them and they decided to continue their journey together. Serbest, Kazu and their families also decided to join them.

It was now late at night and everyone was exhausted. They got ready for rest and sat down together around a small fire. "Auntie, where did you come from?" Agrin said.

"My daughter, we escaped from the city," the woman said. "Almost everyone ran out as soon they attacked us."

"So, all the people of the city escaped?" Agrin asked.

The woman's husband replied in a loud voice, "Yes, my daughter, most of us came to the mountains. But still they came after us and started shooting us. They stopped at the foot of the mountains. We were so lucky because they couldn't drive into the mountains with their cars and tanks. Some of our men who had guns started fighting back, to buy some time so the women and children could escape. We were without food or water for almost six days until yesterday."

"Many people gave up their homes and ran as soon as they got close to the city," Kazu said, as he sat down next to Mevan. He named the neighbourhoods that first fell to ISIS and added, "When they got to those parts of the city, people phoned us from there and told us to run away. But some of our neighbours, no matter what we did, they didn't listen and stayed — like my uncle. He told us that ISIS had no business with us because we haven't harmed anyone. He wouldn't leave his home." Kazu paused for a second, then continued, "My poor uncle, he was so sure about his friends that he said the Arabs of the neighbouring villages promised him that he had nothing to worry about if the village fell into the hands of ISIS. But then my cousin phoned, crying for us to come and help. She said the attackers were killing everyone they could catch, and they had killed my uncle and other men. I went back to help her. On my way to help, her phone went dead, and I couldn't find her. Since then, no one has answered my calls."

When Agrin heard Kazu's story, she cried, and asked him for the name of the neighbourhood again. "Please, Kazu, are you sure? It's where my parents and most of my family lives. My God, you mean they were killed?"

"Don't panic, my daughter. I'm sure many of them escaped, as well as your family."

"Yes, Agrin," Mevan said, "we will find them as soon as we get out of here."

"Yeah, they must have run away, too. I'm sure they did," Agrin said, wiping her tears.

"Mevan, my brother, where did you get those weapons?" Serbest said, pointing. "Look! The bag is full."

Mevan looked at the weapons and said, "They belong to the ISIS soldiers."

Barin said, "Brother Serbest, we were captured by ISIS, then Uncle Mevan came after us and he killed four of them and saved us."

"Yes, he saved me as well, by killing some men who came after me," Agrin said.

Kazu said, "God bless you, brother. I swear to God and my honour that as soon as I take my family to a safe place, I will make them pay for what they have done to us and throw them off my land." Kazu pounded his fist on the ground.

"There is no way for them to live in peace with us after this," Shirin said.

The other men and women agreed.

Suddenly, a scream and shouting was heard, so Mevan, Agrin and some of the others went to see what was happening.

A woman emerged from the dark, running away from a man. She was crying, "No, no ... I won't! He will stay with me. Leave us alone. I swear to God if you take him, I will kill myself – now back off!"

Agrin and Mevan went over to the young woman and saw she was holding a child wrapped in a blanket. She was keeping the child away from the man who was being helped by two other women.

Agrin saw what was happening and ran between the woman and the man. Agrin shoved the man away and shouted, "Who are you? Let go of her child!"

The man pushed Agrin aside and went back to the young woman. "Give me the child – give him to me!" he yelled. "Don't make me force you! Listen, woman ..."

Mevan grabbed the man by the collar and turned him away from the woman. "What are you doing? Why are you bothering her, man? Tell us what is going on."

The man hit himself on the head with both hands and cried, "Brother, let go of me, she is my wife! For the love of God, help me, she is losing her mind. I do not know what to do – I am losing it, too."

Mevan let go of the man's collar and went with him back to the young woman.

Agrin was sitting next to her and put the woman's head on her shoulders. "Calm down, we won't let him take your child away. Stop crying and tell me what happened. Why does he want the child?"

The man came back to sit down next to her and begged his wife, "Please, Naze, give me the baby. You are going crazy. I can't lose you, too. Please, I'm begging you, let me bury him."

Agrin was shocked. She looked again and saw that the child was dead.

One of the two women with them said to Mevan, "Her other child, who was twenty days old, died a few days ago. This one was her two-year-old son. We were without food and with little water for days. Two days ago, their son got sick so bad that he died as well."

The other lady, who turned out to be Naze's mother-in-law, cried, "She doesn't let us bury him. She has been carrying his body for two days. I can't watch her suffering any more. My poor son has lost his children and now … to see his wife like this. Please, you try to reason with her."

Her husband held her hands. "Please, Naze, I don't want to hurt you or force you any more. Look at his body, look at his face, I can't stand to see him like that. Why don't you understand? For God's sake, he is dead, he is gone."

Naze glared at him and said, "Why can't you see my heartache? Let his body stay with me. Please let me take him and bury him somewhere near to us, then at least I can visit his grave. You buried my other baby in the middle of nowhere – her grave is unknown. She will be alone forever. I won't let you bury him like that."

Mevan sat next to her and said sadly, "My sister, it is still not clear when it will be safe to open the road and when we will be able to get to safety. Believe me, it is going to get worse."

Agrin, who understood the mother well, wiped her tears. "Naze, my sister, listen to me. I lost my daughter, too. I didn't even get to hug her one last time. I know how painful it is not having your son in your arms any more, but holding him like this will hurt you and devastate your husband. You must let him be buried somewhere here. Put a sign on his grave so you can come back later and dig him up and bury him close to you."

Her husband said, "I swear to God I will do that. I will bring back our daughter as well, and we will bury both of them together, next to each other – I promise."

Naze accepted Agrin's suggestion, crying silently, as she hugged her son's cold and lifeless body. She kissed him several times and then handed him to her husband. "Khozan, you promise me that you will return to them, you will not let them be alone in this mountain without a grave."

Khozan assured his wife, "I promise you. Now please give me our son."

With the help of Mevan and the other men, Khozan buried his son. Agrin and Shirin took Naze and the other two women and joined Kany and Agid.

Agid started crying, so Agrin hugged him and started breast-feeding him. Naze looked at Agid and called for her children. She began to sing the lullaby she used to sing putting them to bed. Heartbroken, Agrin handed her Agid, "Here! Hold him, hug him, look at his little hands. I know I'm not his mother, but I bet he sees me like one."

Naze held Agid and started rocking him. "Oh, darling baby, I know, I know, sweetie. They are ticklish, aren't they? Yes, dear baby. Oh, how good to see that even tears of a mother can still bring babies happiness."

The men returned. Khozan sat in front of his wife and hugged her, saying, "Enough crying, Naze. Whose is this baby?"

"He is Agrin's," Naze said. "Look how sweetly he is playing."

"Yes, I see," Khozan said, with tearful eyes and a trembling voice. "Sister Agrin, is it okay for me to hug him as well?"

"Yes, my brother," Mevan said, sitting next to Agrin.

Khozan hugged Agid and cried, "Hey, my sweet son, I pray for you and your parents. As a heart-broken father, may God hear that I pray and hope you never see the pain of losing this sweet boy, my sister Agrin." Khozan then handed Agid back to Agrin. He then turned to his wife and said, "Come with me, Naze, and let me take you to our son's grave."

Together, they went to their son's grave, using the light of a phone torch to see their way. The two women who had been with the couple thanked Mevan and the rest of the people for their help, then followed Khozan and Naze.

After they left, everyone prepared a place to rest with their family.

Mevan said, "Let's go — we need to get some rest as well."

"Where?" Agrin asked.

Mevan pointed and replied, "Over there, there is a place among some rocks. I checked — it's like a small cave. Shirin, Barin, please help me with our stuff. Agrin, you can stay with Kany by the fire. We'll make the place ready and then I'll come for you."

When their place at the little cave was ready, Mevan returned for Kany. While Shirin and Barin waited at the cave, two women from another group came to them with a couple of blankets.

"Come, my daughters, you have these," one of the women said. "It gets cold at night."

The other woman said, "Have this small bag, too. There are a few dates and some bread for your baby's mother."

Shirin and Barin thanked the women.

When Agrin was approaching, Shirin and Barin went to her and gave her the blankets and food. "Do you want any help with the baby?" Shirin asked.

"No, thank you," replied Agrin. "I will feed him and put him to sleep. You go and sleep, too."

"Okay, but make sure you eat something," Barin said. "You are feeding the baby so much, you need it. Okay sister?"

"I will," Agrin said.

Shirin and Barin lay down and went to sleep.

Soon afterwards, Mevan came and sat next to Agrin with their bottle of water. "Here, Agrin, please have this water as well."

"No, Mevan, this is your share, I have mine," Agrin said.

"It's for my son. I'm worried you don't have enough food ... please."

"Okay, I'll take half of it, and I promise you that if I need it, I'll ask you."

"Okay," Mevan said. "How is your foot? Let me take a look."

"No, please, it's okay, thank you," Agrin said, while changing Agid.

"The wound was deep. Are you sure?"

"Yes, it stopped bleeding after you bound it, and it doesn't hurt as much — don't worry."

"Okay, if you say so," Mevan said. "You can let Agid stay with me tonight. I will take care of him so you can rest."

"No, he should stay with me. You don't know how to put him to sleep. He will cry all night, otherwise. I'll be fine. You go and sleep."

"Okay, thank you, Agrin. If you need anything, let me know." Mevan lay down on a small rock close to them and settled into sleep.

Agrin wrapped the blanket around her and shifted a little further into the small cave, so that Agid would not wake the others. She waited for him to get tired, playing with him and watching him and making cute noises until Agid got tired and sleepy. Agrin picked him up, lay next to Kany, with her back to the others, then breastfed Agid. The sound of little Agid's feeding and breathing while drinking his milk was so peaceful it calmed Agrin's heart. She began softly singing her lullaby to him.

Mevan hadn't quite fallen asleep and the sound of Agrin's beautiful voice brought tears to his eyes.

Once Agid fell asleep, Agrin hugged and kissed him and closed her eyes. Mevan finally fell asleep with tears in his eyes, after ensuring Agrin and his son had fallen asleep.

They woke early in the morning, packed up and then continued on their way with dozens of others deeper into the mountains.

By noon, helicopters were flying over their heads, dropping water and food packages and blankets. People rushed towards the packages, while many other people ran after the helicopters or sat on the ground to insist they land to take the wounded and children with them.

When Mevan went to approach one helicopter — which was full of women, children and the elderly — it flew off.

A person nearby said to Mevan, "You also have a sick girl needing to be carried on your back. Why didn't you go with the chopper?"

"I couldn't catch up to it," Mevan said.

"Don't worry, brother," said another man, who tapped Mevan on the shoulder. "Tomorrow it will come again and we will help you catch it and save your daughter."

Mevan returned to Agrin and the girls and they all continued walking.

Eventually, Kany said, "Uncle, you can put me down now. I can walk myself. I'm feeling much better now."

"No, Baba, I can carry you. Don't worry about me, darling," Mevan replied.

Kazu said, "If you are tired, brother, I can carry my little sister for a while."

"Please, Uncle, I want to walk. I'm much better, I promise," Kany insisted.

Mevan stopped and looked over his shoulder at her shy face. He hesitated for a moment, then said, "Okay, but when you get tired or can't walk, you tell me, ha?" Mevan put Kany down carefully.

Kany stood next to Mevan and held his hand. "Okay, Uncle, let's keep going."

Around lunchtime, they heard a man shouting as he came running down a hill towards them. Four children were following him, not far behind. He cried, "Help, please, someone help!" He dropped to his knees, breathing heavily, and looked at the people coming towards him.

After catching his breath for a few moments, the man went over to Serbest and Kazu, who were armed with guns over their backs. The four children looked on — three girls and a boy.

Mevan was also walking next to Serbest and Kazu, and was the first to ask, "What's the matter?"

The man replied, "My wife – I have to go after my wife! Please help me out."

"Come, have some water and calm down," Mevan said, "so we can better understand your situation, brother."

The man shook his head and continued, "They were coming after us. My wife was injured, so she couldn't come. I had to hide her somewhere to save the children. Please help me!"

One of the men in the crowd spoke up, "We are coming, brother, but I'm sure they have captured her by now. Even if they didn't know where to find her, they are all fully armed and we can't do anything just yet."

"No, there were not many, maybe five or six of them. They followed the helicopter for the packages and saw us. If you can't come, at least give me one of those guns and please take care of my children, then I will go after her."

"Do you know where she is and how far it is from here?" Mevan asked.

"Yes," the man replied. "I was walking with the children at that stage, but if you and I go there now, we can return by nightfall."

Mevan stood up, grabbed his gun and took another weapon from his bag, then gave it to the man. "Let's go," Mevan said.

"I will owe you for my whole life – thank you, brother!" said the man.

"Does anybody else want to help?" Mevan asked. Almost all of them volunteered to help. "How many of you can fight?" Mevan said.

"We can all fight, but all we have are these three guns," said one of them.

Mevan grabbed his big bag, opened it, then gave them guns

and ammunition. "Come on, enough wasting time, lead us to her," Mevan called out, and they all ran down the hill.

Agrin and Shirin went over to the man's children. "We will look after you until your father comes back, okay?"

After Agrin and Shirin gave the children some water and food, they all continued on their way. After walking for a few hours, they sat down and rested.

Near sunset, one of the women's phones rang. "It's my husband," the woman said before she answered. "Okay, yes ... we are all together ... His children are here with Mevan's family ... Did you find their mother? Okay, okay ... stay safe." The woman hung up.

"So, what's the news?" Shirin asked. "Did they find her? Is she okay?"

"Yes," the woman said, smiling. "She is with them, and they will be here in another hour."

"See, I told you, she would come," Agrin said, hugging the four children. "Now be happy and stop crying and eat something."

After a while, the men and the man's wife appeared over the hill. Agrin and others joined them. The woman was being helped by Mevan and another man. The head and face of the woman's husband was bruised, and his lips and nose were covered with blood. The children ran to their mother, but the woman shouted at them and turned them away. Everyone, including Agrin, was surprised by the woman's reaction.

"What are you doing?" Barin called out, shocked. "Your children were dying of worry about you."

But the woman shouted back, "I do not want them! They are not my children. I don't want to see anyone."

"Stop, Nore! Are you crazy?" her husband shouted.

Shirin went up to Kazu and asked, "What happened? Did you face the enemy?"

"No," Kazu replied, "we saw her alone, limping along with the help of a stick. When we got to her and she saw her husband, she started throwing stones at him and shouted, 'Why did you leave me?' Her husband did everything to calm her down, but she kept hitting him and herself and swearing. Her husband lost his patience and slapped her a few times. Brother Mevan saw him hitting her and became angry with him. Mevan grabbed him to take him away from her. Then she kept cursing her husband all the way here, until she was almost out of breath."

Mevan went over to the woman and helped her to sit. "Calm down, my sister ... Come on, tell me what happened."

Nore, who was angry and shaking all over, picked up a stone and threw it at her husband. "It's all because that jerk left me alone!"

"Stop, please stop, sister, give me the stone," Mevan said, holding Nore's hand. "Agrin, please don't just stand there. Try to do something."

Agrin nodded and went over to sit next to Nore.

Her husband also moved closer and said, "Why are you doing this? Didn't you tell me yourself to take our children and save them first?" He shrugged when she did not reply. "So I made a mistake ... I shouldn't have left you behind, but please stop, for the sake of our children."

Mevan said, "My sister, if he didn't come now, you and your daughters would have been captured, and they would have killed your husband and your son. We do not doubt that."

"I know," she said, and started crying and beating herself.

Her husband sat down next to her and helped Agrin to hold her hands. He begged, "Stop it, please … Look what you have done to yourself. Your whole body is injured. Your head is bleeding. Why are you beating yourself?"

"I didn't do this to myself," Nore said.

"You didn't? Then who hit you like this? Who did this to you?" her husband asked, but his wife did not answer. The man shook her by the shoulders and shouted, "Nore, talk to me! Who did this to you?"

Mevan moved forward again and pulled the man aside. "Control yourself, brother. I swear to God if you touch her, I will beat you up. We just need to find out what the hell happened to her."

"Okay, Mevan, I promise I won't hit her, but let me ask her one question … one."

Mevan said, "Okay."

The man turned to his wife, sat on his knees, then asked, "Nore, please answer my question … Did they find you after we left or not?"

Nore dropped her head on Agrin's shoulder and began crying but said nothing.

"For God's sake, woman, answer me," the man said. "Did they find you or not, ha?"

But Nore kept on crying.

The man put his head on the ground and shouted, "God damn them! Those bastards! Ahhh, God … why am I not dying?" He pounded the ground with his fists.

Another man went to him, trying to calm him down.

Mevan said, "Okay, enough. Compose yourself, sister." He motioned for Agrin to calm her down. "I'm going to take your husband for a little talk." Mevan and the other man led the husband away so the women could talk more openly.

Agrin moved closer to Nore and said gently, "My sister, please calm yourself and tell me if they found you and what happened."

Nore cried, "What can I say? They found me ... There were five of them, they stood over me. I showed them my broken and wounded leg so they would have mercy on me, but they didn't. I begged them to leave me, but they didn't listen. I resisted, I argued with them. I threw stones at them to keep them away from me as much as I could. All of them started hitting me and raping me. One of them pulled out his gun to kill me, and I begged him to shoot, but they told each other, 'Why should we waste bullets on her? Let her perish here.' They humiliated me, laughed at me, they took away the water and food that my husband had left me. I begged them for mercy, but they called out, 'You are an infidel, a devil worshipper – this is your right – but we should not have mercy on you.'"

Agrin said to her, "I know what horrible things you have been through, but this is not the way – like this. You'll hurt yourself and your family more. You still have your kids and husband; they are all alive and with you."

"What are you saying, my sister?" Nore asked. "I have lost everything. Nothing can be the same. I'd rather die than live with this humiliation. I don't want anything."

"Okay, Nore, I have had enough," Shirin said firmly. "Everyone here has been hurt as much as you or even more ... okay? They beheaded my husband and took my child away, then they raped me for days. They killed Agrin's daughter and husband. Look at Kany over there ... she lost her mother, father, all her family, and was in their hands for days. For God's sake, look at her! She is still a little girl. Now if you want to kill yourself, you will hurt your loved ones and your people even more. Those ISIS criminals wanted you to die, anyway. We don't need you like this. So pull yourself together and help your family and your people to get through this crisis."

Nore listened and sympathised with what had happened to the others and what terrible calamities had befallen them. She could see that they still hadn't given up, and despite all their pain, they were trying to help her. She calmed down and hugged her children.

Agrin said to her, "I know what pain you are in, but hear me out on this: don't tell your husband the details you've told us."

"Yes, my sister, he will hurt more," one of the women next to her said.

Barin ran over and interrupted the women. "Agrin, Kany is not well, her complexion is pale and her face is hot."

Agrin hurried to Kany, took Agid from her and put her down to rest.

"Auntie, what happened?" Kany asked. "Where did you all go for so long?"

"They needed help, sweetie," Agrin said. "But you could still have called me. Come on, let's go." Agrin tried to help Kany to her feet.

But Kany put her head on Agrin's lap and said, "I want to sleep. I'm so tired."

Mevan returned and sat next to Nore. "Look, my sister, we have all suffered. I understand the pain you're in, but now you must be strong, for the sake of your children and your husband, okay? Please promise this to your brother ..."

"Okay, brother, I promise. Where is my husband now?"

"I talked to him. He is much better now. He wanted to be alone for a little while, and he will come soon."

Mevan then noticed Kany and went over to her. "Why are you pale again? Did you eat anything?"

"I'm so tired, Uncle," Kany said, in a low voice.

He hugged her. "I shouldn't have let you walk. I will get you to the doctors by tomorrow. Okay, my daughter?"

Kany nodded.

Nore's husband came back out of the darkness and sat next to his wife and children. He asked Nore, "Are you better?"

"Yes," she said tearfully, as she hugged him. "I was terrified. I shouted your name to come back to help, but you were too far away."

Her husband wiped away her tears. "It will be fine. These days will pass, we will fix it together. As long as you are alive and here breathing in my arms that is enough for me. I will make it. Now let me help you and take you to a woman to look at your leg. They say she knows this stuff well."

Mevan came to their aid and helped the husband take his wife to see the woman about her leg. Shirin guided their kids through the darkness.

It was late and most people were exhausted. Many were lying down or asleep already. Agrin and Barin made a comfortable place for Kany and she fell asleep.

A little later, Shirin came back and prepared a place with Barin for them all to get some sleep. Shirin noticed Agrin was still sitting up. "Aren't you going to sleep?" Shirin asked.

"I will after I feed and change the baby," Agrin replied. "But please, I want you to go to sleep." She picked up the baby's bag and moved a little further away so as not to disturb the others.

It was a beautiful moonlit night and so peaceful. Agrin spread the blanket and began to change Agid. She was talking and playing with him, and her heart was warming up as she saw Agid's cute smile and playfulness. She was so happy at that moment. Maybe she was remembering the times with her baby daughter, or perhaps she had forgotten about her death again and had seen her spirit in the little boy's eyes.

Mevan came back and saw Agrin and his son. He stood there for a while and looked at them. He went forward to her and said, "Haven't you slept yet?"

"No, Agid is not tired yet," Agrin said. "But after I feed him, I will put him down to sleep."

Mevan went and sat behind Agrin because she was breastfeeding, then asked, "Agrin, when we get out of here, what do you want to do next?"

"I'm going to look for my family and my husband's family," Agrin replied. "Why do you ask, Mevan?"

Mevan kept silent for a while, then changed the subject without answering her question. "When Agid is finished feeding, you can let him be with me for tonight, so you can get some sleep."

"Okay."

"You take excellent care of him. I was so lucky to come across you. If it weren't for you, he wouldn't have survived."

"Here, he is ready," Agrin said, then handed Agid to Mevan.

"Okay, thank you. Leave him to me, and you go have a nice rest tonight."

"Okay, but … if he gets cold or hungry tonight, you can bring him back to me to sleep. Or at least wake me if he needs me," Agrin said, releasing Agid's hands.

Mevan was encouraged by Agrin saying that she wanted the child to be with her. Mevan felt the attachment he was hoping for between her and his son. He smiled and held Agrin's hands, saying, "Okay, I'll bring him back to you if that happens because I can see it is better for him to be with you. Now, you eat something, then go to sleep. Don't worry, I'll put him in your arms when I come back." He bent down and kissed Agrin on the forehead and left with his son.

Agrin followed him with her eyes until he disappeared in the dark, then she lay down next to Kany and closed her eyes.

Later, Mevan saw Agrin had made Agid's bed ready next to her. He placed Agid, who was now sleeping, in her arms,

"You came back," Agrin said, opening her eyes. "What took you so long? Where did you go?"

"Yeah … Agid is sleeping," Mevan whispered, as he threw the blanket over both of them. "Now, you go back to sleep." He went over to check on Barin and Shirin. He made sure they were okay, then rolled little Agid's cloak and put it under Kany's head. He kissed her on the forehead, then went to his spot for the night, but started thinking instead of sleeping.

11

Early in the morning, everyone agreed to move to a safer place. Mevan tied Kany on his back and asked Agrin and the others to follow him.

Around noon, a helicopter was heard throwing packages of water, food and blankets to people on the ground. People started yelling for the chopper to land. It soon landed in a suitable place, then the men went to help the sick and very young to get on board.

Mevan began running towards the open door of the helicopter. He shouted over his shoulder to Agrin, "Hurry up, come on!" Mevan handed Kany to a man inside the helicopter. Mevan turned and took Agid from Agrin's arms, then gave his son to the man in the cabin. "Okay, Agrin," Mevan roared, over the noise of the chopper, "now it's your turn. Go up."

"What about you and Shirin and Barin?" Agrin asked, in bewilderment.

"The helicopter is almost full, and there are still more children and elders to go. We will come next time."

"No, you should go. He's your son — he needs you, not me," Agrin insisted. "Why should I go? What if we don't find you?"

"Agrin, listen to me," Mevan pleaded, "my son and Kany need you more than me. We will catch up soon."

"Okay," Agrin said.

Mevan took Agrin's hand and helped her aboard. He said, "Take care of them for me."

"I will," she said.

As the helicopter rose, Mevan could see Agrin taking Agid from Kany. He waved his hand until the helicopter disappeared into the blue.

Inside the cabin, the man sitting next to Agrin said, "Don't worry, my sister, we are going to the camp now. They will take care of you there. Soon enough, your husband and the others will come, too."

When they arrived at the camp, they were helped off the helicopter. Kany and Nore couldn't walk, so a few nurses came and took them on stretchers to a doctor.

Agrin, with Agid in her arms, followed Kany inside a large tent. They placed Kany on a bed.

A doctor came over and asked Agrin, "What happened to her?"

"She escaped from ISIS."

The doctor checked her temperature and asked the nurse to take Kany's dress off. When Kany overheard that request, she hid behind Agrin.

"All right," the doctor said, "I see you're not comfortable with me being here, and that is okay, my daughter. I'll pull the curtains around you and move away. The nurse will examine you, then, if it is necessary, I will come in to help you, okay?"

"Okay," Kany said, nodding.

The doctor asked, "Do you want this lady to be here with you?"

"Yes," replied Kany, "I want my aunt Agrin to stay." Kany reached out with her shaky, weak hands to hold Agrin's hand.

"Very well, my daughter," the doctor said. "Now, be comfortable and don't be scared." As soon as he moved away, Kany burst into tears.

The nurse asked her, "How old are you?"

"I will be thirteen in two months."

"Let me take off your clothes and look at your injuries."

Reluctantly, Kany agreed.

The nurse was horrified to see Kany's wounded and bloodied body. She asked the doctor to come quickly and look.

The doctor rushed over and examined Kany. "My daughter, how many men raped you?" he asked.

"I don't know, I don't remember," Kany cried, scared.

Agrin handed Agid to the nurse, then held Kany in her arms and said, "Sweetheart, don't be afraid. Just tell the doctor whatever you remember."

"I do not remember the first night because I was unconscious. Then I was imprisoned in the bathroom, and I was harassed until I was unconscious again. Maybe ten men ... over several nights. I do not remember more than this." Kany began crying.

"Enough, that is enough," said the doctor, his voice trembling with great sadness and anger. He started treating Kany and asked the nurse to fetch her clean clothes. The nurse gave Agid back to Agrin before she went for the clothes.

When he had finished, the doctor said to Agrin, "My sister, please come to my room. I have to explain her situation to you."

With Agid in her arms, Agrin followed the doctor inside a small office. The doctor closed the door, offered her a seat, then sat down on his chair. "She has a lot of infection. There are signs on her body that she may have caught some disease. Still, I cannot be sure until we get her test results back."

"Okay, what will happen now?" Agrin asked.

"She is in a lot of pain right now, but don't worry, she is going to be fine, even though we will have to send her to the hospital."

"Okay, send her — do whatever she needs," Agrin said. "But I'm going with her as well."

"You and your baby should stay here," the doctor said. "It's not a safe place to take a baby."

"But her uncle left her in my care. I can't send her alone."

"You can still go to visit her, then, after she gets better, we will bring her back to the camp to be with you. But you can't stay with her while you are caring for a baby, so please do as I ask. Kany has been through a lot and, as I see it, she will have a hard time trusting new people, so if you will please talk to her and make her feel comfortable to come along, it will be easier for us as well as her."

"Okay, I'll talk to her."

The doctor looked at Agrin and said, "You have a cut head, I see. Is your foot bloody as well? I'd like to take a look."

Agrin handed Agid to the doctor, saying, "I was captured by them, too, but could you see to Agid first?"

"How old is baby Agid?" the doctor asked, as he took off Agid's clothes.

"Three months," Agrin replied.

"Are you breastfeeding?"

"Yes, but he is not my baby. His father left him with me until he gets here."

"What about his mother? Where is she?"

"She is dead," Agrin said, sighing sadly.

"How long since he's been fed?"

"Not too long ago," Agrin replied. "I breastfed him in the helicopter on the way here."

"So, where is your baby?" he asked.

"They killed her."

"I am so sorry to hear that. To hear such horrible news ... I can't find any words to tell you the depth of my sorrow, my sister."

Agrin nodded, holding Agid's hands, while tears fell down her cheeks. "How is Agid? Is he okay?" she asked.

"His weight doesn't match his age, but after all that this poor baby has been through, it is understandable. In a couple of weeks, bring him back and we will re-check his weight. If we don't see any improvement, then we will have to find out what is going on with him. Okay now, let me see your head. I will clean up the dried blood so I can see how deep the wound is. If it starts hurting, let me know."

"Okay," Agrin said.

The nurse appeared at the door to the office. "I did all of Kany's tests and she is ready now."

"Very well," the doctor said. "Please come and take care of Agrin and see to her foot and also her shoulder. I ordered some tests for her to make sure she is well. I'm going to contact the hospital to check Kany in."

"Yes, doctor," the nurse replied, and stepped inside the office.

By the time Agrin had been treated, the doctor had returned and he took Agrin to see Kany.

Kany looked up from her bed. "Where did you go, auntie?"

"Sweetheart, the doctor says that you should go to the hospital. There are not enough facilities here to help you. I wanted to go with you, but the doctor says it's not a safe place for a baby because Agid might get sick. After they treat you, they will return you here. Mevan will come to visit you as soon as he can. So, what do you say?"

"I don't know," Kany said, worried and scared.

"Okay, Kany, don't cry, sweetie," Agrin said, holding Kany's hand. "If you want me to come, then I'll go with you — whatever you say."

Kany paused to think for a moment, then said, "That's okay, I'll go by myself. I don't want Agid to get sick."

The doctor said, "That is brave of you, my daughter. Please try not to worry. I will be with you all the time and, anytime you ask for Agrin, I will bring her to visit you. I will now leave you with Agrin and Agid until we are ready to leave."

"Thank you," Kany said.

After Kany had been taken to the hospital, one of the camp officials took Agrin and Agid to a dormitory tent. He explained to her, "My sister, you and your baby are safe here. I will bring you food and everything you need. If you want anything else, you can come to the same office that you were in earlier, and we will help you out."

"I will, thank you," Agrin said. "Also, will I be able to call the hospital later so I can talk to Kany?"

"Oh, don't you have a phone?" asked the official.

"No, I don't."

"Okay, sister, whenever you need to phone, you can come to the office. For now, this is the tent you can stay in. They are all women here, so I hope you feel comfortable."

"Thank you," Agrin said.

The official stood at the opening of the tent and called out, "Aunt Marjan! Are you inside? Auntie, where are you?"

A middle-aged lady came out of the tent and said, "Hello, son, how can I help you?"

"I brought you a guest," he replied. "This is Agrin, she has arrived today. We have just come from the doctor. If you have enough space for her, she would like to stay in your tent until she finds her family."

"Yes, of course," Marjan said, with a heart-warming smile. "We will look after her, don't worry, son."

"Okay, thank you, auntie. I will go and bring the necessary things for her and her baby," he said, as he walked away.

Marjan came forward and invited Agrin into the tent, saying, "Come, my daughter, let's go inside, you must be exhausted. Please sit down, darling."

Agrin thanked her and sat down. There were another two women and two children inside.

Marjan sat next to Agrin. "As you heard, my name is Marjan," she said, then pointed to the others. "This girl is my daughter Kajal, and this one is my daughter-in-law Galavij. Over here, we have my granddaughter Rondek and my grandson Hozan."

"Hello, nice to meet you all. I'm Agrin and this is Agid. Thank you for letting us stay with you."

"Of course, my daughter," Marjan said. "You must be hungry. Kajal will make something for you to eat. Do you need anything else for yourself or your baby?"

"Well, I haven't heard anything about my parents and family, and I haven't been able to call them yet," Agrin said.

"Do you want a phone?"

"Yes, that would be wonderful, Aunt Marjan."

Marjan handed her phone to Agrin and said, "Here, call your family to find out where they are."

"Thank you," Agrin said, as she took the phone. However, as she went to dial the number, she stopped.

"Why don't you dial the number?" Galavij asked.

"I'm afraid," Agrin replied. "I heard that the first area of the city that fell is still in the hands of ISIS and that is where my family lived."

Kajal said, "My father and brother had also gone there for business. When ISIS attacked, my brother phoned and told us to leave the house as soon as possible and run to this mountain. He was talking to us and guiding us on the phone until we reached the foot of the mountain, then his phone went dead. We haven't heard from them for more than a week now."

Agrin was now certain that something terrible must have happened to her family. Her hands started trembling, and she put the phone down.

"But, Agrin, you have to call. What if they are looking for you?" Marjan said. "Pick up the phone and call."

Agrin picked up the phone again and dialled the number of her father's house. No one answered.

She dialled her father's mobile number, but it was turned off.

She began to weep while she dialled her older brother, whose phone was also off.

As she dialled her younger brother's phone number, she cried, "Please, Rezgar, answer the phone." The phone started ringing, but it rang out with no answer. "He is not answering, either. Why is no one picking up their phone?"

She dialled Rezgar's number again. "Please, little brother, answer the phone. I'm begging you," she mumbled, as she waited.

Finally, her call was answered, but nobody spoke.

"Hello, hello, why aren't you talking, Brother? It's me, Agrin," she said. "Where are you now? Are you in the city?"

The voice of a stranger speaking in Arabic replied, "Who are you?"

Agrin was shocked to hear this voice and began shaking as she asked, "Where is my brother? Why do you have his phone?"

The man said in a commanding manner, "First, tell me where you are – are you inside the city?"

Agrin did not reply.

The man continued, "Your brother has joined us and I will bring him to you if you tell me where you are."

Agrin knew enough Arabic to understand what he was asking, and she did her best to reply in his language. "If you are telling the truth, let me talk to my brother first – put him on the phone," Agrin said as assertively as she could, even though she sensed the situation was hopeless.

The man paused for a second, then said, "He says he does not want to talk to you. You are an infidel to him now. He will talk to you when you're here."

"Okay, tell me his name. Tell me, what is my brother's name? Then I will come to him right now."

The man did not reply.

Agrin cried, "I know you are lying! Please tell me the truth, what have you done to him?"

The man now knew Agrin would not believe any more of his lies, so he said, "Your brother is dead. Now, you better come to us by your own choice and become a believer so that you can be married to one of our Jihadis like a free woman. Otherwise, we will get you sooner than you think and you will be enslaved for rest of your life." He hung up.

With that, Agrin lost all hope for every member of her family. She shed tears and cried in disbelief, "It's impossible! I can't lose *all* my family. I cannot lose all of them – my parents, my brothers ..."

Marjan held up her hands and called skywards, "God, hear us out! Why has this happened to us? How we will cope with this hell? You must help us, God!"

Marjan wept along with Agrin and hugged her.

Galavij took Agid from Agrin, and Kajal brought her some water.

Marjan said, "What can I say, my daughter? Maybe he is lying, and your brother is still alive. Don't lose all hope; God will help us."

"No, auntie, he didn't lie. They have killed him," Agrin sighed. "I have seen them, I know how they are."

"Don't say that, my daughter, you don't know. Maybe he has escaped."

Long, painful hours passed as Agrin sat motionless, deep in thought, tears continually running down her face.

"Come, my sister," Galavij said, as she offered Agrin some food, "you have to eat something and feed your baby. He is crying and must be hungry."

"Yes, my daughter, God will help us out somehow," Marjan said, as she made Agrin a bite to eat.

"God?!" Agrin exclaimed, with a heavy heart full of anger. "God didn't help us and will not help us."

"Don't say that, my daughter," Marjan said in tears. "God is my hope, the one pillar I have counted on, the reason that I'm still waiting for my son and his father to come back."

Agrin, who had lost everything and had no hope left, didn't want to carry on any further. "You are right, auntie, I hope they come back. Don't lose your hope." For the rest of the day, Agrin couldn't eat anything, but she cuddled and fed Agid.

The next day around noon, Agrin left Agid sleeping inside the tent and slipped outside.

Marjan saw her and was concerned. She followed Agrin to the door of the tent and asked, "Where are you going, my daughter? Let me come with you."

"I can't just sit here and wait. I am going to see if Agid's father has arrived or not."

"Okay, my daughter, let's go together. I can't let you go by yourself," Marjan said, as she quickly put on her shoes.

Agrin and Marjan walked all over the site, but there was no sign of Mevan and the girls. After quite some time waiting at the gate to the compound, they both returned to the tent.

When they arrived back at their tent, Agrin said hello to Nore, her son and three daughters.

"Oh, thank God, my sister, Agrin, I was looking for you," Nore said. "I asked them to take us to you until my husband gets here."

Agrin said, "Yes, my sister, I was at the gate waiting for them, but they didn't come. Maybe they will get here tomorrow."

"Are you ill, Agrin? Have you seen a doctor?" Nore asked. "Where is Kany? Has something happened? You don't look good."

Marjan answered for Agrin, "My sister, how can I say this ...? Agrin called her family yesterday. Her brother's phone was in the hands of an ISIS soldier. He told her that they had killed her brother and her family. The poor girl has not eaten since yesterday." Marjan shed more tears.

"My poor sisters," Nore said, holding Agrin's hands, "I wish I knew a way to help you cope with this tragedy, but you have to eat something. The baby needs you, you are all he has."

Agrin looked at Agid's innocent little face as he was busy playing with her hair. She sighed, "You are right." She kissed his little hands and started feeding him.

The next day, a man came to their tent and called out, "Is Agrin here? Come out, please, you have guests."

Agrin ran out of the tent and found Shirin and Barin waiting for her. "You made it!" Agrin cried, as she hugged them. "But where is Mevan?"

Barin hesitated to answer. Instead, she peered inside the tent, then asked, "Where are Kany and Agid? I don't see them."

"Kany is hospitalised," Agrin replied, leading Barin and Shirin inside the tent. "I talked to her and her doctor yesterday – she is much better now. Agid is sleeping over there next to my new friend's kids. Now, why are you alone? When will Mevan get here?"

Shirin looked down at her feet, then said, "Agrin, Uncle Mevan ..."

Agrin gently tilted Shirin's head upwards and looked her in the eyes. "Uncle Mevan ... what?" Agrin frowned. "What happened to him?"

Shirin couldn't speak and looked at Barin.

Barin blurted out, "He will not return. He joined the Kurdish forces. He gave me this phone. Let me play his message for you."

Agrin couldn't believe this news and grabbed the phone from Barin to listen to Mevan's voice message: "Agrin, I couldn't come with the girls. We have lost everything. And now enemies who killed our loved ones and raped our girls and women are living on our land and in our homes. I can't run away. I'm sorry I didn't tell you my plan, I knew you would never accept it. Agid is all I have left in my life. Please be his mother and I promise you, up to the last second of my life, I will fight ISIS till the last one is dead or out of our land. Take this phone with you, and I will call you. Take care of Agid and Kany, Shirin and Barin. They, like me, also have no one but you. Look after them, stay safe."

Shirin took out a green necklace and handed to Agrin. "Uncle Mevan said this belongs to Agid's mother and you should keep it for him."

Agrin didn't know what to say or do. She let out a long, slow breath as she took the necklace and sat back on a nearby pillow.

At the same time, Shirin's phone rang. "Hello ... Yes, she is here, yes, they are fine ... Okay, one second, I will pass the phone to her." Shirin handed the phone to Nore. "It's your husband."

Nore grasped the phone and asked anxiously, "Where are you? Why haven't you arrived yet?"

"I can't come," her husband replied. "I'm going to the war with the rest of the men and women who are going now."

"What are you saying? You can't leave us alone here like this! Please come back – they will kill you," Nore said, crying and begging.

"I know it's hard, but you and the kids are safe there, so please stop crying and be strong."

But Nore didn't want to let him go and cried, "Please, how can I take care of the kids without you? What if you never come back and something happens to you? I swear, I will kill myself."

Her husband replied grimly, "Listen to me, woman — stop your crying. What do you mean they *will* kill me? Are you listening to yourself? They already killed me the day they started killing and raping my people and my family, taking whatever we had. Now it's their turn. I'm going to war and I won't come back until they are dead or I am. Now, pull yourself together, otherwise I will not call you again until I return or the news of my death comes to you. This unjust war will not end if we all try to stay safe."

Nore wiped her tears and said, "Okay, you're right. Don't get mad, I'm sorry."

"Okay, sweetheart, I won't. Now, don't cry. I contacted my uncle and he is coming to take you and the kids to his house. I must go now."

"All right, but please take care of yourself and be safe," Nore said.

"I will. Kiss the kids for me and I'll call you tomorrow," he said, then hung up.

A few days passed, then Nore and her kids left the camp with her husband's uncle.

Two weeks later, Barin hurried into the tent one morning and announced, "Kurdish forces have entered the camp. They want to give military training to the women and men. I am going to register for training. Are you coming as well?"

Shirin said to Kajal, "Let's go and see what's going on." They got ready without delay and strode out of the tent behind Barin.

Agrin picked up Agid and followed them.

When they arrived at the recruitment tent, an armed woman enthusiastically welcomed all the new arrivals. Then she said to them, "I know you have been through difficult and painful days.

Still, it is not yet over. We don't want you to fight against the most dangerous enemies that we all have faced, but we want you to learn how to fight to defend yourself and your family. After you have been trained, it will be your choice what to do next."

Kajal and Shirin, along with Barin, wrote their names on a recruitment list they were offered. It committed them to a training roster across the coming mornings. Agrin wanted to put her name down, but she couldn't because of Agid.

One of the military women came up to Agrin and asked, "Do you want to learn as well?"

"Yes, very much, but I can't because of the child. I can't leave him with someone. He is too little."

The woman looked at Agid and tickled his tummy, then said to Agrin, "You don't have to do the training each morning. If you learn the basics of self-defence, you will have done a lot. When you have free time, come down and I will personally teach you. So you will still be able to take care of this cute baby of yours as well."

Agrin accepted and thanked her.

Two months passed and Kany returned. Her physical condition was much better, and she was improving mentally every day – her nightmares were becoming less frequent.

Mevan contacted Agrin several times and reported the advance of the Kurdish forces and the enemy's defeat. Everyone was praying for the freedom of the city and good news.

One afternoon, a few Kurdish soldiers came to the women's tent. One of the soldiers called out, "Aunt Marjan ... Aunt Marjan ..."

"Yes, what has happened?" she replied, as she walked out of the tent.

The soldier was standing next to a woman and her daughter. He said, "Aunt Marjan, this is Ronak. She and her little daughter Havin would like to stay with you until we can find a place for her."

One of the camp officials was standing next to the soldiers. He looked apologetic as he said, "Aunt Marjan, I know you don't have enough space, but we are out of tents. We had no choice, but I promise you we will find another place that will take them as soon as we can."

"That is okay, son, they can stay with us," Marjan said kindly. "Don't worry, we will take care of them."

She turned to the young woman and held her hand. "Come, my daughter, come in. You and your daughter must be hungry."

Shirin picked up Havin and followed the two women into the tent. The official called after them, "Thank you, Aunt Marjan, and you others, so very much. God knows, if our people were not so kind and didn't care for each other like this, then we could not help as much with the little facility that we have."

Marjan smiled and replied, "I know, son. We all need to help each other and take care of each other all the time, especially in this situation. If there is still someone left, bring her to us. It's a small tent, but we can still fit a few more people in with us."

The official considered her words, then said, "Yes, Aunt Marjan, I'll keep that in mind, thank you. Now we have to go. If you need anything, let us know."

"Son, wait … I gave my husband's and son's names to check for them a long time ago, and I haven't heard anything yet."

"I know, auntie," the official said, "but unfortunately, we haven't heard anything yet. I assure you the names of all of you are on the list. We will inform you if we receive any news. All my hopes are on God to return them safely."

"Okay, son, you can go now, thank you," Marjan said.

Everyone inside the tent made Ronak and her daughter feel welcome.

"Eat some food, and I'll feed Havin," Agrin said, putting Agid down next to her. Agrin started giving food to the little girl.

"I'll give you a pillow," Kajal said, as she picked up a pillow. "You look so tired. Rest a little."

"No, I'm okay, thank you," Havin said.

Galavij brought a tray of tea for everyone and sat next to Ronak. "So where do you come from?"

"We lived in a village near the city. The day our village was attacked, they killed the men and enslaved the rest of us, including my daughter and me, but we escaped," Ronak said mournfully.

Shirin held Ronak's hand and said sadly, "God knows what calamities have befallen you, like us, my poor sister — we all sympathise. At least you have your daughter with you. I can't pass a second in my life without thinking about my poor son who they have taken away."

"Each one of us has horrible memories and pain that kills us inside every day," Marjan said. "But at least talking about it together helps us to cope better, my darling daughter."

Everyone fell silent, lost in their thoughts.

After a while, Kany asked, "Ronak, how did you escape?"

"When they caught us, they separated us all. They took two of my daughters from me. Sheller, nine years old, was put on the bus on the first day and taken away. Nalan was seven years old. She was with me, but a month ago, they took her away as well. They said she doesn't need me any more, now she has grown up. I don't know where my daughters are now. They imprisoned me in the barracks with some other young women and harassed us. They gave us so little food that even my little daughter could not get enough to eat. They raped me many times in front of my daughter's eyes – horrible times that tear my heart apart. But I got lucky one day. They locked me inside a room and didn't take me back to the others. After they left, I got up in the middle of the night and saw that I could open the window. I grabbed my daughter and we jumped out of the window. Without looking back, we kept running. When we entered the city, my daughter was crying. I knocked at several houses, but no one opened their door. Finally, someone opened their door, but, when he realised that I had escaped, he closed the door and asked me to leave. He threatened to hand me over to ISIS again. I was so scared that I kept running again until a car stopped next to me and a man got out and called, 'Hey! Stop! Did you run away?' I was terrified and told myself that everything was over, but made myself face the terrible punishment coming my way. They had already showed us videos of burning girls alive in cages and I still remember their tortured faces and hear their cries ... So, I backed away from this man, step by step, looking into his eyes and begging him to let me go. It was my last chance either to escape from him or kill myself, but I had nothing in my hands to finish myself before he could get to me, so I ran into the darkness, hoping he would shoot me. I didn't get far before I fell over some rocks and cut my daughter's head. She was so scared, but she held her mouth to stop herself from crying out. The man shouted at me, 'Stop running! Are you okay?' He came closer and asked, 'Is that a child you have under your clothes?' Frightened and shivering, I said, 'Yes, please let us go.' He came forward and lifted me, then said, 'Don't be afraid, stop struggling, calm down. I will help you, sister, I promise. Come and I will drive you.' He took me to his house. He and his wife were so kind to my daughter and me. Then two weeks later, he took me out of the city, pretending I was his second wife and handed me to the Kurdish forces. That was what I have been through. And now I can only think about what has happened to my other two girls. I am desperate to get them back. I wish they would have been killed when they beheaded my husband." Ronak couldn't continue and covered her face with both hands and started crying.

Shirin got up and hugged her. "Do not cry, my poor sister, we can't bring them back by crying. It's not the time for grief. We are training with Peshmerga to learn how to fight and you can come, too. When our training is over, we will join the Kurdish forces and go after our children."

Ronak wiped her tears and nodded. "Okay, I'll come with you. Can I take my daughter with me?"

"Let her stay with me," Agrin said warmly. "I will take care of her."

One day at noon, Shirin, Barin, Kajal and Ronak entered the tent after they had finished training. Kajal said, "Agrin, mother, come, we have good news. They liberated the city. Now our city is free again. Can you believe it – in three months, we took it back?

"Oh God, that is the best news I could get ..." Agrin exclaimed.

Everyone was happy and hugged each other.

Kany then asked, "So why didn't Uncle Mevan call us and tell us? He said he would call whenever they were successful."

"I haven't heard from him for a while now," Barin said anxiously.

"Let me call him," Agrin said. She tried ringing him a few times, but Mevan didn't answer.

"What if something happened to my uncle?" Kany said nervously.

"Don't think that way," Marjan said. "I'm sure your uncle is fine and he will call soon."

"Yes, he must not have his phone with him," Agrin said, trying to calm Kany. "Didn't he say not to call him and wait for him to call?"

The next day around noon, the phone rang. Kany hurried to answer it. "Hello …?" Then a beautiful smile beamed across Kany's face. She quickly said to Agrin, "It's Uncle Mevan." She continued talking on the phone, "Uncle, why didn't you answer our call? We were so worried about you!" After a few seconds, Kany had to say goodbye, then ran to Agrin. "Uncle is coming back in a few days!"

12

One morning later that week, Agrin put Agid down for a nap in his sleeping spot inside their tent, then handed Havin to Kany. Agrin said to Kany, "I gave Havin her breakfast, but she is still tired and needs to sleep some more. I think you should also try to get some more rest because I know you didn't sleep much last night with the nightmares you were having.

"You're right, Aunt Agrin, I will try to sleep some more," Kany said.

"I'll go and wash the kids' clothes," Agrin said, then went outside the tent.

An hour later, Agrin was busy hanging out clothes to dry, when she saw Marjan coming towards her with a big smile on her face.

"Agrin, I have good news for you, sweetheart," she said.

When Agrin heard these words, she stopped what she was doing and said, "I knew, auntie, I knew my family weren't all dead."

But the smile disappeared from Marjan's face when she realised Agrin was expecting a member of her family to show up. Marjan looked Agrin in the eyes and waited a few moments. "Well, it's ..."

Agrin heard a voice call out, "Hello, Agrin." She looked behind Marjan to see Mevan approaching. Agrin's face fell and tears began to form. She was disappointed in her wish for at least one member of her family to return. But she quickly put a smile back on and walked towards Mevan. "Hello, Mevan, welcome back. I am thrilled to see you!"

"Thank you, Agrin," Mevan said, with a broad smile. "It's so good to see you!"

Mevan introduced the two men who were following him and Agrin welcomed them. Marjan then introduced herself, welcoming them all with the warmest of smiles.

Mevan had noticed that Agrin had tried to cover her first reaction to his arrival. He sensed the reason and said sympathetically to her, "I'm sure we will soon find out some news about your family as well."

Agrin put on a brave face and replied, "I'm sure we will, too."

Mevan nodded, then looked around. "Where are the girls and Agid?"

"Agid is having a nap inside the tent with Kany," Agrin replied.

Marjan added, "The other girls went with my daughter to do military training. They will return around sunset."

"Excellent," Mevan said, "I can hardly wait to see them."

Marjan led them all over to the tent, then pulled back the door so they could go inside.

"Thank you, mother," Mevan said.

"It's so good to see you finally, Mevan," Marjan said. "The girls talk a lot about you, and they have missed you so much."

"I have missed them deeply, too," Mevan said.

Marjan went over to a little stove to boil water for tea. "Now, you and your friends must be hungry."

"Thank you, Mother Marjan, we are," Mevan replied, then went to his son, who was still sleeping in the corner of the tent. Mevan sat next to Agid and looked at his beautiful face. He pushed the mosquito net away from Agid and held his little hand.

Agrin whispered to Mevan, "Do you want me to wake him up? He has been sleeping for more than an hour."

Mevan looked at his son, smiled and said, "No, let him sleep." He turned to Agrin. "My son has changed a lot and grown so much already – thank you, Agrin."

"Yes, he has," she said, returning his smile.

"Where is Kany?" Mevan asked.

"Oh, she is sleeping over there. Ever since she heard you were coming back, she has been so excited. Every day she has been waiting for you at the gate, saying, "Today must be the day that my uncle will come."

Mevan stood up, with a laugh, and said, "Okay, I think she's had enough sleep." He sat down next to her bed and whispered in her ear, "Hey, my sweet daughter, it's almost noon. Don't you want to wake up?" He gently shook her shoulder and said, "Come on, big girl, time to get up, Kany ... Baba."

Kany opened her eyes and, seeing Mevan, jumped into his arms with joy. "Uncle, I missed you very much, I was so worried about you."

"Why, silly? I told you not to be, that I would be fine. My sweet daughter, how glad I am that you are better," Mevan said, hugging her tightly.

Marjan looked to the sky with a prayer in her heart and, with a beautiful smile, said, "Oh, Kany, how good for you to see your uncle again. I pray to witness this joy for all of us who hope to see their loved ones come back one day soon."

Mevan silently appreciated Marjan's words for a moment. Then he joked, "Okay, Kany, can you make a nice tea for your uncle and his friends? Let me see how good you are at making tea."

Kany smiled at his good humour, then got up and went to make tea.

Agrin began to spread a tablecloth and put out some simple snacks.

"What about the city?" Marjan asked. "How is the city?"

"We liberated the city, Mother Marjan," Mevan replied proudly.

One of Mevan's friends, Bapir, added, "But the city was destroyed. The enemy had dug themselves into trenches in many places, but cannons and tanks were a great help to us."

"What about the people who stayed in the city?" Agrin asked.

Mevan's other friend, Hawal, said, "When we got there, most of the houses in the city were empty. In some houses there were women and children, but there were no men. We were told they killed all males over nine years old. But most of them left the city and ran to the mountains, which was the right decision. We were still able to save many of our women and daughters who had been kept in their prison."

Bapir raised his head and said, "Brother Hawal, you should mention that the women helped us a lot, even when they were prisoners."

Hawal nodded and continued, "Yes, Bapir is right – they gave us all the information we needed to attack the enemy. Some of our women and girls, as soon as they were released, armed themselves and started fighting. The motivation that our fearless women gave us was one of the main reasons we were able to defeat those occupiers and thieves."

Mevan looked at Agrin, who was deep in thought, and asked, "Agrin, have you got any news about your family yet?"

"No, I haven't," replied Agrin sadly.

Marjan said, "The first day she arrived, she called her brother's phone, but an ISIS soldier answered the phone and told her that her brother had been killed."

Agrin's tears started falling.

"Hey, hey, please don't cry, Agrin," Mevan said. "You still don't know, they might be still alive. We have seen many of them come back."

"Yes, my sister," Bapir said, "don't lose all your hope."

At this moment, Havin woke up and sat on the edge of her bed with her cute, sleepy face and curly hair. She rubbed her eyes and looked at the strangers in surprise. Her eyes drifted to Agrin, then Havin put her dummy in her mouth and walked with her little blanket in her hand and sat on Agrin's lap.

"Who is this beautiful little girl, Agrin?" Mevan asked. "Is she your relative?"

Marjan looked at Agrin, chuckled, then turned to Mevan. "No, my son, she is Ronak's daughter. Ronak is training with the other girls. When they come back, I will introduce her to you. She escaped from ISIS not long ago. Oh, you should have seen that poor woman, she was so miserable about her two young daughters who are in ISIS's hands. But she is much better and stronger since she started to train. She has built up so much hope of finding them. And Agrin is taking care of her daughter until she comes back. But I have to say that our little Havin loves Agrin so much that, even when Ronak comes back, she doesn't go to her – she stays with Agrin, even at night."

Kany said, "She calls Aunt Agrin 'Mummy', and calls her mother by her name."

"How old is she?" Mevan asked.

"Two-and-a-half," Agrin replied, as she picked up Havin. "I'll go wash her face and change her outside."

After Agrin left, Marjan said to Mevan, "My son, please do something for the poor girl. No one from her family has been found yet, neither mother nor father. She returns with tears in her eyes every time she goes for news in the camp office. Please search and ask your friends, maybe you can find some hope for her."

Bapir asked, "What happened to her family? Where did they live?"

Marjan said, "She was in her yard when a rocket hit her house, and she pulled out her eight-month-old daughter who was dead under the rubble. Her husband was a school teacher who fought ISIS when they attacked. He killed some of them after he was captured. Oh, it's hard for me to even say it … the poor girl said that their commander killed her husband in front of her eyes, and the same commander took Agrin to rape her. She said she killed him that night and ran away for help. Then she came across Mevan." Marjan finished her story with a sigh, then turned to Mevan, who was shocked and heartbroken. "Mevan, my son, take care of the poor girl. All she has now is you – help her."

"I will, mother, I will do everything I can for her. I will keep looking for her family until we find them. Till then, I will take care of her as my family, I promise you." He paused when Agrin entered.

Agrin said to Havin, "Okay, now you sit here next to your Mother Marjan, then I'll get you some food." Havin sat down and Agrin went to prepare her food.

While Agrin was feeding Havin, Agid woke up. Kany went over and hugged Agid, then took him to Mevan.

"Hello, Baba, how are you?" Mevan said. "Look at how you have grown up so much. You have become such a strong young man." Mevan kissed Agid, hugged him, then put him on his lap. Mevan was so happy and his heart was so warmed to see his son happy and healthy. Mevan started playing with him and he took the red dummy out of Agid's mouth. "Put this away, boy. You are a grown man now — you are six months old," Mevan joked. But Agid went red all over his face and tried to put the dummy back in his mouth. Mevan laughed. "Okay, Baba, sorry ... Come, you can have it back. No need to fight, sir."

"Look at the way he grabbed Mevan's hair," said Hawal, laughing. "He is a good fighter, like his father."

The beautiful and loving scene of father and son brought a smile to everyone's face, including Agrin. Mevan saw Agrin's smile, hugged Agid, then went closer to her and said, "Agrin, I promise you, I will keep looking for your family. I'm sure that we will find them. Until then, I will take care of you like my family, like Kany and the girls, okay?"

"Thank you, Mevan, you are a good man," Agrin said, looking into his eyes.

Agid was grabbing onto Agrin's scarf and wanted to go to her. "Look at him," Mevan said. "You got tired of your father this quick, huh? You naughty boy." Mevan laughed, then handed Agid to Agrin. "Here, Agrin, have him before he pulls out all my hair."

Agrin hugged Agid, and he immediately calmed down and started laughing and playing with Agrin's hair. This was what Mevan had hoped for: to see his son this happy.

Kany said, "Uncle Mevan, Shirin and Barin are going for training every day. Agrin also went for a month and learned a lot. I want to go, too, but Aunt Agrin says I have to ask for your permission first."

"No, Kany, it's too soon for you," Mevan said, in a serious tone.

"But I also want to learn, so I can fight if we are attacked again," Kany insisted.

"I told you, Kany, it is too soon for you to take up arms. When it's the right time, I will teach you myself – how to defend yourself. Please do not say that they might attack again. It is nearly over, and we will finish this fight soon. We will never have such a disaster again, I promise you."

"Okay," Kany replied sadly. "Don't get upset, Uncle. Whatever you say."

"Sweetheart, I don't want you to think about these things. You deserve to have your childhood and enjoy life, darling," Mevan said calmly.

"Oh, Uncle, I forgot to tell you, Agrin says I can go to school instead – and I do like studying and going to school."

"Well, that is the right thing for you to do. I couldn't agree more, for my daughter to go to school and be a doctor or teacher or whatever you want to be." Mevan smiled and kissed her on the forehead. He stood up and said, "Thank you for the food, Mother Marjan. We are going to take a tour around the camp and see how things are. From there, we will go to the training place for a while, and we will return with the girls."

"You're welcome, son. By the time you and the girls come back, we will have a nice dinner ready."

Bapir and Hawal thanked them all as well, then the men left.

At dinner time, everyone sat on the ground around the tablecloth, which was full of simple but tasty food. Everyone started eating.

Bapir said, "Mother Marjan, your cooking is fantastic! Your food is so delicious. I have not eaten such good food for a long time."

"You're welcome, my son, but I did not prepare the food – Agrin did."

Bapir turned to Agrin and thanked her.

Kany said, "Agrin does everything here. She takes care of the kids and organises them all."

"Yes," Shirin said, "she has even made rules for everyone to follow, such as nobody has the right to yell at the kids no matter how much they are stressed."

Barin added, "After a few arguments, she told Galavij and Ronak that if they don't feel good or they are stressed, to put on a red scarf and she would take care of the kids. And so many more rules like this – which at first didn't make sense to us – but now we can see how useful those rules are."

Kajal laughed and said, "Yes, and ever since then, I have not seen my smart sister-in-law Galavij without a red scarf."

Everyone started laughing. It was a joyful time for everyone after such a long time of hardship and pain.

After dinner, Mevan thanked them, then said, "Well, Mother Marjan, you are all tired now. It's time for my friends and I to leave so you can rest."

"Where are you going, my son? Is there a place for you to stay?" Marjan asked.

"Yes, we will go to our comrades. They are in the place where the girls are training."

"Okay, son. Do you want to take some blankets and pillows?"

"No, thank you, we will be all right," Mevan replied, before he kissed Agid and gave him to Agrin.

As he was about to leave, Marjan said, "My son, kiss the rest of the children as well. Their eyes are on you. They haven't seen their fathers for a long time."

Mevan, Hawal and Bapir looked at all their faces. With love and good humour, they hugged everyone. Galavij's little boy Hozan held onto Hawal and did not want to let him go. No matter how much his mother tried, the little boy wouldn't listen and kept holding onto Hawal.

Hawal looked at the little boy and said, "It's okay, let him stay with me for a little while. I'll take him out for a nice walk. Then I'll bring him back again. I don't want him to cry."

The following day, the girls trained and Kany went with Galavij. Her two children went to the camp's temporary school, which had recently opened, as Mevan and Agrin had wished.

Agrin and Marjan remained at the tent, working and taking care of Agid and Havin.

It was almost noon when Mevan came to the tent alone. He hugged Agid and sat down next to Marjan. He asked Agrin, who was bringing tea, "Agid looks healthy and good. Has he ever been sick?"

"He has been fine. Thank God he hasn't been sick. When we first arrived, he was underweight and crying all the time, which made the doctors worried. They said his weight was no match for his age, but, after a while, he improved. Now that Agid is almost seven months, the doctor said I can start him on some solid foods, but I haven't tried this yet."

Mevan was relieved to hear Agrin's words. "Thank you, Agrin, you are an amazing mother."

Marjan turned to Mevan and said, "Yes, my son, I assure you, she did no less than a mother would for your son and the same for Havin. She takes care of everyone here; we are blessed with her."

"I know, mother, and I'm very thankful for her," said Mevan.

Agrin smiled and took Agid's mother's necklace off her neck and offered it back to Mevan. "Here, now that you have come back, you can keep it for him." She put the necklace in Mevan's hand.

"But, Agrin, I have come back to visit you for only a couple of days," Mevan said.

"What? You're returning to fight even though we got our city back! Didn't we?" Agrin asked. "Mevan, I will no longer accept this responsibility. You have to stay with your son, and Kany needs you as well. You have been away long enough."

"But the fight is not quite over yet," Mevan said. "They can gain power again, they are still a big threat to our people. I have to go back."

"Okay, go back," Agrin said. "But this time I won't take responsibility for Agid and Kany."

"But you are the only one I have," Mevan said, standing up. "Who else can take care of him?"

"You! You are his father, you take care of him yourself. I must go after my family."

"Go where? There is nothing but war out there. How are you going to look for them?"

"I'm in training like everyone else. I don't want to sit here and do nothing while everyone is going to fight them. I feel helpless, useless."

"Agrin, please, I have to go back. They need me over there." Mevan moved closer to her.

"I can't stay here, please understand, Mevan. Agid can eat normal food now, he doesn't need me any more. I told you, there is no way I can stay – end of discussion, okay?" Agrin left the tent.

Mevan handed Agid to Marjan and said, "Please take the baby, mother. Let me see if I can change her mind." He followed her outside and asked her to wait, but Agrin didn't want to listen, she just wanted to be alone.

Agrin walked around the camp for a while and then headed to the training centre. A trainer saw Agrin coming and went over to sign her on. Agrin was writing her name down when she saw Mevan and the others coming towards her. Agrin looked at them with a frown.

Mevan approached her and said, "Agrin, in my life I have this child left for me. If you don't take care of him, I can't go to war safely."

"Don't go – stay with your son. I am not his mother, and he has no one but you. He deserves to be with his father. I gave my word, Mevan – I want to go to war like everyone else."

"Oh ... why don't you try to understand the situation? You know how dangerous it can be going to war. You could get killed."

"I do understand, and I don't care if I die, okay?" Agrin said, raising her voice.

Mevan's friend Hawal saw him losing his patience and said to Mevan, "You go, Mevan, let me talk to my sister Agrin." He walked towards Agrin and asked her to sit. "We are all under his command. If it were not for him, our troops and I would have been trapped and killed several times by now. He knows all the places and knows how to fight. We need his war skills."

"I know he is smart," Agrin replied. "I have seen him. He saved my life, but, if I am trained, I can fight and be helpful to my people the same as he is."

"No doubt you will," Hawal said. "If you both could come, it would be ideal. But if you come, he has to stay. He can't leave his son and Kany alone. He is already skilled, and we don't have time to spare, my sister."

The female commander, who was training Agrin one hour a day, nodded in agreement.

Ronak, who had come with the men, added, "Agrin, you are an educated woman, you know how to help people and how to talk and give comfort. If it was not for you, your words and care, none of us could stand up and be like this again."

The female commander said, "The front line is now in two places: one here, one where Mevan will go. We don't have enough time. You have to stay where you are best suited now, where you can help the most."

Hawal said, "Agrin, we do not want to bother you and force you. Now that you have heard us, it's your choice, and we respect whatever decision you make."

Agrin looked at Mevan, who was standing over by a car, watching her. She thought for a few seconds. "Okay, you're right. Me staying here is more helpful. I should go back to the tent to Agid and Havin." With that, she left.

Ronak and Hawal went to Mevan and told him that Agrin had changed her mind and would stay here. After hearing their words, Mevan ran after Agrin and said, "Agrin, wait for me."

Agrin stopped. "I will take care of your son and Kany until you come back. I won't let anything happen to them, now you can go."

"Please don't cry, Agrin. I also don't want anything to happen to you as well, you are just as important to me. I want you to be safe, I don't want you to put your life in danger."

"But I don't want to live any more, I don't want this cruel world, I want nothing to do with this life – I miss my husband and my daughter so much that I want to die. The reason I'm still breathing is that I don't want to give up my life like a loser. But as you said, it's not the right time to think about myself when my people need me, so I will stay here and do what I'm responsible for."

"You can't say that, you can't think of death. Our war will not end by defeating ISIS because it will come again – as it has more than seventy times in the past. It will end when we make sure these tragic massacres never happen to our children and us any more. That day will become true if we get to work and learn why this keeps happening to us. You lost Evin, but you still have hundreds of children like Evin that need a mother like you. How can you look in their eyes and say you have nothing to do when there is a child dying for your hug as a mother?"

Agrin looked at him in stony silence.

"We need our fighters, for now," Mevan said, "and we need to keep you, and people like you, safe so you can raise the new generation to make them see reality. So please don't give up. Keep fighting your way – with passion – and give them the knowledge that you have and are yet to learn." Mevan's eyes were full of emotion.

Agrin said with a sad smile on her face, "You are talking like my husband, Delovan. He would say all the time: 'The way to save our people and have a peaceful life, with the respect they deserve, is knowledge.'"

"I, ahh …" Mevan didn't quite know what to say.

Agrin didn't really want an answer. "I need to go back to Agid," she said. "He must be hungry by now. You go back to your friends."

"No, I'll accompany you to the tent." Mevan caught up with her. "Agrin, I have heard about your husband from Mother Marjan. He was a brave man. I'm so sorry for your loss."

"Yes, he was. I do miss him so much." Agrin stopped, tears began trickling down her cheeks.

Mevan stopped and hugged her. "I know how painful it is. I feel the same way about Henan. But I promise you it will get better, and you can still enjoy life. We will stand up again."

"I hope so, because now things just seem to get harder and harder," Agrin said, wiping her tears.

When they reached the tent, they saw Marjan holding Agid and trying to calm down Havin. Marjan saw Agrin and said, "Oh, Agrin, my daughter, where did you go? Havin has been crying for you since you left, and I think Agid is hungry. Please come and do something about it."

Mevan picked up Agid and tried to calm him. Havin soon quietened and started playing next to Agrin.

After a few moments, Agrin turned to Mevan. "Let me have Agid. He must be hungry, and it's almost his nap time." She held out her hands for Agid.

"Yes, he does look tired. Here, my boy, go to Agrin. Your baba has to go." Mevan handed Agid to her.

"Where are you going, son?" Marjan asked.

"I will go to my friends, then I'll come back later in the afternoon."

After a few hours, Agrin heard Mevan outside talking to Kany.

"Hello, Kany! How was school?"

"It was great, Uncle," Kany replied.

"That is good, my daughter. Is Agrin inside?"

"Yes, she is cooking dinner for us."

"Can you call her? I need to talk to her."

Agrin overheard, picked up Agid and went out to see Mevan. "Hello, you came back early. Is everything okay?"

"Yes, the schedule has changed, we have to leave the camp tonight. Let's have a walk, I need to talk to you." Mevan hugged Agid and waited for Agrin to get ready.

"Kany, sweetheart," Agrin said, "please look after Havin – she is sleeping. And please let Mother Marjan know that I left so that she can keep an eye on the food and it doesn't burn."

"Okay, Aunt Agrin, don't worry, I'll let her know," Kany said.

Agrin put Agid's little hat on his head and left with Mevan.

Mevan took the necklace out of his pocket and gave it back to Agrin. "Here, I'm giving this back to you, and here is some money – you will need it."

Agrin took the necklace and thanked Mevan for the money.

"Agrin, I'm sorry that I can't bring back your husband and daughter. I will look for your family. I wrote their names down with people everywhere so they could keep an eye out for them. I will not give up fighting ISIS until they all go back to where they came from or are dead. This time our operation will take us deeper into enemy territory, so I can't visit you. But we will be in contact by phone. I want you to take care of yourself and the others."

Agrin, who had been silent until that moment, raised her head. "Okay, I will, I promise you, but you also have to promise to take care of yourself. If something happens to you, I do not know what I would do. None of us do."

"I will come back – have no doubt – I promise you. If something happens, I know you will be fine. Now I have to go and get ready to help the group get prepared. Shirin, Barin and Kajal will also come with us, now they have finished their training."

"Yes, they have been preparing for a long time," Agrin said.

"Okay, then, I'll see you at dinner time. Do you need anything?"

"Maybe some bread and salt for tonight," Agrin said.

"Okay, I'll get them on the way back. Here, please hold Agid and go inside," Mevan said, then left.

At dinner, everyone was silent.

Eventually, Marjan spoke up, with tears in her eyes, "My daughter, Kajal, I don't want you to go. If your father or brother come back, they won't be happy. Can you please change your mind and stay?"

Kajal replied with a sharp tone, "Mother, we talked about this. I will go. If they come back, by any chance, I'm sure the first thing they would do is arm themselves and go to war, and you know it. Now please be supportive – that is what I need now."

Marjan, who didn't want to upset her daughter, said, "Okay, darling, whatever you say. May God protect you and everyone else who is fighting our enemies."

After dinner, everyone helped pack up, then said goodbye to each other.

Mevan kissed Kany and said, "Okay, my sweet daughter, I'm going now. I want you to be strong and promise me you will take good care of Agrin and Agid – and, of course, yourself – until I come back, okay?"

Kany hugged him with tears in her eyes. "I'm going to miss you so much."

Then their soldiers got into the car and drove away.

Agrin went back inside with Kany and the others. The tent felt so empty and depressing. Ronak helped Galavij and Agrin get the beds ready.

"Why have you put Havin's bed over there?" Agrin asked.

Ronak replied, "I could see how tired you became today while taking care of Agid. So please let Havin stay with me, and you rest tonight."

"Okay, but at least put her here — over there is cold," Agrin said.

"Okay, it's good that she is sleeping. Otherwise, she would want to be with you more than me."

"Don't say that. You are not around her as much as I am — that is all."

Ronak smiled and said, "Well, I am so thankful for you."

"She is such an angel — I love her so much, too."

"Thank you, sister. Now go and have a nice sleep because tomorrow we have work to do," Ronak said.

The following day Agrin woke up to feed Agid. She saw that Ronak's bed was empty and said to Galavij, "Ronak has left early for training — did they change the time?"

Galavij looked at Agrin several times, like she wanted to say something but thought better of it, and did not say anything.

In the afternoon, Marjan and Galavij sat next to Agrin. "Agrin, we want to tell you something," Galavij said.

"Okay, tell me, what is going on? You have been acting strange all day."

"Well, yesterday Ronak took us aside and said, 'I can't stay here, I have to go after my daughters.' Then she left during the night, around 3 am, with the second troop."

"What!? She left? But how? What about Havin? Did she leave her here alone?" Agrin cried.

"Yes, she left Havin here with us," Galavij replied.

"Has she gone crazy?" Agrin said, with a raised voice. "And tell me, did Mevan know about this?"

"No, Ronak didn't tell Mevan, either," Marjan said. "She was worried that he wouldn't let her leave Havin. She said that she would call him later to explain."

"She didn't even complete her training," Agrin said. "How did they let her go?"

"Yes, she did, she finished it sooner than expected," Galavij said. "She wanted to tell you but didn't because when she saw you did not want to accept Agid, she was afraid to tell you. That's why she asked us to ask you to take care of little Havin as well. And if anything happens to Ronak, she said that she wants you to be Havin's mother and raise her."

Marjan reached out and held Agrin's hand. "I know it's a big responsibility, and Ronak should have asked you, but — that poor woman — God knows how much she has suffered from having two little girls in ISIS's hands."

Galavij tried to reassure Agrin. "But you are not alone — you have mother and me. We will help you."

"Well, there is no other choice left for me," Agrin said, downcast. "I understand her, and I pray for her to come back safely with her daughters."

*

Months passed. Mevan and the young women, along with other Kurdish forces, were still at war with the enemy on the battlefields.

One day Agrin's phone rang. She did not recognise the number but answered the call. "Hello …?"

A girl's voice asked, "Are you Agrin?"

"Yes, I am! Who are you?"

"It's me, Siber. I called and talked to you when ISIS had taken me hostage."

Agrin was so happy to hear from her. "Siber, where did you go? Why didn't you call again? I called you so many times. We were worried about you. Where are you now?"

"I had to turn off my phone and hide it again. That man sold me to someone else a month later."

"Where are you now?"

"I was saved a week ago. Our forces attacked ISIS and rescued us. I want to return Narin's phone to your camp and see you. Where is the camp?"

Agrin gave her the location of the camp address, then said, "Okay, I will be waiting for you. When you arrive at the camp, let me know."

A few days later, Siber came to see her. Agrin greeted her and invited her into the tent, along with her companions. She sat them down and offered them all something to eat. "Siber, so tell me, did you find anyone from your family?"

"Yes, this is my brother," Siber said, as she gestured to the man next to her. Then she turned to her two other companions. "And this is my mother, and this is my brother's wife. However, we still haven't got any news about my older sister and cousins yet. Just like you asked me, I made notes and memorised all the names of the girls and women I came across and gave them to the authorities." She took out a phone and gave it to Agrin. "Here, this is Narin's phone, it still has all the photos."

"Thank you," Agrin said.

"Thank you very much, my daughter," Marjan said. "Her brother will be so happy to see her photos because he can use them to look for their family."

After they had all chatted for a while, Siber said, "Okay, Agrin, I think we better leave. Thank you for helping me, your words helped me a lot. Anytime you need anything, let us know, okay?"

"Yes, my sister, when anyone needs anything, call Siber," Siber's brother said. "We also have some milk and eggs that my mother-in-law sent you." He went to his car to get them.

"Thank her very much," Agrin said, "that was so thoughtful of her. Thank you all for coming and saying hello, and please give our regards to your mother-in-law and her family."

Agrin accompanied the others to their car, where Siber's brother gave her the milk and eggs.

After they had gone, Agrin went back inside the tent with the others, turned on the phone and looked at the photos. Marjan cried when she saw the pictures, saying, "Look at Narin and her beautiful smile! How happy she is with her family in these photos. And that one is Mevan — the lady next to her must be his wife!"

"Yes, mother, she was his wife," Agrin sighed.

Galavij said, "Look how proud and happy he was, but now what? God knows what is happening to Narin right now. I doubt if she is even still alive. Oh … poor Mevan!"

A few days passed. One evening, when everyone was chatting over dinner inside the tent, one of the phones rang. Agrin answered it. "Hello …?"

"Hello, Agrin, how are you?" Mevan said. "How are the kids? Is everything going well?"

"Yes, we are all good and doing well. How are you? It's been a while. Why you haven't called?"

"I know, I can't. I'm on the front line, but I'm okay."

"Mevan …" Agrin said.

"Yes?"

"Do you remember we talked to a girl named Siber? She had your sister's phone."

"Yes, did she call again? Did she say where she is now?"

"No, wait a second," Agrin said. "She came here and visited us with her brother. She returned your sister's phone and there are photos of her and your family still on the phone."

"That is excellent news," Mevan said. "Please send me some pictures, so I can get help to look for them."

"I will," Agrin said.

"Tell me, how is Agid? Last time I called, you said that he was sick."

"He is much better now. We couldn't find what the problem was, so I'm more careful with what I feed him now, to make sure he won't get sick again."

"I can't thank you enough, Agrin."

Agrin said, "Kany is here as well, and she wants to talk to you."

"Okay, but before I talk to her, you should know that I might not be able to call for a while, so don't get worried, and take care of yourself and the others. Now you can pass the phone to Kany – and please say hello to Marjan and Galavij as well."

Kany grabbed the phone and started talking to Mevan.

They had a good chat and eventually said goodbye.

Then Agrin asked Kany, "My daughter, please send some photos of Narin, and all the members of the family, to Mevan. And please remember to send the photo of the wedding that you and your mum were in. Photos will help him to find your family."

"Okay, Aunt Agrin, I will send them now," replied Kany, with hope and excitement.

13

A few months had passed since Mevan's last call. Agid was getting sicker and more unsettled every day, but the doctors could not find any reason for it.

One day while Agrin was cooking, she saw Agid lose his balance for no reason at all, then fall to the ground and hit his head. Agrin immediately picked him up and hugged him, then turned to Marjan, who had seen this as well, and said, "Mother, this cannot be normal, there must be something wrong with Agid. I will have to take him to a good doctor to get some answers."

She prepared Agid and went to the clinic tent. She walked straight into the doctor's room and said, "Please, doctor, every time I bring Agid here, you say you can't find anything wrong, but his condition and growth is getting worse. He has been restless and has been crying for a few days now. I have given him every medicine you said, but nothing has helped. You have to give me some explanation."

The doctor asked Agrin to describe Agid's behaviour over the last few days. Agrin looked at Agid in her arms and said, "He is not well. Today he was walking and he fell on the ground for no reason."

"You will need to go to a specialist in a well-equipped hospital," the doctor said. "They will find the problem, my sister. We do not have many facilities here. We can send for tests. If there were an immediate and obvious danger, then we would send the patient to the hospital. But your son's tests have not shown anything so far. I will make an appointment with a specialist. I will write his address and name on this paper, then please take him home. In this bad weather, he shouldn't stay out, okay?"

"Okay, doctor, I will take him to the specialist as soon as possible." Agrin then took Agid back to their tent.

"What did the doctor say?" Kany asked anxiously.

"We have to take him to a specialist to find out what is going on," Agrin said, with a trembling voice. "Now, let me put him down for a nap."

That night Agid didn't stop crying for hours. Agrin and Marjan took him straight to the doctor again. After the examination, the doctor said that it would be better to take Agid to the hospital immediately. "Please go back to your tent and pack some essentials for you and Agid, then we will send you both by car to the hospital."

Agrin and Marjan returned to the tent to pack, then Agrin and Agid left the camp with the doctor in a car. As soon as they arrived at the hospital, the doctors took Agid and examined him.

A few hours passed while Agrin sat in the waiting room on a chair. Eventually, the camp doctor came into the waiting room and said, "My sister, come, follow me. The specialist wants to talk to you."

They entered the doctor's room, and the specialist asked Agrin to sit down. The specialist looked at his notes, then said, "My daughter, exactly how old is your son?"

"Eighteen months."

"Okay, when you were pregnant and even before you became

pregnant, did you have any problems or anything that you think I might need to know about?"

"I do not know. I am not his real mother so I do not know anything about it," Agrin said.

"Okay, then. Where is his mother?" the specialist asked.

"His mother died and his father is on the front line of the war with ISIS."

"Is there any family or someone who could give me some information? Do you know if they have other children or not? How old is his father?"

"No, this is their only child. His father is about thirty-eight or near that age. I do not know exactly, but his niece is in the camp and she should know. Let me call her and ask her your questions."

"Thank you," he said.

Agrin took out her phone and called Kany.

Kany told her, "Yes, they did have some problems. Henan became pregnant a few times, but each time she had a miscarriage two or three months later. But somehow Agid eventually made it through."

Agrin hung up the phone, then passed the information on to the specialist.

He added the details to his notes, then said, "Unfortunately, as I suspected, it might be a deeper reason for the child's health problems. We have made some early diagnoses about the child's condition. Still, we are not sure until the test results come back from the laboratory. But it seems most likely the child's parents shouldn't have had children."

"What now?" Agrin asked. "What will happen to Agid? Is he going to get better?"

"I do not know, my daughter. We have to wait to see what the main problem is. Your son is in intensive care now, because of his serious condition. He has to stay there to be properly taken care of."

"His father left him in my care," Agrin said. "I promised him that I would not let anything happen to him. Please save him – do something, doctor."

"I can't promise you anything. We have to wait and see, but we'll do our best. You try to contact his father and inform him."

Agrin began to cry, so the specialist gave her a glass of water. He said sympathetically, "My daughter, don't cry. Let me take you to him."

Agrin followed the specialist to the intensive care unit. They stood behind glass and watched a nurse attend to Agid on a bed inside the unit.

After a little while, Agrin phoned Kany.

"Hello, Aunt Agrin, how is Agid? What did the doctor say?"

"I don't know, Kany. Is mother there?" Agrin asked, with a trembling voice.

"Yeah, let me give her the phone."

Marjan took the phone. "Hello, my daughter. What happened – how is Agid?"

Agrin broke down and cried. "I don't know, he is in the intensive care unit and the doctor says he is not well. Now, what should I do, mother? I can't lose another child. What if I lose him? What if he leaves me as well? Please, mother, I'm scared to death ..."

Marjan was upset and became even more worried about Agrin when she heard her words. "My daughter, be patient. He will get better soon, I'm telling you. Did you call Mevan?"

"Yes, but he doesn't answer."

"Okay, my daughter, go and wash your face and get some water. If anything happens to you, it won't get easier – not for Agid, not for any of us. So please be strong and don't lose it. I'll try to call Mevan and see if Kajal or Shirin know how to contact him."

"Okay, mother." Agrin hung up the phone and started crying.

One of the nurses came and sat next to her. "Don't cry. God willing, he will be fine. Let's go and rest for a while and eat something."

A week passed. Agrin went back to see the specialist in the hospital. He wanted to explain Agid's condition. At the very moment he went to speak, Agrin's phone rang. She looked at the phone and said, "Doctor, it's Agid's father."

"Okay, answer it," he said.

"Hello ... I called you so many times. Where were you?" Agrin cried.

"I know, I'm sorry," Mevan said. "I was on the front line and didn't have my phone with me. Mother called! Now how is Agid?"

"His specialist is here. I'll pass the phone to him."

The specialist took the phone and said, "Hello, brother, I'm Agid's specialist ..." While he was talking, he moved away from Agrin.

She couldn't hear what he was saying, so she waited, worried sick.

After the call was over, the specialist called Agrin over to him.

Agrin asked anxiously, "Now, how is Agid? Is he any better? Please, doctor, tell me what we can do. I'll do anything."

The specialist hesitated, then said, "I told his father – and I'm about to say it to you as well – it's a miracle that Agid is still alive and grown to this age. I do not want to disappoint you completely, but it is possible your son will not be able to continue living."

Hearing the specialist's words made Agrin's nightmare of losing another baby real again. She could not stand and sat on the floor and started crying.

The specialist sat next to her. "Darling, I understand how hard this is, but there is still some hope, your son is a little warrior. There still might be a chance for a miracle to happen. Now come, let the nurses take care of you and give you a sedative, so you can get some rest."

A few days later, Agrin was still hoping for a miracle. She was standing in the hallway outside the intensive care unit, looking through the glass window at Agid. She was praying from the bottom of her heart for his health to improve, for him to open his eyes and for her to hear his voice again.

A nurse came to check on Agid, but rushed out immediately. Agrin's heart was pounding, as she stood watching more nurses running to Agid. The specialist ran past her and entered the room. He pulled the curtains while he checked Agid's condition.

Agrin waited and waited, then began walking the corridors of the hospital until she was out of energy. After what seemed like hours, she returned to the intensive care unit and sat on a bench outside the glass.

She waited until the nurses all left the unit, but no one spoke to Agrin until the specialist came out. Agrin got up as the specialist approached her, with sadness in his eyes. As gently as he could, he said, "We couldn't save your son. I'm sorry."

Agrin sank to the floor, feeling helpless.

The doctor held Agrin's shaking hand as he lifted her. "Please be strong, my daughter, and try to get up. Do you have anyone to come and stay with you?"

"No, he was all that I had left in this world, and you are telling me that he's gone ..."

"I know, my daughter, I'm so sorry."

"Now, what do I do without him, and how can I tell his father that his child died? I promised him I'd take care of Agid," Agrin cried.

"I saw your connection with this little boy. I'm sure he had a good life, and he was fortunate to have you. Now let me take you to the nurse to take care of you. I will inform Mevan myself. You need to be taken care of now." The specialist called for a nurse to come immediately.

The nurse took Agrin to a room and gave her some medicine to make her sleep for a while.

Agrin woke to the sound of voices – a nurse talking to the specialist. The nurse asked, "Doctor, did you talk to his father?"

"No, he hasn't answered my calls yet."

A few days had passed since Agid's death. Agrin was sitting in the hospital yard next to the morgue, as she had been doing for the last few days, waiting for Mevan to call or answer his phone.

Finally, Mevan called and Agrin answered, dreading how to break the news.

"Hello, Agrin, how is Agid doing?" Mevan asked.

Agrin started to cry.

"What! What happened? Is he not good? Agrin, please say something."

"He's gone, Mevan ... we lost him."

Mevan went silent for a moment, then said, "I ... I'll call you back." He hung up.

Agrin ran to the specialist's room. "Agid's father called. I told him what had happened, but he couldn't talk and hung up the phone."

"I'm sorry you had to do that," the specialist said, as he offered Agrin a seat. "I called him a few times, but he didn't answer. Now, when is he coming back?"

"I don't know. He said he would call me back, which is why I have come to you, so that you can talk to him."

"Okay, my daughter, now don't cry and please take it easy on yourself. You did the right thing coming here. I'll talk to him."

Agrin's phone rang again and the specialist answered it. He confirmed it was Mevan calling, then said, "I'm so sorry for your loss, brother, and I'm sorry that we couldn't save Agid ... Yes, your son has been cold for a few days now ... We told Agrin to return to the camp, and we would keep him until you came back, but she has insisted on sitting in front of the morgue every day ... Her mental and physical health is deteriorating every day. Please come back soon, you are needed here."

"I can't come back anytime soon. Please tell Agrin to take my son and bury him in the camp."

"Okay, do you want me to pass the phone to her?"

"Yes, please."

"Hello, Mevan, I need you here," Agrin said.

Mevan couldn't reply, he was torn by divided loyalties.

Agrin tried again. "When are you coming back?"

After some long moments, Mevan said, "I can't come back now, we are in the middle of a difficult military operation. Please could you take Agid home for me and be with him for the last time? I'm sorry I can't be there."

Agrin passed the phone back to the specialist without saying anything.

"Yes, brother," the specialist said.

Mevan said sadly, "Please send them both home and make sure Agrin will be okay."

"Okay, brother, I understand and don't worry, I will take care of everything. My condolences to you again, and be safe, brother." The doctor hung up the phone, turned to Agrin and offered her a glass of water. "My daughter, Mevan requested that you return Agid to the camp and bury him there."

"He said he can't come back ..." Agrin said, still not believing his words.

"Yes, my daughter, but you and Agid can go home now."

"We will have to."

They prepared Agid's body, and Agrin held him in her arms for the long drive back to the camp.

Marjan, Kany and Galavij were ready for their arrival, waiting with tearful eyes by the clinic's tent. Their hearts sank even further when they saw the car coming through the gate. They ran forward, crying.

Agrin stepped out of the car, and Marjan hugged her, crying.

A few men took Agid's tiny body to the cemetery next to the camp to bury him. Agrin followed and watched them with a bleeding heart. Once again, she had lost all her hopes and seen all her happiness buried under a load of dirt. She bent over Agid's little grave, heartbroken, tired and numb. She put her head on the cold dirt and hugged it.

Marjan, Galavij, Kany, and several neighbourhood men and

women had accompanied her. After a few hours, Marjan said to Agrin, "My daughter, let's go, it's getting dark."

"You go, mother, I want to stay here a bit longer," Agrin said, still staring at Agid's grave.

"Okay, my sweetheart, you can stay as long as you need." Marjan turned to her daughter-in-law. "Galavij, you go home with the children and Kany. I will stay with her."

They stayed for a while because Agrin couldn't bring herself to leave Agid alone.

"At least you know he's not in pain any more, my daughter," Marjan said, trying to soothe her. "This is life. If you don't let it go, you'll suffer more. Let's walk home, you can come to visit him again tomorrow."

Agrin raised her head from the grave and Marjan wiped the dirt from her face, saying, "My poor daughter, look at you."

"Mother, I can't take all this pain any more – it's not fair."

"I know, my poor baby, nothing in this world is fair ... nothing. Now let's take you home," Marjan said. They started walking away and returned to their tent.

When Havin saw Agrin, she ran to her and threw herself into Agrin's arms. She had been yearning to see Agrin, and began wiping her tears away while she said in a sweet, childish voice, "Mother, don't cry any more. I missed you so much and I'll take care of you."

Agrin put her head on the pillow and hugged Havin tightly. "Okay, my baby girl, I won't cry, and I missed you, too. Now let's go to sleep."

*

A few months had passed since Agid's death, with no news from Mevan, and his phone was off most of the time.

One afternoon, Marjan asked Kany, "My daughter, call your uncle again, he hasn't called since Agid died. I'm worried, we don't know if he is okay or not."

"No, auntie, I have called several times and left a few messages, but he hasn't replied. Once, one of his friends picked up the phone and said, 'Mevan is fighting and can't talk – he'll call you back.'"

"Yes, mother, it's better not to call, and to wait for him," Galavij said.

"Okay, as you say. I hope he is all right," Marjan sighed.

Agrin was unbearably upset because she felt that Mevan might never forgive her. She hugged Havin and went out of the tent.

"Where are you going, Agrin?" Marjan asked.

"Nowhere ... I'm just going to take a walk with Havin to Agid's grave. I'll be back soon," Agrin said in a calm, mournful voice.

On the way, Havin said excitedly, "Mother, look! See how many stones I am collecting. You can collect some, too. Now we can go to my brother Agid's grave and finish what we started yesterday."

Agrin looked at Havin's beautiful face, leaned towards her, and said, "You are right, darling, let us collect beautiful stones. We could also cut some of the branches off the bushes and make a nice bunch out of them, like flowers, and put them on Agid's grave."

"Yes, mother, and I am going to make a smiley face for Agid."

"That is beautiful, sweetie."

Agrin and Havin decorated Agid's grave for a long time. Finally, Agrin said, "Okay, Havin, I think it's time to go home now. You look so tired. We will come back another time."

14

A few weeks later, around noon one day, Marjan and Galavij were busy cleaning up the area outside their tent. Galavij looked up, pointed and said, "Mother, isn't that Mevan coming towards us?"

Marjan straightened, put one hand on her forehead and peered into the distance. After a few seconds, she said, "Yes, it's him! It's Mevan!" She hurried to him.

She was still a few steps away when she opened her arms to Mevan, then hugged him. "Thank God you came back safe and sound, son! I thought I would never see your face again."

"Hello, mother, how are you?" Mevan said. "Please don't cry. I don't want to see you cry. It is so good to see you." Mevan bent down and kissed Marjan's hand as a sign of respect and gratitude for the love and affection of her greeting and welcoming.

Marjan said kindly, "My son, give me your bag, let me carry it for you — you must be exhausted." She grabbed his bag and walked along with him.

"How are you doing, mother?" asked Mevan, as they walked.

"I'm doing okay, son. Now that you've come back, I'm much better."

"How are Kany and Agrin?"

"Kany is a lot better. She doesn't have nightmares and hasn't been crying or beating herself for a long time. She goes to school and Agrin is helping her a lot."

Mevan smiled. "That is so good to hear. And Agrin herself?"

Marjan stopped and sighed. "What can I say, my son? As long as your son was alive, she was full of hope for life again ... laughing, planning the future for him, she was getting better every day. But after Agid's passing, she was all sad again. She is quiet most of the time. She is going to his grave almost every day and returning with swollen eyes from her crying. She is beating herself up, wondering how she can face you with Agid buried, instead of holding him in her arms. I don't know, son, I have almost lost hope of seeing her smiling again. At least, thank God, she has Havin around to keep her busy."

"Okay, mother. Where are they now?"

"Kany has gone to school. Agrin is inside the tent feeding lunch to the children."

When they reached the yard outside the tent, Galavij welcomed Mevan. "Hello, brother! Thank God you are okay. We were worried about you."

"Hello, my sister, thank you," Mevan said, smiling and hugging her. "How are you and your children?"

"Yes, thank God, we are all okay," Galavij replied.

Mevan stood in front of the door to the tent for a few seconds, then went inside. "Hello, Agrin," Mevan said.

Seeing him, Agrin put down the bowl of food she was feeding the children and stood up. She dropped her head and said nothing, wondering about Mevan's reaction.

Mevan walked towards her. "How are you, Agrin?" His voice was filled with compassion.

She burst into tears and looked at Mevan. "I don't know …"

Mevan went to her and hugged her tightly, tears flowing from his eyes.

"I'm sorry, Mevan, I couldn't take care of him, and now he's gone."

"It's not your fault," Mevan said softly. "I know you have done all that a mother could do. Now, please don't cry."

Galavij and Marjan hugged Mevan and cried on his shoulder.

Agrin raised her head and asked, "What is this blood? Why are your clothes bloody? Are you injured?"

"I was wounded in the war. On the way here, one of my friends bumped into my chest by accident and my stitches opened up. I took care of it, but it's starting to bleed again." Mevan put a hand over his chest and compressed the wound, trying to stem the bleeding.

"My God! How and when did you get injured, son?" Marjan said, checking his shirt. "Why didn't you tell us anything?"

Agrin said, "You can't close it yourself, it's dangerous. What if it gets infected? You have to go to the clinic – now."

Marjan agreed and said, "Yes, my son, it's still bleeding. You have to see a doctor."

"Okay, you're right, I'll go," he said.

"I'll come with you, too," Marjan said, already putting on her shoes.

An hour later, Agrin and Galavij were waiting outside the tent for Mevan and Marjan to come back. When they finally spotted Mevan and Marjan in the distance, they could see Marjan was slapping her legs and mumbling under her breath.

When the two reached the tent, Galavij asked, "What happened, mother?"

Marjan turned to Mevan. "Oh, my poor son, what do you want me to say?" But Mevan did not reply, so Marjan continued, "We went to the doctor, he took off Mevan's shirt ... Oh, your mother dies for you, my poor son! What have you been through, huh? His whole body is full of scars and shrapnel from mines or bombs. And besides that, he was shot twice – once in his shoulder and once in his chest." Marjan shook her head in disbelief, then asked Mevan, "Why didn't you tell us? Why didn't you say you were shot?"

"Please, mother, stop. I don't want you to do this now. I'm okay and, if I had told you, it would have made you more miserable."

"But ..." Marjan said.

Mevan didn't wait for her to finish her protest. "There were so many warriors and young heroes who were wounded and lost their lives every day in front of my eyes that I was ashamed to talk or even think about mine. Now, please stop worrying. You were at the clinic, you heard the doctor say that it's not so bad. I'll be fine."

"Okay, son. Thank God that you are back. Now let me get you something to eat," Marjan said and wiped her tears.

"No, mother, I'm not hungry now. I want to go and visit my son's grave," Mevan said sadly.

Marjan sighed. "Okay, son, let Agrin take you there. While you are there, I will prepare some food."

Mevan waited for Agrin to pick up Havin and join him. On their way to Agid's grave, Mevan said, "Agrin, please tell me about my son, about his last moment. Was he in a lot of pain?"

"In the few weeks before he went to hospital, he kept getting sicker more quickly, even though I took him to the doctor regularly. After he fell on the ground and kept crying, the doctor and I took him straight to the hospital." Agrin could not stop herself from crying while she was walking along the middle of the road, with Havin holding her hand. "I'm so sorry, Mevan. I still can't look directly into your eyes. I made a promise to you, and I couldn't keep it."

"It's not on you, Agrin. Don't beat yourself up like this." Mevan looked at Agrin. He wasn't certain whether he should continue, but he did. "Henan and I were married for more than ten years. She got pregnant several times and had a miscarriage each time. Then the doctors told her that we should not have children and, even if we had one, the child would not live for long. Being pregnant could also put Henan's life in danger. After many years, Henan became pregnant unintentionally because we did not expect it to happen. When we found out, it was too late. The baby was about two months, but the doctor still said that losing it would be the best outcome, before it grew more. However, Henan couldn't bear to lose another child that she had always dreamed of. By some miracle, Agid was born alive and he was fine. After Henan gave birth, the doctor reiterated that we might not have the baby for long. Still, the sweetness of his existence in our lives was so great that we put all our hopes for a second miracle on him. After Henan's death, I was sure that he had no chance of living, and I had been waiting for the day for him to depart this life. The first time I came back to visit you from the war, when I saw Agid growing up and laughing, I assured myself that you were the miracle that my wife and I were hoping for, but …" He wiped Agrin's tears.

"I'm so sorry, Mevan."

"You have no reason to apologise to me. I was the one who was not here." He paused for a moment, then said, "In this war I have carried the bodies of dozens of children and babies ... uhhhh ... even newborn babies as innocent and beautiful as my son. Their bodies were in my arms because they either died under the rubble of the war or because of hunger, cold or heat. They were motherless and lost. Agrin, I am so thankful that at least my son was in your arms until the last moments of his life and did not suffer. I owe you for this for the rest of my life. I know I should have told you, and I was about to warn you about Agid's situation, but seeing Agid growing and happy, I believed that the danger was over and my son would live with you and grow up. I did not doubt that I might lose him, but I did not want to worry you."

Agrin said, "I don't know if it would have been better if I had known or not, but thank you for telling me. Let's go to him ... we're almost there."

When they got there, Mevan sat next to his son's grave. "I hoped for him to stay with me and see him grow up to be a young man." Then he looked at Agrin and said, "You go home with Havin."

"Okay," Agrin said.

While Mevan watched Agrin walking away, he could not stop the tears falling down his cheeks from the deep pain he was feeling. He started to sing a mournful song that gave voice to his broken heart.

Hey li vay, vay, vayê, Mêvanê, jarê reben û ...
Tu mayî tenê dîsa, Şivanê bê kepen û ...
Ne halê ne malê, vê jiyanê ...
Ser da girtin, li kuştin Brîvanê ...
Hewî dana bî li ser gula evînê ...

Nezani berfêji dibare nîva havînê ...
Bibarine lavo, derdê te giran ey ...
Eve resma jiyanê van nemêra ey ...
Ser agirê malê me dê giran ...
Van neyara pê çênabe, hêlîn ava kirin ...
Li hevarê ay hevarê, hevar, derengê ey ...
Xwîn rijiya se axa sar, dinya he bêdengê ey ...
Hey li vay, vay, vayê, Mêvanê, jarê, reben û ...
Tu mayî tenê dîsa, Şivanê bê kepen û ...

(Oh, you poor man, Mevan, you are all alone again, with no
feeling, no home, no life, I put all my hope on the flower of
love, didn't know that it would snow in the middle of summer,
cry, you beautiful soul, your pain is exceptional, this is the
way of a coward's life as he can't make a home for himself, he
starts to destroys the man's house, shouting for them as deep
as it is too late already, the blood of so many lives has been
shed in this cold dirt, and the world is still quiet, oh, poor
man, Mevan, you are all alone, again.)

After a while, near sunset, Mevan left his son's grave in distress.
He approached the tent and saw from a distance that Kany was
coming towards him with haste and excitement. Mevan pulled
himself together, put a smile on his face and opened his arms.

Kany's eyes were full of tears as she reached Mevan and placed
herself in his loving arms. "My dearest Uncle, I missed you so
very much. I worried about you till it hurt. Please don't leave
us again."

"I know, Baba. I am back now and, see, I am fine. Now don't cry, sweetheart, let me look at you ... Oh God, look at you ... what a beautiful young lady you have become, my sweet daughter." Mevan kissed her forehead.

"Uncle, I'm so sorry about losing Agid. I miss him so much."

"Thank you, Baba, I miss him so much as well."

"We are heartbroken for you because we know he always reminded you of Henan."

"Yes, you are right," Mevan said. "He had his mother's eyes, and it warmed my heart each time I looked into his eyes. Uhh ... my darling daughter, what can you do? He is gone now, like thousands of other children of Sinjar who have passed away and left their families heartbroken. You can't change what has happened already. Now wipe your tears. I don't want to see you cry. At least I still have you to live for, my daughter."

"And Aunt Agrin, you have her as well. She doesn't have anyone else," Kany said, with her kind heart.

"Yes, of course, you are right. I have Agrin as well – who is now waiting at the yard for us to go home," Mevan said, with a smile.

Mevan and Kany walked towards the tent together. Agrin, Galavij and Marjan were waiting for them outside the tent. Galavij's son ran over to Mevan and Kany, then Mevan bent down, hugged him and went inside.

"Come and sit down, my son, the food is ready," Marjan said. "My daughter Kany, please set the table while Agrin pours some tea for Mevan."

After dinner, Kany went to Mevan, who was deep in thought. She said hesitantly, "Uncle, do you want to see videos and photos of Agid? Aunt Agrin has been looking at them a lot because it helps her to cope."

Mevan paused for a second, then replied, "Yes, I want to see them, but not now. If you give me the phone, I'll look later."

Agrin picked up her phone and said, "Here, I saved them all in this file with Agid's name on it."

Mevan took the phone and thanked her. "I will return the phone tomorrow," he said.

"That's okay, don't rush, I don't need it," Agrin said.

"Okay, son, come and sit at the table," Marjan said.

Mevan sat next to Agrin, and they started eating.

Marjan asked, "Son, when will my daughter and the girls come to visit us?"

"They can come back anytime they want, mother, but now they are needed there," Mevan said. "I spoke to them today, on the way here. They are all okay and doing well."

"Uncle, how is Barin? Is her injury better now?" Kany asked.

"Yes, Baba, she is okay, it wasn't serious. I asked her to come back with me and rest for a while, but she was happy to stay there." Mevan finished what he was eating, stood up and said, "I must go now." He then started preparing to leave.

"Where are you going, son?" Marjan asked. "You are injured, don't go. I will make a bed for you here to stay with us."

"Yes, Uncle, can you please stay?" Kany asked. "We have plenty of room here."

"No, my daughter, I will go to my friends tonight; they are waiting for me. I will think of something else for tomorrow." He turned to Marjan. "Mother, don't worry, I'll be fine. I will see you all in the morning. Goodnight." Mevan left the tent.

Mevan met up with his friends and sat around a campfire with them.

After a while, Mevan moved to a place to sleep and took out his phone. He searched for Agid's folder and opened it. The folder was full of photos and videos of Agid. In one video, Agrin was trying to teach Agid how to say "Baba". The sound of Agid's voice trying to say this word again and again brought a bitter smile to Mevan's face. In all the photos and videos of Agid, he was laughing. He seemed so happy with Agrin. Seeing all those photos assured Mevan even more that he had made the right choice to leave Agid with a kind mother.

The following day, Mevan went to the tent with a few packages and some food.

Marjan welcomed him and said, "Hello, son, good morning. Let me prepare breakfast for you."

"Morning, mother, I have some food and necessary items for you, and this is a small tent that I picked up. If it's okay with you, I will set it up beside your tent."

"Yes, son, you certainly can. For now, let us go inside and make you some breakfast."

Mevan entered their tent and was soon eating breakfast. Afterwards he said to Kany, "Do you want to help me set up my tent?"

"Yes, I do," Kany replied, and stood up with excitement to help.

15

A couple of months passed. Each morning, Mevan and some of the other men would usually leave the camp for work and return later in the day.

One afternoon, Mevan returned to the tent and said to Marjan, "Today Kajal called and she asked me to tell you that —"

Marjan interrupted and asked anxiously, "Is she okay? Why didn't she call me? Is it bad news? Has she found her father and brother?"

"No, no, mother, wait for a second … She is okay and there is no bad news. Kajal was promoted yesterday because she is a brilliant girl and she has made a lot of progress. She told me that she would stay with Shirin and Barin in the military in Kurdistan. They will not return."

"But she can't stay. How can she leave us here and not return? That is not what she promised me."

"She will return, mother," Mevan said. "She can come and visit all the time, or you can go and see her anytime you want. However, Kajal said, 'I have made my decision, I will stay. But I don't want my mother to be upset and heartbroken, I want her to understand me.' And, mother, I know she will be so successful there."

Marjan sighed sadly, "What can I say, my son? The girl is as crazy as her father was. She never listens to me. Let her stay ... I pray to God to keep her and the others safe."

"They will be fine," Mevan said. "The war is almost over, and they are well trained."

"And what about Ronak, son?" Marjan asked. "We haven't heard from her for a long time and I'm so worried about her."

"*Now*, this is what I'm about to tell you: Ronak is on her way here, she will be here by night, and she has found one of her daughters."

"Oh, my God, she found her! Oh, that is the best news! I'm so happy for her."

"It is, mother," Galavij said. "I can't believe she found her after all this time." Galavij hugged Marjan, then Agrin and congratulated everyone.

"See, my daughter, Agrin, I told you yesterday to never lose your hope," Marjan said. "Good news is always around the corner, but you can't see it until it pops into view."

"Yes, mother," Agrin said, "I guess you were right."

They sat down for tea and started talking. "Agrin, I think that Havin won't go to her mother," Marjan said, with a smile. "She loves you more than anything."

"Yes, you are right, mother," Kany said, laughing. "Even Havin calls her 'mother'. Aunt Ronak will have to work hard for Havin to call her mum again."

"I dare her to take Havin away from me," Agrin joked. "I think I'll also take her other daughter when she comes back."

Galavij laughed and said, "Yes, you are right, my sister. I'm with you on this."

Towards sunset, Ronak arrived at the camp's central tent and greeted Mevan, who was waiting for her. They returned to their own tent. Everyone was waiting outside their tent and welcomed them warmly.

Ronak saw Agrin, ran to her and hugged her. "My beautiful sister, Agrin, I missed you so much."

"I missed you, too, Ronak," Agrin said, as they hugged each other tightly. "Welcome back, my sister."

Ronak pointed to a little girl and said, "This is my little daughter Nalan."

Everyone started welcoming Nalan, but she hid behind her mother, and scratched her nails while looking at the ground.

Ronak turned to her daughter and said, "Come on, my daughter, why are you hiding? Say hello to everyone."

But Nalan didn't want to say hello, and was uncomfortable with her mother urging her to talk. Nalan's hands were shaking, she looked frightened and on the verge of tears.

Agrin sat down next to her and said kindly, "Do you want to see your sister Havin? You must have missed her so much."

Nalan shyly nodded.

"Okay, let's go see your sister — she's sleeping inside," Agrin said calmly. "Do you want to hold my hand?"

Nalan shook her head.

"That's okay," Agrin said. "Come on, we'll go inside."

Nalan followed Agrin inside and walked over to Havin's bed. Havin was sleeping. Nalan sat next to her.

Agrin whispered, "Let me wake her up so you can play with her."

Ronak entered the tent, and the others followed her inside.

Ronak looked at Havin, then tears began falling from her beautiful eyes. "Oh, my God, look at her, she has grown up a lot. Oh God, I missed her so much. Agrin, I don't know how to thank you."

Agrin smiled and gently said to Havin, "Hey, sweetie, look who's here. Your mama and your sister. Come on, my baby girl … open your eyes."

Havin woke up, and Ronak hugged her tightly.

Nalan remained silent and sitting still.

Agrin said, "My daughter Nalan, why don't you say something, sweetheart? Do you want to go out with Kany and the kids and walk or play a little before it gets dark?"

Nalan said nothing.

Kany walked over and gently took her arm. "Come on, Nalan, let's go outside. Let's play together."

Nalan looked at her mother.

Ronak sighed. She turned to Kany and said sadly, "If a man or young boy comes close, let Nalan come inside." Nalan went to her bag, took out a large black scarf, then threw it over her face and went out with Kany.

"What was that for?" Galavij asked. "Why shouldn't Nalan stay outside when a man comes in, and what is that black scarf? She can barely hold that over her head. How is she going to play?"

Ronak looked at their surprised faces and sighed. "I do not know myself, either. We attacked one of the ISIS residences and won. We found twenty or more prisoners in a house. Nalan was one of them. I took off her niqab but still couldn't see her face because she wouldn't look up. Although she was standing right next to me and knew me, she wouldn't come to me. Whatever we did, she would not take off her chador, and we didn't push her as I couldn't stand her tears. But every time I see her like this, it kills me inside."

"Be patient with her," Agrin said. "God knows what horrible things she has been through."

Ronak said, "A young woman who was among them told me they had harassed her a lot. She said that they were fighting over the younger girls under ten years, and my daughter has suffered so much." She started crying and hitting her lap. "God knows now what terrible situation my other daughter is in. I couldn't find her anywhere. They said she must have been taken to other cities or even another country. I wonder if I will ever see her again."

Mevan said, "We will also see her back to us one day. I gave her name to several groups looking for our girls and women in their cities. They are looking for them in the markets where they sell them. I hope they might give us a call soon. Some of my friends were found and returned to their families."

Then he looked at Agrin and said, "I wanted to be sure before telling you, Agrin, because I received a call last night to say that a forty-nine-year-old woman named Sourgol Meraz was sold in the market last week. They couldn't take a photo of her, but they took a picture of the sales list and it also had your mother's name on it."

"What!" Agrin exclaimed in shock. "Are you saying that my mother might be alive? I can't believe it!"

"Come here, let me show you the picture," Mevan said.

Agrin sat next to Mevan and looked at the picture. "Yes, yes, this is my mother's name – my mother is alive!" She hugged Mevan. "I thought she was gone as well … Thank you, Mevan."

"As long as they are alive, wherever they are, I won't stop looking for them until they return home," Mevan assured Agrin. "Now don't cry – smile. Because one day soon, your mother will be with you."

They were all happy and congratulated Agrin.

Marjan said, with tears in her eyes, "My daughter, I am thrilled! I prayed a lot to God to find at least one of your relatives. My sweet daughter, I'm so happy for you."

"Thank you, mother," Agrin said, then turned back to Mevan. "I didn't think you would look for them like this and send people inside their community to find our families and people."

"I didn't send them. It was too risky, and the chance of success would be zero because we don't know much about them. Otherwise, I would have gone myself. These are the people who live there. They are looking for them and trying to save them or buy them and send them back to us. Many of them are doing it for humanity, but some see it as a business. Hopefully, we will come across good people. Now for your mother, she has been sold recently. They say we might be able to find out who bought her and get close to her. Or, if we can't, we'll wait for them to put her on the market again."

"Well, at least my mother is alive," Agrin said, even though she was now very worried about her mother's safety.

"And I will find her and bring her back to you," Mevan said. "Now please don't be upset and trust me." He kissed Agrin's forehead.

A few days passed and everyone became more concerned and worried about Nalan's behaviour. She wasn't an ordinary little girl any more. Her mother couldn't understand her and how much she had changed.

Very early one morning, a loud commotion from Ronak woke everybody in the tent.

"What's happening?" Kany shouted in fear.

Agrin got up and went to see what was going on.

A frazzled Ronak was trying to pull Nalan's scarf from her head. Nalan was crying as she tried to hold onto her scarf. Ronak exclaimed, "Why are you torturing me like this? Give me this damn thing! What are you doing so early in the morning? Doing *their* prayers, ha! Have you become one of them? Do you want to be heartless and full of hatred? Do you want to kill and enslave? Why can't you see this, Nalan?"

"No, leave me alone! I have to do it. Stop it now, please, mummy – leave me alone."

Agrin became angry. She grabbed Ronak's hands and pushed her away. Agrin shouted, "Back off her, Ronak! What the hell are you doing? Are you crazy?"

Mevan heard the ruckus from the other side of the tent door. "What happened?" he called out. "What's going on in there?"

"Come in, son," Marjan said. "I don't know what to say about this madness."

Mevan entered and said, "What is all this? Be quiet – people are sleeping."

"Ask Ronak," Agrin growled, "she is out of her mind."

Ronak cried and hit herself on her hand. "After all that pain I went through, finally, I got her out of their hands and promised myself that I would never lose her again. But now look at her! I'm not even sure whether I found my little Nalan at all – she has become one of them." Ronak looked at Nalan and pleaded, "Don't you remember what they did to us, huh? They killed your father in front of your eyes? Your sister is still in their hands! Please, Nalan, I'm begging you, be the same Nalan you once were."

217

"Okay, Ronak, that is enough," Agrin said. "They have been forcing her to become what they wanted, and now you are doing the same thing. What should the poor child do? She is barely eight years old, for God's sake. Didn't I tell you to let her be free, let her feel safe again?"

Ronak cried and said, "Why don't you understand me, Agrin? How can I upset her? All I want is for her to laugh again, dance, rejoice, play, but look at her ... I would rather see her dead than like this. It's too painful; I can't take it any more. I don't know what else to do."

Agrin could see the hurt and confusion in Nalan's crying eyes as her mother scolded her. Agrin said in a steely voice, "You don't have to do anything, Ronak, other than shutting your mouth. How dare you say that to her face!"

"Hush, Agrin ... calm yourself, please," Mevan said, pulling Agrin away.

"But you look at Nalan – look at her," Agrin protested. "How can Ronak wish for her death? How can she say that?"

Agrin's reprimand made Ronak realise how much she was scaring Nalan. Ronak said nothing for a moment, then began crying.

When Agrin saw Ronak crying, she calmed down and sat next to her. "I love you like my big sister, Ronak, and I feel your pain. Still, I swear to God, if you don't control your anger, I will have nothing to do with you."

"Please don't say that," Ronak sobbed. "If you leave me, sister, who else do I have? Please help me save my little daughter."

"You can start by leaving her alone," Agrin said. "Don't tell her what to do or what not to do. Let her feel like she has a choice. If you can't understand her choices, then, please, the least you can do is respect them. All this is coming from somewhere in her past year living with them. She has been through a lot; she will never be the same Nalan as before. None of us will, but she will get better. I promise you she will eventually start talking, laughing and dancing – she just needs time and freedom. As a mother, you must love her no matter what."

"It's so hard to accept," Ronak said, "but I promise you that I will do as you say."

"I know it's hard, I understand. That is why I told you yesterday to leave her to me. If you do as I say, then I'll help you."

Ronak wiped her tears as she looked at her frightened daughter. "Okay, I promise I will listen to you."

Mevan said calmly, "Okay, Agrin, take Nalan to my tent and stay with her. Kany, you go, too."

Agrin took Nalan outside and helped her wash her face and hands with water from a small bucket. Agrin led Nalan into Mevan's tent. "Don't cry, Nalan ... your mother is just worried about you. She was wrong getting mad at you, sweetheart, but you should know she loves you so much. You heard her promise not to push you to do anything." Agrin kissed Nalan, then helped her to tie her scarf and secure it the way she wanted.

Kany came into Mevan's tent with a pillow and a blanket, then sat next to Nalan. Mevan came in and sat beside them. He said to Nalan, "Sweetheart, you should know your mother doesn't want to hurt you. She is worried about you, and she promised me that it will never happen again." He kissed her on the head.

"See, she promised Mevan, too," Agrin said. "Now don't be upset.

Tell me, my daughter – it is still so early and dark – why did you wake up?"

With tears in her eyes, Nalan began to speak for the first time, "Because if I do not wake up and pray, my master will punish me. They will not feed me, and he will take me to the market and sell me again."

"What master? Nobody owns you here," Mevan said, concerned. "We are your family and nobody is master here."

"Yes, I have a master because God made me to be owned by a man," Nalan replied. "That is my duty in life: to make him happy, make children for him and worship God."

"Do you like that belief?" Agrin asked. "Do you want your life to be all about that?"

Nalan started crying again. "No, I like what my father taught me. But what if my owner comes after me? What if he attacks us and kills Uncle Mevan, like my father, and takes me with him again? If I don't practice, I might forget my prayers. Then he will say that I have become an infidel again. And if I become infidel again, I won't be forgiven this time … That is why I shouldn't forget to worship."

Agrin held Nalan's hand and said to her firmly, "They can no longer reach you, and you have your Uncle Mevan here. No one would dare to come near you. Isn't that right, Mevan?"

Mevan had been hit hard by Nalan's words, but he came to his senses and said, "Of course. Anyone who comes near you and wants to take you must face me and get through me."

Nalan said anxiously, "But they have guns and big knives, and they kill people with those knives. If they didn't have those, they couldn't fight my father. He was empty-handed, and they got him. Uncle, do you have any to protect us?"

Mevan raised his voice and said, "Of course I have." He went to his bag and opened it. "Everything I need is always by my side to defend you and the family." He smiled warmly at Nalan. "Come and see … These are my weapons, these are my daggers and guns. I'm stronger than all of them."

"Yes, Nalan, he is right," Kany said. "Uncle came and saved me from their prison and killed all four of them."

Nalan's face brightened and she looked at Mevan with her eyes full of hope. "Uncle, you do look powerful … even stronger than my owner. He was big, but that was because he was fat," she said with a smile. "He can't beat you."

"Yes, my daughter," Mevan said, returning her smile. "Now, please sleep comfortably with Agrin and Kany in my bed, and I will go outside."

"Where are you going?" Agrin asked. "It's still dark. Why don't you stay here with the girls, and I'll go back to my bed?"

"No, I can't sleep," Mevan said, then left the tent.

Agrin could see how worried he was, so she settled the girls down, then followed Mevan outside. She found him sitting on a rock and sat next to him. He looked devastated. She gently asked, "Mevan, are you okay?"

"With this pain, how can I be?" he replied. "Did you see her little hands shaking while she was talking about those bastards? And still, we have thousands like Nalan left in their hands! What should we do? What can we do to bring them back?"

"I don't know, but we will do whatever we can. Until they all come back home, we won't stop trying."

"Yes … this can be the reason for all of us to live from now on." He paused when he saw tears in Agrin's eyes. "I'm sorry, I didn't mean to make you sad."

"I'm okay," Agrin said, wiping her tears.

"Now, you go inside and make sure Nalan is okay. It's cold out here so I'm going to go for a run."

"Okay, be safe." Agrin went back inside and settled down with Nalan and Kany. "Now, let's go back to sleep and rest a little more."

Nalan thought for a moment and then sat up again.

"Do you want to do something?" Agrin asked softly. "If you do, that's okay, be comfortable and do it."

Nalan looked at Agrin for a few seconds, then said, "No, that's okay, I'll do it later." Nalan put her head on the pillow and closed her eyes.

Agrin pulled the blanket over Nalan and Kany, put her head on Nalan's pillow, and looked with tearful and pitying eyes at Nalan's innocent sleeping face.

In the morning, Agrin woke to Mevan's voice calling, "Nalan, my daughter, wake up, come outside. I've got something for you."

Nalan got up and went outside the tent with Kany and Agrin.

"Good morning, Nalan," Mevan said, "come see what I've got for you, sweetheart."

Ronak, Marjan, Galavij and Havin were standing just behind Mevan. "Nalan, sweetheart," Ronak said, "come and look what your uncle has brought you."

Nalan looked inside the colourful bag that Mevan was holding out to her. A smile broke across Nalan's face when she saw he had brought her a doll and some other toys. She picked them up with joy and excitement and gave a toy to Havin. Nalan hugged the Barbie Doll and started laughing.

Mevan had another small bag in his hand, which he opened. "Wait, Nalan, I also got these for you."

Nalan peered inside and discovered it was full of beautiful, coloured bracelets, hairbands and necklaces. "Ooh ..." was all she could say.

Mevan grinned and handed the bag to Nalan and kissed her. "These are all yours, my daughter. Okay, now go and play."

"Thank you, Uncle Mevan," Nalan said, as she went off to play with her presents.

Mevan turned to Kany. "And I also have a gift for my beautiful daughter who is going to school and becoming a brilliant student." He pulled a package out from underneath his jacket. "Here, go and try it on."

"Oh, thank you, Uncle Mevan!" Kany said, with a beaming smile. She excitedly opened the wrapping and her eyes nearly popped out when she saw it was a beautiful new dress. "This is so nice, Uncle! I can't wait to try it on." Kany rushed off to the tent with her gift.

Mevan then turned to Galavij and handed her two bags. "Here, sister, you can give these toys to your kids when they wake up."

Galavij was delighted and said, "Thank you, Mevan, that is so kind of you."

Marjan said to Mevan, "Thank you, son, for making their day. I haven't seen them this happy for a long time. Now let's go and have an excellent breakfast together."

A few weeks later, Mevan returned early from work one day. He went to the women's tent and found Marjan near the entrance with some of the others.

"Hello, mother, I have something to tell you," Mevan said. "Please gather everyone inside."

"What's happened, son? Is it good news?"

"Yes, mother, it's good news."

When everyone was gathered, Mevan said, "The last time I came back, Shirin, Kajal and I went to the site office and wrote down everyone's names so we could leave here for another safe country. Now we all have been accepted. We have to wait a few weeks for Nalan to get her visa and then we will leave."

"Where are we going?" Ronak asked. "And what about Sheller, my other daughter? How can I leave her behind? As soon as Nalan gets a little better, I would like to go after Sheller."

"Most of our land has been reclaimed from ISIS," Mevan said. "Not much is left for them. Soon the Kurdish forces will get rid of them all. If, by chance, our forces find any of our families, then they have our names and addresses to bring them to us."

Galavij asked, "But by going away, how is that going to help us find the rest of our families?"

Mevan replied, "Most of the women and children who have not yet been found have been sold in markets in their cities or even other countries. The best thing to do is to leave here. Most importantly, you and your children will be safe. We will start work in a new country and make money. The person who informed me about Agrin's mother said that if we do not have enough money to buy back our family members, then someone else will buy them. And if he calls us now, we don't have enough money saved, and we can't buy them back. We can't do anything to help them. The only hope of us ever seeing them again is to work with those groups who are looking for them. If they do find our loved ones, we need to be ready because they can't do anything without money."

"You are right, my son, but what about the girls, aren't they coming back?" Marjan asked.

"I talked to Kajal," Mevan said. "She asked me to send you and Galavij with the kids because she doesn't want to come. She will call you herself. Shirin and Barin also want to stay in the military with our Peshmerga force."

"But what can we do?" Ronak asked. "We don't know anything about another country. How are we going to survive there alone?"

"You will not be alone," Mevan said. "I will come with you because of my injury. They won't let me go back to fighting for a few years, and they don't need me as much any more."

"So how far away is this new country?" Galavij asked. "Is it a good place?"

"I asked about it and was told the new country will accommodate us and take care of us."

"Okay, son," Marjan said, "we will do whatever you think is best."

Mevan looked at Agrin. " So what do you say, Agrin? You have been quiet."

Agrin raised her head and said, "Yes, I think that is a good idea, especially for the kids. But I'm not sure if right now is the time. I still have some work to do here. Let me see what happens and I'll let you know."

"What work?" Mevan asked. "We still have two or three weeks, so if you tell me about it, perhaps we can work on it together."

Agrin said uncertainly, "Not now, I'll explain it later. Let's drop it for the moment because I have some washing to do." She picked up a basket of washing and left the tent.

After Agrin left, Mevan turned to Marjan and asked, "Has something happened? Is there anything going on that I don't know about? Tell me, mother!"

"I do not know, son, she hasn't said anything to us," Marjan replied.

"Okay, then, if you say so, mother." Mevan hesitated. "I'll rest a little, then I'll go back to work."

He went inside his own tent to think about Agrin. After a while, he spotted her through his tent's window, returning with the basket of clothes.

Agrin went over to her tent and said, "Mother Marjan, I've finished my work and I have something to do for half an hour in the camp office, so I'll be back soon."

"Okay, my daughter, don't be late," Marjan said.

Mevan overheard Agrin, then waited a few moments before following her from a distance. Agrin went inside the site's main office.

After a while, she came out, thoughtful and upset. Mevan did not understand what Agrin was doing there, and he became anxious about her as she was on her way back to her tent. However, Mevan decided to leave her be, then turned to go back to his work. Only a few steps later, he stopped to watch a man go up to Agrin and talk to her for a few minutes.

That night, after eating, Agrin was sitting next to Mevan, and asked him, "Can't we wait a few months and then leave?"

Mevan looked at Agrin and said, "They could give us a few months, but why should we wait? It is better to leave as soon as possible. What do you need a few months for?" Mevan was still wondering about the man Agrin had been talking to earlier.

Agrin lowered her head and mumbled, "Nothing."

"Are you sure?" Mevan said.

"Yes, you can go," Agrin replied. "When I'm done, I'll follow."

Marjan interrupted. "What is it, my daughter? Tell us – maybe we can help you."

"No, I don't think so, mother. I just need some time and would like to stay a bit longer, if that's okay. I will come afterwards."

"No, you won't," Mevan said. "We will all go together. Whatever you have to do, either tell us so we can help, or finish it soon."

"If you could help, I would tell you, but it's personal," Agrin said.

"Whatever it is ... we are all going together," Mevan said sharply.

"Why are you raising your voice at me?" Agrin asked.

"Because you are being unreasonable," Mevan said. "How are you going to stay here alone? Why don't you tell us what is going on?"

"I don't want to, okay? It's my problem," Agrin said, then abruptly left.

Marjan said to Mevan, "Why did you lose your temper so quickly, son? Agrin has never been unreasonable. I'm sure there is something wrong. We will talk to her tomorrow and find out."

"But, mother, you tell me, can she stay here alone? Is it safe for her to be alone in this situation? Uhhh ... I don't understand her. Anyway, I'm going to apologise. I didn't mean to upset her." Mevan went out into the night to look for Agrin.

He couldn't see her, so called out softly, "Agrin, where are you?"

"I'm here." Agrin was sitting on a big rock beside Mevan's tent.

"It's cold outside; you better go inside," he said, as he sat next to her. "I'm sorry, I shouldn't talk to you like that."

Agrin didn't say anything.

Mevan continued, "Well, if you want to stay, I'll stay with you as well."

"No, you can't send the others alone, they need you. I will wait for a couple of months and then I'll come after you. It's not a big deal, Mevan. I'm not a child, I can take care of myself."

"Do you have anyone to stay with for a couple of months? Do you know any family that you can stay with?" Mevan was thinking about the man he had seen with Agrin.

"No, but I'll be okay. As I said, I don't need anyone."

"But, Agrin, it's not about that," Mevan said. "Why don't you try to see the other side of the reality we are facing?"

"I know you are worried about me, but I can take care of myself. So enough, please ..."

"Will you just ...?" Mevan trailed off, then took a deep breath. "Uhhh God, you are so hard to ..." He stopped himself again, then said, "Okay, I think it's better to talk about this another time. I'm going for a walk now. Do you want to come?"

"No, thank you."

"Then you should go inside. Don't sit out here. It's cold." Mevan stood up and left.

A week passed. One afternoon, following lunch, Agrin carried a basket full of dirty dishes out of her tent to wash them. Mevan was a few tents away, standing in the sun, talking to a friend. He noticed a man approaching Agrin as she walked away from her tent. It was the same man who had followed her after she had left the camp office a week earlier. Mevan said goodbye to his friend and went to investigate.

The man stopped a short distance from where Agrin was washing the dishes alongside another woman. The other woman soon finished her work and said goodbye to Agrin. When Agrin was alone, the man walked over to her.

Mevan stayed out of sight, but moved a little closer so he could hear their voices.

"How are you, Agrin?" the man said.

Agrin raised her head and answered, "I'm good, thank you. Why have you come to see me again?"

"My sister told me what your answer is."

"Then what else is there to say?" she asked.

The man, staring at Agrin, said, "I wanted to tell you myself. I like you, you are so beautiful and I want to marry you."

Mevan became angry when he heard these words, but did not allow himself to interfere. He waited to hear Agrin's response.

"I don't want to get married," Agrin said. "I told your sister as well. So, please don't ask again and leave."

The man ignored Agrin's words. "But you don't even know me. At least give us a chance to get to know each other for a while. If you still don't want me, then … I'll go."

Agrin became angry at his insistence and raised her voice. "You haven't listened to me at all. I don't want to — now go away!"

Then man stepped forward and grabbed Agrin's arm. "No. I know you have no one. You have to have a man to take care of you."

"I don't need your care or any other man's. Now let me go, or I'll call out for Mevan."

The man leaned into Agrin and said loudly, "Who is Mevan? Is he the guy who lives with you? I know he's not your relative, so it's none of his business."

Mevan ran out of patience and came out from behind the wall. He shouted, "Let her go, or I will kill you."

The man froze and said nothing as Mevan strode over.

"What the hell are you doing?" Mevan yelled. "Didn't you hear her?"

Agrin pulled her arm away from the man and went to Mevan.

The man was shocked to see Mevan and took a step back. "Nothing! Nothing! I swear to God, I didn't want to hurt her or be disrespectful. But I do want to get married because I like her."

"Right ..." Mevan scoffed. "That's no excuse to be this horrible. Why can't you understand? Her husband was killed in front of her eyes; her child died in her arms. She still doesn't know if her parents and the rest of her family are alive or not. And you ... don't you feel disgusting making her feel unsafe and bringing tears to her eyes?" Mevan grabbed the man by the collar.

"I'm sorry, brother," the man said.

"Mevan, please let him go," Agrin said, crying and pulling his arm. "Let's go home."

"You should be ashamed of your behaviour," Mevan growled. "This is not the path of a real man."

The man looked at Agrin and lowered his head. "I'm sorry," he said and left.

Mevan turned to Agrin and pleaded, "Please, Agrin, it is not safe for you to be alone at this time. Please understand what I am saying ... I don't want to force you to come with us, so I will stay with you. That is my final word. Now come, I'll carry the basket for you — let's go home."

Agrin was silent as she walked back to her tent with Mevan.

When they approached the tent, Marjan appeared out the front and asked anxiously, "Where were you, son? I made tea."

Agrin took the basket of dishes from Mevan and she went inside the tent.

Marjan kept Mevan outside and asked, "What happened, son? Why is she upset? Did you upset her?"

Before Mevan could answer, an older man and woman came bustling towards them. The man came right up to Mevan, shook his hand and said, "Hello, my son Shiro has just told us what he did a few moments ago. We were so upset with him, we came here to apologise. That was an inexcusable thing for our son to do."

After hearing the man's apology, Mevan invited them inside the tent. "Come in, tea is ready, Agrin is also inside."

Shiro's parents entered and immediately apologised to Agrin. They promised her and Mevan that it would never happen again. After having a friendly chat, Shiro's parents said goodbye and left.

Marjan reached for Agrin's hand and said, "My daughter, you should come with us. I am not saying that our people are bad, but bad people can be found everywhere. Come with us, it will be hard for you here on your own."

"Mother," Mevan said, "I told her while we were walking back with the dishes, if she doesn't come, then I'll stay with her."

"No need for that," Agrin said. "You are right. It's better for me to come, so I will come with you, too."

"I'm happy to hear that, my daughter," Marjan said.

Mevan asked, "If you'd like to, would you please tell us why you wanted to wait? Maybe I can do something about it."

"I went to the office and told them that I wanted to go to my village and visit my house, but they said they wouldn't let me because they haven't cleared the mines yet. It may take two or three months for the mines to be cleared, before it is safe for people to go back there." Agrin's tears began to fall. "I don't have anything from my family. The only thing I have left is Evin's red dummy and this little knife from my husband. I miss them so much. At least a photo or ... I don't know anything." She wiped her tears.

"Oh, my poor daughter ..." Marjan said, hugging Agrin. "Why didn't you tell us sooner?"

"There was nothing you could do, so I didn't want to upset you."

"Don't cry, please," Mevan said. "Even if we go, we can still come back and visit. But right now, let me go and see what I can do, okay?"

16

A few days passed. Agrin was inside the tent when she heard Mevan outside as he said hello to Marjan. He then asked her, "Mother, where is Agrin?"

"She is inside, making lunch," Marjan replied. "Let's go and have a cup of tea until the food is ready."

Mevan entered the tent with Marjan. "Hello, Agrin," he said brightly, "would you please sit with me for a moment? I would like to talk with you."

Agrin put the lid back on the pot she was stirring, then lowered the gas. She went over and sat next to Mevan.

Mevan said, "I was able to arrange a time for you to go to your village sooner than expected. I convinced the people in charge to clean up your village over the next few days. Then they will allow me to take you there under my supervision. So you have to promise me that when we go there, you will do as I say in order to be safe."

"Okay, I promise. Thank you very much," Agrin said, and hugged him. "Now, when can we go?"

"I don't know yet, but they will let us know soon."

A few days later, at sunset, Mevan went to Agrin's tent and asked her to get ready. "They called me," he said, "and we can leave in an hour."

Marjan asked, "Why are you leaving at night, son?"

"It's a long way, mother, and we will leave with some of my friends who are going there. They started to clear the mines yesterday, so most of the road is under control. But it will still take a long time for us to travel there, so, if we leave at night, we'll get there tomorrow around noon."

"Let's go," Agrin said, "I'm ready."

Mevan and Agrin said goodbye to everyone and walked to the camp centre.

A driver was waiting for them next to his battered utility vehicle. They quickly said hello to each other and drove off. The driver was one of Mevan's friends. He said to Mevan, "Brother, I haven't seen you since you were shot on the front line. Thank God that you look to be better now. Will you come back and join us again?"

"No, I can't," Mevan said. "After the second time I was shot in the chest, they wouldn't allow me to return. At least not for a whole year, possibly longer. During this time, I would like to look for my sister and the rest of my family, but if you need me, then let me know. I will come to help immediately."

"I know, brother," he replied, "I know what you are saying. I hope we find them all and bring them back home as soon as possible. Is this your village, the one we are going to now? And why are you taking our sister with you? It's dangerous there!"

"We have to go," Mevan said, "she will be leaving the country soon and she has lost all her family. She wants to see her home for one last time. Don't worry, I'll be with her the whole time."

After a few hours on the road, the driver stopped for a brief rest and to eat a little food before continuing on their way.

As they neared the village, Agrin scanned the landscape out the window. The mountains and the areas around them revived a lot of memories for her. The closer they got to the village, the more panicked she became. She began breathing heavily, her hands started shaking and she drummed her feet.

Mevan noticed and held one of her hands. "You okay? Do you want to stop the ute?"

"No, I'm okay," Agrin said.

The driver said, "I understand her, brother. She is going to see her home – it is hard. I wish you didn't bring her here, it's too much." The driver passed Mevan a bottle of water for Agrin.

"Calm down and hold my hand," Mevan said. "Agrin, look at me … Do you want to not go any further and stay here? I can go and get your stuff."

"No, I want to go," Agrin said. "I'll be fine."

"Okay, I'll be with you the whole time," Mevan said.

The utility stopped at the entrance to the village, and a guard came towards them. "Can I see your ID and permits to enter the village?"

Mevan handed the guard their papers.

He looked through them, then handed the papers back to Mevan. The guard said, "Be careful because the whole village has not been cleared yet."

Mevan assured him they would be careful, then they drove inside. There were a lot of cars and troops in the streets. Mevan looked at Agrin and said, "We will have to pull over and walk from here. Is your house nearby?"

"No, it's on the other side of the village," Agrin said, pointing.

After they stopped and got out of the ute, one of the military men came over with special tools and equipment. He said to Agrin, "Okay, sister, show us the way to your house, but stay next to Mevan and follow in my footsteps."

It was a long and tense walk through streets of ruined houses. When Agrin finally saw her family's house, she was heartbroken. Almost everything was destroyed. The closer they got, the more heavily Agrin breathed. Her legs weakened so much that she could barely walk. She held onto Mevan's arm and, with his help, started up the steps to what remained of the house.

Evin's cradle was still there. Agrin groaned deeply as she went to it and hugged the sides. She touched Evin's pearls and once more felt the little pillow, now covered in dust, which Evin used to lay her head on.

Everything that remained was dusty and ruined by sunlight, humidity and rain. Agrin made her way to what was left of her room and pushed the door open. The room's furniture was in better condition than outside.

Mevan followed her into the room. He spotted a photo hanging on the wall of Agrin and her husband Delovan at their wedding. He had never seen such a beautiful smile on her face – so full of life.

Agrin touched the torn curtains and smashed photo frames. Their valuables had been removed, along with most of her clothes. There were still some of Delovan's clothes hanging in the wardrobe. She took them and hugged them. The sound of Agrin's slow, painful cries brought tears to everyone's eyes.

Agrin then pulled out a sack from under the rubble. It was full of Evin's little clothes and belongings. Mevan went towards her, but his foot crushed a small photo frame. He picked it up and cleaned the dust from the edge with his hand. The photo was of a beautiful baby with big black eyes, curly hair and the cutest smile.

Agrin looked over to him and held out a hand. "Let me see." Mevan passed her the photo. "Oh, my sweet daughter," Agrin cried, hugging the photo. "She was six months old in this one. We had to tickle her to make her smile."

After a few minutes, Agrin sighed deeply, took a look around her, then found a suitcase and opened it on the floor. She packed it with all the remaining clothes belonging to her, Evin and Delovan. She put all their pillows and blankets onto a big sheet, then started tying them together.

Mevan said gently, "I don't think we can take these with us."

"These are still useable," Agrin said. "The people in the camp are going to need them. It's getting cold and there is not enough bedding."

Mevan shrugged and nodded.

Agrin continued to gather any valuable items she could find. Under one of the blankets, she found their family photo album. She opened it to look at the photos, but quickly regretted it, closed the album and put it in the suitcase. Mevan, the driver and soldier helped her to pack.

Agrin went to the wardrobe and tried to turn it around, but it was too heavy. The three men went over and helped her move the wardrobe. Hidden behind the wardrobe was a wrapped package. Agrin pulled it out and opened it. "My wedding jewellery," she said. "Thank goodness they didn't find it."

Suddenly, they heard a loud noise outside. Everyone stopped

what they were doing and rushed out. Agrin went over to a high place and looked into the distance. "What is going on?"

"I'm not sure," Mevan said.

Agrin then realised some soldiers were digging up the area where Delovan and her daughter and others were buried. She ran towards them as fast as she could.

Mevan called out, "Stop, Agrin! Don't ... it's dangerous!" He ran after her. Halfway there, he grabbed Agrin's arm. "Stop, stop! Where are you going? I told you it's dangerous."

"They are digging up there, don't you see?" Agrin said, panting. "Delovan and my daughter were buried there. Let me go, please." Agrin tried to get her arm out of Mevan's grip.

"Okay, okay, calm down, wait a minute, please. Sit down, hear me out first." He sat on the ground and pulled her down with him. "Let me go first. You stay here until I call you."

"For the love of God, Mevan," Agrin cried, pointing ahead, "those soldiers are right now digging where my husband and my daughter were buried. Please let me go, I have to go over there."

"I see, now I understand," Mevan sighed. "But stop for one second and listen. I helped dig up the mass graves at our village so I could find my father and brothers and ... now I regret it. I wish I had not seen them like that. I wish the last picture of them I had in my mind was their happy faces, their smiles. So, please ... trust me on this. You won't be able to stand the pain. There is no way I will let you go. I can't see you suffer any more."

"Yes, my sister, he is right," the driver added. "Don't go, it's for your own good."

Agrin stopped struggling and didn't say anything.

"I will go and dig them out," Mevan said. "I will prepare them, then I will take you to them."

"Sister," the soldier said, "do you have any proof of identity or anything that could help him? If not, they will take DNA."

"They buried them in that closest corner," Agrin said, pointing. "The grave is not that deep. The woman who had Evin's body put her next to Delovan, under his shoulder. Delovan has long, brown hair and got shot in the head. He has a necklace with Evin's and my name on it. Evin's clothing is red, and she also has a small bracelet on her hand ..." Agrin couldn't continue and dissolved into tears.

"Okay, that is enough," Mevan said. "I'm going. Still, you promise me, you will stay here until I come and get you, okay?"

Agrin nodded, sat back on the ground and stared at the soldiers digging about one hundred metres away.

After a few minutes, more cars came and stopped near the grave, blocking Agrin's view. She couldn't see them any more, so she waited, gazing at the sky and losing herself in memories of her family.

A few hours later, Agrin was clutching one of Evin's small hand-kerchiefs, while leaning her head against a wall. She opened her eyes when she heard Mevan's voice next to her.

"Agrin, Agrin ... open your eyes. Are you okay? Let's go." He helped her stand up and they started walking.

When they were almost at the site of the graves, Mevan said, "Agrin, wait." She instantly stopped. Mevan said, "Here are Delovan's necklace and other things that belong to your family." He put them in Agrin's hands.

"Thank you," Agrin said, before she rushed to look for their bodies.

Several other men were standing over the graves. Mevan pointed to two small bags, one much smaller than the other. Agrin asked, dumbfounded, "These! Is this all that's left of my husband and daughter?"

"Yes, my sister," one of the men said sadly.

Agrin sat next to the bags. She looked back at Mevan and said, "I thought their bodies would be the same as the day I last saw them. Then I would be able to clean the blood off Delovan's face with this handkerchief, and hug him. I imagined picking up my daughter and kissing her with all my heart. I have missed the last embrace of my husband and my baby so much that I did not even notice the time that has passed. They have been gone for more than a year. I didn't realise that my beautiful daughter and my beloved Delovan would now be nothing more than these two small bags." Tears were rolling down her cheeks.

"My daughter, I wish we could bring them back to you," an army officer said to Agrin. "I don't know what words to use to sympathise with you over this tragedy." He sat next to Agrin, clearly heartbroken at her loss. "Our people have suffered too much, my daughter."

"Why does this keeps happening to us, uncle, huh? Why does our suffering never end? How many more times do mothers have to sit and see this, huh, uncle? Please tell me."

"I don't know, my poor daughter, I'm so sorry," he said.

They all waited long enough for Agrin to have her time to mourn.

Mevan and the others took the remains of Delovan and Evin to the village cemetery and buried them. Agrin sat by the graves.

After a while, Mevan stood up and said, "Agrin, I'm going to let you have some time alone. I'll go with the driver to get the ute."

Agrin raised her head and said, "Okay, you go."

Mevan and the driver were a few steps away from Agrin, when Mevan looked back at her. "Brother," Mevan said to the driver, "you go and start to organise the stuff and get ready. I will stay here with her because I am afraid to leave her alone. What if she does something foolish?"

"Yes, brother, I agree, you better stay with her," the driver said, as he pulled a small packet from his pocket. "And, here, you can give her these sedatives to help her calm down."

Mevan accepted the pills and went back to Agrin. He sat on a rock a few metres away from her and waited.

Two hours later, he sat down next to Agrin and asked, "Agrin, are you ready to go?"

"It's hard to leave them here. I feel like my sad story should end here as well. I belong with them, right there," she said, pointing to a place beside Delovan's grave. She put her hand on Delovan's grave, running her fingers through the cold soil. "I miss him so much – so, so much." She put her face on the stone.

"I feel for you deeply," Mevan said. "Don't rush … you can stay as long as you need."

Agrin sighed as she looked at the graves. "No, I think we better leave." She wiped her tears, stood up and they walked away together.

As Agrin was about to get into the utility, a voice called out, "Mrs Agrin, Mrs Agrin, wait!"

Agrin stopped and turned to see a boy running towards her. She didn't recognise him at first, but, as he got closer, Agrin remembered and shouted, "Jiyar!" She ran to him and hugged him tightly.

"Mrs Agrin, I have missed you and Mr Delovan so very much."

"I know, sweetheart. I missed you, too, and have worried about you so much."

"I'm okay, but I miss Mr Delovan. I wish he was still alive."

"I know, but ..."

"Yes, Mrs Agrin, I know," Jiyar said sadly. "That day, we were preparing for school when they attacked. Mr Delovan fought with them a lot, but a coward seized Henar and said that if he did not surrender, they would kill her. So Mr Delovan put down his weapon and surrendered. He was fearless; I will never forget him."

Agrin nodded her head. In tears again, she said, "Yes, he was. What about you, son? Didn't they force you on to a bus and take you away?"

"Yes, they took us to an intensive training camp. They told us that, from then on, we were their soldiers, and we had to fight for them. Most of us had bombs strapped inside our clothes and were taken to the front line to fight and explode. Many boys were killed. Once, when I was readying for an attack with the others, I hid in the building at night and waited for everyone to leave, then I ran away."

Agrin hugged him again and said, "Thank God that you are okay. Who are you with? Did you find any of your family? If not, you can come with me."

"Yes, son," Mevan said, "if you haven't found anyone yet, come with us."

Jiyar thanked him and said, "My mother is with us, and we found two of my sisters a few months ago. I came with my cousin today to identify bodies and help." Jiyar then gave his mother's phone number to Agrin. He added, "Mrs Agrin, can I ask you for something?"

"Sure, son, what?"

"Can I have a photo of my teacher Mr Delovan?"

"Yes, of course, let me get my album."

Mevan took the album out of her suitcase and handed it to Agrin. She looked through it and took out a photo. It had been taken the last day before the summer school holidays. Delovan, Agrin, Evin and all the kids were in the photo.

Jiyar thanked her and hugged her again, saying goodbye as he headed back to his cousin.

It was near sunset when Agrin, Mevan and their driver got into their utility to leave the village. However, a soldier ran towards them and shouted, "Wait! Stop that vehicle!"

"What's the matter?" the driver said.

"Please take these two men with you." Behind the soldier, two other figures were struggling towards the utility. The soldier waved at them and said, "One needs help with an infected wound, the other's blood pressure plummeted after finding the bones of his son and brother. He has to go to a clinic somewhere. We will not finish our work for a few hours, so, if you can, please take them with you."

Mevan said, "I will sit in the back of the ute with one, the other can sit inside out of the cold with Agrin."

Agrin said, "No, let them both come in here. I want to sit in the back as well. I need fresh air." She jumped out of the cabin and climbed into the back and rested her head on her things.

As they left the village behind, Agrin stared at its ruins. She remembered the faces of Delovan and Evin and their laughter. It all seemed to be only a few hours ago. Now, all those dreams for their future happiness had turned into nothing but a bitter memory of their bloody faces and makeshift graves. She was leaving in a veil of tears to travel far away to an unknown destination.

Mevan was sitting next to her. He put a blanket over her and kept silent until she closed her eyes. Seeing her beautiful innocent face so sad tore at him inside. He couldn't do anything more to help ease her devastation. It was too late to do anything. Too many mothers of his land had become childless; too many orphans had been buried; too many loved ones had been killed; too many lovers were doomed to the torment of horrific separations by death or kidnapping; too many families had been broken into pieces; too many girls had been abducted and raped. Any hope for their return was futile. Devastated, Mevan stared at the stars. How could he build hope for an unknown future again? How would it be possible to stand up again after these horrible downfalls? Why did these things keep happening? After enduring more than seventy massacres, he wondered how his people could survive another disaster. How could he make sure that his people would never see such horrible days again? He had to find a way. He leaned against the corner of the ute and eventually fell asleep under the weight of his sorrow.

Early next morning, Mevan opened his eyes and saw Agrin had woken and put the blanket over him. "Morning, Agrin. How long have you been awake?"

"A few hours. Nightmares didn't let me sleep."

"Why didn't you wake me? How are you doing now?"

"I do not know," Agrin said.

"Do you want to talk? Maybe it'll help you to find peace."

"I can't find any reason to live ..." Agrin sighed. "Living this life isn't worth the pain."

"Don't say that — we have to be strong. Time will make it better, I promise you. You will find your reason."

The driver stopped the utility next to a clinic. The two other men got out, thanked them and left. The driver turned back to Mevan, "Morning, brother, let's have a rest and eat something."

"Good idea," Mevan said.

The driver said, "You know, while we were driving, I tried to offer our sister Agrin some food or a cup of tea, but she said she wanted to wait for you to wake up."

Mevan looked at Agrin, but she didn't say anything.

After they had eaten and rested, they finished driving to their camp.

When they arrived inside the gates of the compound, the driver realised the track ahead was too muddy for them to drive across. Mevan spotted Kany and called out, "We're back, Kany! Can you please tell Ronak and the others to come and help. The road is muddy and our car can't get through."

Kany was delighted to see them and quickly ran off to fetch the others.

They were all there within a few minutes to help. Marjan saw Agrin and went to her. "Oh, my poor daughter, welcome back! How are you coping?"

"I'm okay, mother," Agrin replied. "Let's help take these things home."

Mevan said, "No, you go home with mother, and the girls and I will take care of it all."

"Yes, my daughter, you can hardly stand," Marjan said. "How can you help, sweetheart? Let's go home." Together, Agrin and Marjan left for their tent.

Agrin went inside, sat in a corner, put her head on a pillow, and closed her eyes. Marjan placed a blanket over her to make her comfortable, then said, "Yes, my daughter, rest a little, you must be exhausted."

A few moments later, Mevan appeared at the door of the tent. He was carrying a large bag. Marjan quickly went over to help him and said, "Here, let me help you put it down outside on this rock so it won't get muddy."

"Thank you, mother," Mevan said, as he placed the bag on the rock. "What happened to Agrin?"

"She is sleeping. What happened there, son? Why is she looking so upset and sick?"

Mevan peered inside the tent at Agrin, then pulled down the door-flap and walked back to Marjan. He lowered his voice and said, "Her whole house was destroyed. It was heartbreaking. We buried her husband and daughter yesterday. She was in a terrible state, and I gave her a few sedatives to help her rest for a while."

"Oh, my poor, poor child," Marjan said, sitting next to the bag on the stone.

"Please, mother, take care of her," Mevan said. "Don't let her be alone for too long. I don't want anything to happen to her."

"I will take care of her, my son, I will."

Two hours later, Agrin raised her head from her pillow.

Marjan saw her and said, "You woke up, my daughter. Come, let's have lunch together."

"I'm not hungry," Agrin said.

Ronak came over and said, "Don't say that, my sister, we were waiting for you to wake up to eat together. Now, come and sit down. Otherwise, we will not eat, either."

"Yes, mother Agrin, and I'm so hungry," Havin said, sitting next to Mevan.

Agrin smiled and said softly, "Okay, you start eating. Let me go wash my hands and face, take in some fresh air, and then I'll come."

"Wait for me, auntie, I'll come with you," Kany said, and left with Agrin.

After lunch, Agrin opened the boxes, the suitcase and bundle of bedding she had brought back from her village. She put some things in a bag to keep for herself, then picked up the rest of the bedding and clothes and said, "I'm going to wash these. They need to be clean before I give them to the camp office to pass on to those who need them the most."

Galavij said, "Let us come to help you, too."

"No, I want to wash them myself," Agrin said, then left.

Mevan followed her out and asked, "Why won't you let them help you?"

"I want to be alone."

"But ... okay, if you say so."

"Stop worrying, Mevan," Agrin said.

"I want to make sure you are okay and you won't ... I mean you ..."

"I won't follow the path of Henan, I promise you," Agrin said. "I will be okay."

"Okay, thank you. I'll go back to work now. Let me know if you need anything," Mevan said, then left.

17

A few days later, Agrin was sitting in front of her tent, watching Nalan play with the other children. She called her, "Sweetheart, come here."

"What is it, Aunt Agrin?"

"Come with me, I want to show you something." Agrin took Nalan's hand and went inside. From the suitcase, she took three beautiful pieces of material and said, "Look at the colours and touch them. See how soft they are. Can you tell me the colours?"

"This is green, and this one is blue, and this is red," Nalan said.

"Yes, excellent. Now choose one of them to let me see which colour is your favourite."

"Well, I like purple more than anything, but you don't have that, and I like this one, too." Nalan put her finger on the blue fabric.

"What a beautiful colour."

"Yes, it is like the sky."

Agrin smiled. "Yes, it does have the same colour as the sky."

Nalan said, "But when it's happy, not when it's crying or angry, because then it turns into dark and grey colours, and I don't like that at all."

"I know, right. Sometimes it also scares me, especially when it starts crying loudly," Agrin said, with a smile.

"Oh, auntie, you are like me," Nalan said, smiling.

"Now, let me measure your size, then I will sew a beautiful dress for you, okay?" Agrin said.

Nalan nodded while rocking herself.

"Okay, now you are all done, you can go and play with your dolls."

Nalan went off to play with her dolls, then Agrin called for Kany, "Come, my sweet daughter, now you choose a colour."

Kany went over to her and said, "Aunt Agrin, I love red, it's always been one of my favourite colours."

Galavij overheard, while she was getting the tea ready, and said, "Red, well that is a beautiful colour, especially for a pretty girl like you."

Agrin looked over at Rondek and Havin and called to them, "Now, what about you two? I can sew two more cute little dresses. Come on, hurry up, choose your colours."

The girls ran to her and started touching and playing with the fabrics. After measuring them, Agrin went to Marjan, who was sitting next to Mevan outside. "Mother, I'm going to borrow our neighbour's sewing machine."

"Okay, my daughter. You should sew yourself some clothes."

"I don't need any, I have enough. We are about to leave the country, so I would like the kids to have nice dresses."

"Do you want me to come and carry the sewing machine for you?" Mevan asked.

"No, it's not heavy – I'm good. I'll come back in a minute," Agrin said.

After she finished sewing, she called out to the girls, "Come inside, your dresses are ready. Let's try them on to see if they fit nicely or need some changes."

Kany was the first to try on her dress. "Oh, my God, auntie, I love it – it's perfect!" She twirled around.

"Come here, Kany, let me fix your hair as well," Ronak said.

"Uncle Mevan, do you like it, too?" Kany asked.

"Yes, my beautiful princess, it suits you so much," Mevan said.

Rondek and Havin were so excited about trying on their dresses that they were jumping around Agrin while waiting for their turn.

"Okay, okay, you two be patient," Galavij said. "Come bring your dresses here and let me help you put them on."

However, Nalan was holding her dress in her hand and didn't want to try it on.

"Darling, why don't you try it on?" Agrin asked. "Come here, I'll help you."

Nalan stayed still and quiet.

Ronak said to Nalan, "Aunt Agrin has been working the whole day and she will be upset if you don't try it on."

"What is it, Nalan? Don't you like it?" Agrin asked.

"Yes, I do like it," Nalan said softly, rocking herself.

"Then why aren't you trying yours on like the others?" Ronak asked.

"Shush …" Agrin said to Ronak, then turned to Nalan. "I won't be upset if you don't wear it. Maybe you want to keep it clean for a special day. You know what? Put your dress in that suitcase. You can wear it anytime you wish to – how's that?"

"Okay," Nalan said, relieved. She put her dress in the suitcase and went out to play.

Ronak sighed. "Will I ever see the day when she is free and happy like the others?"

"I'm sure you will," Agrin said. "You will see her blooming like the most beautiful flower and, until that day, you don't have to do anything but make her feel safe and loved."

"Yes, I hope you are right," Ronak said.

Agrin began resetting the sewing machine. "Okay now, does anyone have anything they would like me to sew?" she asked.

"Yes, my daughter, here is Mevan's shirt," Marjan said, handing her the shirt. "Could you please re-sew the sides. I did it with a needle, but it doesn't look nice."

After Agrin had finished Mevan's shirt, she picked up the sewing machine, ready to return it to her neighbour, but she was not wearing her shoes.

"It's dark outside," Mevan said. "Let me take care of that." He took the sewing machine from Agrin's arms.

*

Finally, the day to leave their homeland arrived. They gathered all their necessary items and said goodbye to the neighbours. They got in the car and drove to the airport.

"Son, how far away are we going?" Marjan asked. "I'm a little nervous about my daughter Kajal — she should have come with us."

"I don't know exactly how long our trip will take, but I have been told it might be around the whole day before we arrive," Mevan said. "I'm sure Kajal will be fine. I talked to her an hour ago to check on her and the girls."

Ronak heard what Mevan said, and asked, "That long? I didn't realise it was so far away. Couldn't we go to a country that is much closer to us?"

"We could," Mevan said, "but this one accepted all of us as a family, and those who are already there told me that we can find a job there."

Kany said, "What if the people over there don't like us because we don't look like them and don't know their language and so much more? I'm afraid, Uncle."

Mevan went silent and looked at Agrin to say something.

Agrin took her cue and said, "Well, I don't think it will be like that, Kany. I think they want to help us. Let's not be worried about that, because we don't really know much about the place yet, but, whatever happens, we have got each other."

They arrived at the airport and boarded the plane. Galavij and her children sat together, Ronak and her daughters were together, Mevan and Agrin were next to Kany and Marjan.

Agrin looked down from the window as the plane took off. She felt calm but also so strange at not being on the ground any more. She didn't know why, but somewhere deep inside her a sound whispered: "This is going the right way."

After a while, Marjan said to Mevan, "Son, my leg is becoming sore from sitting for so long on this seat. How much further?"

"Mother, get up and walk a little," Mevan said.

Marjan sighed. "I left my daughter Kajal alone. I wish she was here with us. How long do you think it will be before I see Kajal again, my son?"

Mevan helped Marjan to her feet. "I know what you are saying, mother, but think about your two grandchildren – they deserve to have a safe place to live and grow. Besides, you can always go back and visit Kajal."

"You are right, son," Marjan said.

"Now, we have a long way to go. Please walk a little, then try to have some rest." Mevan sank back into his seat and took a deep breath.

"Mevan, are you okay?" Agrin asked.

"Yes, I'm fine."

"Are you?" Agrin asked again.

Mevan made sure that Kany was sleeping, then whispered, "I don't know how to say this, Agrin, but … how are you doing with all this — going away from everything we know?"

"I am very nervous. I mean, my hands were shaking for hours earlier. It's a big change, but I feel we are heading in the right direction."

"You really do?"

"Yes, I do," Agrin said. "No doubt we will have some troubles because it's a new environment, but as long as you are with us, I feel safe."

"Of course, I will protect you and the family with my life. However, I'm not absolutely sure leaving our home was a wise choice."

Agrin was surprised. "Why are you in doubt?"

"I don't want to see you and the others suffering any more and lead you into new challenges that might be devastating. I want you to have a peaceful life, finally."

Seeing Mevan stressed like this, Agrin held his hands. "I know it's a big responsibility for you, but you have all of us beside you — I'm beside you. We will get through this together."

Mevan smiled. "Thank you, Agrin."

When they arrived at their destination, several people were waiting for them at the airport. Among them was a man who came forward and said, "Hello, welcome, my name is Diyar. I'm here to help you."

They all exchanged greetings while Diyar translated for the others in his group. Then he said to the new arrivals, "My friends and I are so happy to welcome you all to Melbourne, Australia. We have prepared a place to make you feel welcome. Now, you must all be exhausted, so please follow me to a minibus waiting outside for us."

"Where are you taking us, brother Diyar?" Mevan asked.

"We will take you to your house," Diyar said.

"Our house?" asked Ronak.

"Yes, my sister," Diyar said. "Due to your situation, they got you a home. They wanted you to be comfortable and stay together. There is a large number of our brothers and sisters there, too – they came during the war. Your house is in their neighbourhood so that you can be with your community."

When the minibus stopped, Diyar got out and opened the door. He said to Marjan, "Come out, mother, this is your new home. Let's go inside and I will give you a small tour."

"Thank you, son," Marjan said.

They entered and saw everything had been organised, from gas and electricity to beds, food and clothing.

"Oh, my God, this is a nice house," Ronak said.

"Yes, sister, it is," Diyar said. He turned to Mevan. "There is a separate room outside, Mevan, that I think will be comfortable for you. Let's go out and I'll show you."

"Thank you, my brother," Mevan said.

After showing Mevan his room outside, Diyar came back inside and said to Marjan, "Okay, mother, I guess that is about it for this evening. Tomorrow I will come back to see you. Have a nice rest. Good night."

"Thank you for everything, my son, and good night," Marjan said.

"Let me walk you to the minibus," Mevan said.

"Okay, thank you," Diyar said.

When they were outside, Mevan said, "Brother, we don't have much money to pay for our expenses. Can you find me a job?"

"I know what are you are saying, brother, but don't worry, the Australian government will support you and your family," Diyar said.

"They have already done more than enough, and I'm so thankful for that, but if you can find me a job, that would be helpful."

"Sure, brother, every morning many of our people are going to work. It's on a farm not too far from here, if you want."

"Yes, brother, whatever the job is, I want it," Mevan said.

"Okay, I will call one of my friends to come and pick you up tomorrow morning, then you can go and see if you like the work."

"Thank you very much."

"No problem, have a nice night," Diyar said, then left.

Mevan went back inside and smiled when he saw how excited everyone was about the house. The kids were busy checking everything out.

"Come over here, son," Marjan said. "What did you talk about with Diyar? Is there something you are worried about?"

Mevan sat next to her, Agrin and Ronak. "No, mother, I asked him if I can find a job."

"So, what did he say?" Ronak asked.

"Yes, I will go to work with them tomorrow. He said there is enough work for everyone."

"Then we will come, too," Agrin said.

"No, not yet," Mevan said. "I'll go tomorrow by myself to see how it is."

"If there is a job for us, why wait?" Ronak said.

"No, you are not coming," Mevan insisted. "I won't take you there until I make sure that the environment is safe and secure enough for you."

"Yes, my daughter, he is right," Marjan said. "Let him go and see it first. Some jobs and some places are not suited to everyone."

"Okay, brother, whatever you say," Ronak said.

The doorbell rang.

"Who could that be?" Kany asked.

"Maybe it's Diyar," Galavij said.

A man's voice called out in Kurdish from behind the door, "Hello, we are your neighbours."

"Let me open the door," Mevan said.

On the doorstep was a man with a big smile. "Hello, brother, I'm your neighbour and I've come to welcome you and get to know you."

"Hello, brother, please come inside," Mevan said.

"Oh, how good to meet you, son, come in, please," Marjan said.

A young lady followed the man in with a pot in her hand. "Hello, mother, I'm Sharmin and I've come with my husband to welcome you, too." She then turned to Ronak and said, "Here's some food I cooked. Be careful — it's still hot."

"Oh, thank you very much," Ronak said, taking the pot and

peeking inside. "My daughter Nalan hasn't had anything on the way, and this is her favourite food."

Sharmin explained the living conditions to Agrin and the others, and how everything worked. Her husband sat down with Mevan and started talking. "My name is Miran. My family and I have been here for a few months now. Diyar called me to take you with me to work tomorrow. I said to my wife, let's go and see them to make sure they are comfortable."

"That was very thoughtful of you, brother," Mevan said.

After Miran and Sharmin had left, everyone got ready for bed, then went to sleep.

Early the next morning, Mevan woke up in his room and pulled the curtains open. "Time to go to work," he said to himself, then went inside the main house.

Ronak, Marjan and Agrin were already in the kitchen. "Breakfast is prepared," Ronak said, putting a bowl of food on the table.

"Morning, everyone, I didn't want to wake you – it's still so early," Mevan said, as he sat down at the table.

Marjan poured him a cup of tea. "Did you think I would let my son go to work without breakfast?"

"Thank you, mother, this food looks delicious."

"You're welcome, son, but Agrin made it," Marjan said. "She wouldn't let me do anything but the tea."

"Thank you, Agrin, I appreciate it."

"No problem," Agrin replied.

That afternoon, Mevan came home with a small bag of fresh fruit. He walked in the front door, but couldn't see anyone, so he called out, "Hello, where are you all?"

"Here, Uncle, in our new backyard," Kany called back.

Mevan went out the back to find Marjan and the girls sitting under a large tree. "Hello, everyone," he said, beaming.

"Hello, son, welcome back," Marjan said.

"So, how was work?" Ronak asked.

"It was perfect," Mevan said. "We were picking fruit and vegetables. It's a wonderful place and they pay you at the end of the day."

"Uncle, did you pick the fruits in the bag?" Kany asked.

"No, sweetheart, I bought them on the way home. Go wash them and bring them back for the kids."

"Okay," Kany said, taking the bag and going inside.

Mevan said, "Mother, if you make a list of the things we need, then I'll get them tomorrow after work."

"What about us? Are you going to take us with you tomorrow?" Agrin asked.

"Yes, tomorrow you and Ronak can come," Mevan said.

"What about me, brother? I do want to come, too," Galavij said.

"But what about your kids?" Mevan asked.

"Well, I will take care of them," Marjan said. "Nalan and Kany are here, too, and they are old enough to stay away from their mother for part of the day."

"Yes, and most of the time, they play together and don't make any trouble," Galavij added.

"Okay, then," Mevan said, "tomorrow morning we are all going, but remember we have to take our lunch with us."

"Okay, we will take care of everything, Mevan," said Galavij.

"Very good, now let's have dinner," Mevan said. "I'm so hungry and the food smells so delicious."

18

A few months passed with life going very well. The children were going to school to learn, Marjan stayed at home and took care of the house, while Agrin, Mevan, Ronak and Galavij went to work every day of the week.

One night when everyone was at the dinner table, Ronak asked, "Mevan, did you hear back from the man who you sent Agrin's mother's name to?"

Mevan looked at Agrin and said, "We talked last week and he said that the days of the sales markets are limited. We have to wait and be patient."

"I'm sure we will find her and the others," Galavij said.

"Yes, that is what he said," Mevan said to Galavij. "I gave him both Agrin's number and yours, in case I missed his call."

"Maybe they killed her, or she committed suicide," Nalan muttered under her breath, as she lowered her head.

Marjan sighed and said, "My daughter, why are you saying this? Don't think like that."

Nalan said, with uncertain sadness, "I don't know, Granny, I'm sorry." She sighed.

"Why did you think of that, Nalan?" Agrin asked.

"Mmm ... well, once one of my friends was returned to the room at midnight. She was hurt and in a lot of pain. Nobody helped her and she died the next day. Another time, a man bought me along with an older girl like Kany. This girl was telling me all the time, 'I will take care of you. We will get out of here one day soon.' She was kind and so brave. A few times, she stood up to my master and didn't let him hurt me. Once, she hit back at his wife, who called us infidels and started hitting me. This girl promised me if she succeeded in finding a way to escape, she would come back for me, but they caught her and took her away for a few days. When she returned, she was like another person. She was screaming at night and kept cleaning herself all the time, crying so hard, and she was full of anger. I was terrified of what she had become, but I was still taking care of her, and doing all of her work so she wouldn't have to face them as much. I liked her very much and tried to help her get better. She was sleeping next to me until one morning I woke up and saw my clothes and our bed were all bloody. I got up and saw that she had cut the vein in her arm and killed herself. After that, I was lonely for so long."

"Oh, my poor daughter, what have you been through?" Ronak cried.

Nalan lowered her head sadly.

Agrin, who was sitting next to her, hugged her tightly, kissed her, raised her head, looked into her eyes, and said, "I'm sure they'll all be back one day. It will take time, but we'll find them and bring them back here with us – my mother, your sister Sheller, and Kany's mother and sisters. Every one of them will come home one day soon, like you did."

"Yeah, maybe they are alive and waiting for us to save them," Nalan said.

"Of course, and we will never give up – no way," Agrin said, as she handed Nalan some food. "Have this to eat. Then I want you to go and draw me one of your beautiful pictures."

"Auntie, do you want me to draw you a picture of a flower? I learnt a new one at school," Nalan said.

"Yes, please," Agrin said.

"And you can hang it over your bed like the others," Nalan said, before she left the room.

"Did you hear her?" Ronak said, as she began crying. "The hell that my poor daughter was in ..."

"I know, my sister, it's so painful," Agrin said quietly, "but please control yourself. She is on the couch in the next room and might hear you. If you cry, she might never say anything of her dark past and keep it to herself so as not to make you sad. She gets sensitive when you cry, and blames herself."

"Okay, Agrin, you are right," Ronak said, wiping her tears.

After eating dinner, they were at the table talking and having tea when someone called for Agrin at the door. Agrin opened the door, greeted her friend and told her to wait so she could get ready to go out together. She picked up her bag, said goodbye and left.

"Who is this woman, mother?" Mevan asked. "Hasn't she come here a few times for Agrin? And where is she taking her this late?"

"She is our neighbour from a few blocks away, son," Marjan said.

"They go to the community building," Kany said. "There are other people there as well. They talk and have a good time together. My teacher says it can be helpful in a new neighbourhood."

"Why at night — can't they go earlier?" Mevan asked. "I don't want her going out at night. It's not right and could be dangerous."

"Oh no, son, her friend's brother takes them in his car," Marjan said. "But if you are worried, I will talk to her."

"No, leave it to me, mother," Mevan said, as he stood up from the table.

"Where are you going, Uncle?" Kany asked.

"I'm going to bed. I'm so tired. Thank you for the tea, mother. Good night, everyone." Mevan went out the back to his room.

A couple of nights later, Mevan saw Agrin waiting at the door. "Are you waiting for your friend?" he asked.

"Yes, she should be here by now."

"Last time you came back so late, I was worried. Try to get home sooner this time. After a long day of work, you have to have rest."

"I know, I'm sorry," Agrin said. "We talked a lot and had so much fun that I forgot about the time. It won't happen again."

"Fun! What fun? What do you talk about for hours?"

"All kinds of stuff. You know, we are new here, and learning about a new culture and language can be challenging. We have to get through so many troubles and some of them turn out to be so funny."

"Who else is there?" he asked.

"A lot of people, but most of the time my friend and I sit somewhere quiet, so that she can teach me what she has learnt at school."

"Like what?" Mevan asked. "I do want to learn about this culture and language."

"Why don't you come to see how it is yourself?" Agrin asked.

"Okay, then let's go," Mevan said, and they went out the door together.

Agrin said, "Let's walk, it's not that far. Mother Marjan asked my friend's brother to take us, to be safe, but I will be fine with you."

"Okay, if you want to," Mevan replied.

On the way, they started talking. "So, what are you learning here?" Mevan asked.

"Their language. If we learn their language, then life and communicating will be far easier. Also, we learn about so much other interesting stuff."

"Such as?" Mevan asked.

"Their culture is so different to ours. Did you know this country is only around 200 years old? It is amazing they built it in such a short period of time. They have so many different languages and other beliefs, and so much more besides all these differences. Look how peaceful this land and life here is."

"I see," Mevan said. "If I can find some free time, then I will come to learn, too, or I'll wait for you to teach me."

Agrin laughed. "Ronak and Galavij asked me the same thing."

"Agrin, did you go to school?"

"Yes, I finished university."

"Very good," he said.

"What about you?"

"I also went to school but couldn't go to university. Still, I always wished to go," he said.

"You can go to university here," she said.

"I don't think it would be that easy."

"I'll help you, step by step. If you start, we will get through it, one day."

"Okay," he replied, "maybe one day, but for now I have to make sure that the family are taken care of and heading in the right direction in this new environment."

Agrin smiled. "Mother Marjan is right ..."

Mevan stopped. "Right about what?"

"That without you, we wouldn't be this happy here, you know. Everything is excellent, but I still feel frightened sometimes. So, to have you with us, well ... it's ... uh – I don't know how to describe it to you – but you should know we are all so thankful to have you, Mevan."

Mevan smiled and kept walking with her.

When they arrived at the gate, Agrin said, "Here, this is the building, let's go in. I think everyone is in there and, look, that's my friend's car."

Agrin introduced Mevan to her friend, then they sat down to enjoy their time together.

The following day they went to work as usual. Agrin's hard work and energy attracted the boss's attention. He called her over and introduced himself.

Agrin said, "I can't understand you very well."

The boss called over one of the other workers to translate.

A man joined them and translated for Agrin. "He is telling you not to be so hard on yourself, and to rest a little."

Agrin thanked him and said to the translator, "Tell him I'm not tired. This is not heavy work and I need it."

"Aren't you supported?" the translator asked.

Agrin sighed. "Yes, but my mother is still in the hands of ISIS. She is being traded back there as a slave. If we find her, I have to be able to buy her or help to bring her back."

The translator relayed this to the boss, who replied, "I'm so sorry to hear that. I hope you find your family as soon as possible – good luck to you." The boss paused for a moment, deep in thought, then said, "But still, I want you to take it easy and be careful with your health."

Agrin thanked him and went back to where Mevan was working.

Mevan asked, "What was he saying to you?"

"He wants us to not work this hard and have some rest."

"He is right," Mevan said, "you and Ronak are working too hard. Sometimes you do not even eat lunch. I'm worried about you two."

"Well, you are working even harder!"

"Yes, but I'm a man and it's different for me because I am used to heavy work and can handle it. For now, let's go and we can both rest and drink some water."

The next day after work had finished and the workers had been paid, the translator went to see Agrin before she left. Agrin was talking with Mevan, Ronak and Galavij. The translator interrupted and said, "My sister, the boss wants to see you in his office."

Agrin and the translator walked to the office. They went inside where the boss was waiting for them. He said, "Hello again, come and have a seat."

"No, thank you, my friends are waiting for me," Agrin replied, through the translator.

"Oh, okay," the boss said, then told the translator, "you go and bring them inside as well."

The translator nodded and left the office.

The boss turned back to Agrin and said, "Please, have a seat." They sat down to wait, and soon the translator returned with Mevan.

The boss said through the translator, "I couldn't stop thinking about your situation. Since yesterday, I have talked to my family. I have two beautiful daughters a little younger than you. I'm so sorry for what has happened to your family. My family and I want to help you. If you find your loved ones, then we can help you buy them back."

Mevan turned to the translator and said, "Tell him, that it's kind of him and his family – we appreciate it. But we still haven't received any news, and we don't know when we will. If we find them, there are some organisations that will help us. He is already helping us a lot by giving us these jobs."

The boss replied through the translator, "I understand and I do hope you find them soon. Please remember that I'm always here to help. We share the pain of this heart-breaking tragedy with you. Rest assured, you and your family are not alone."

"Thank you very much, brother. We appreciate all your support, it gives us hope and strength to get through this," Mevan said, and hugged him.

*

A few months passed. One afternoon, Mevan entered the front yard of their house to find Marjan and Agrin sitting and talking on the balcony with one of the women from next door. He said hello to Agrin and Marjan, greeted the guest, then went inside.

After the woman left, Agrin went to wash the cups. Marjan went to Mevan and asked, "Do you know why she was here?"

"No, Mother, why?"

"She was here to propose marriage to Agrin for her brother."

"Oh!" Mevan said. He paused, then asked, "So what did Agrin say? Was she interested?"

"No, son," Marjan said. "She didn't accept; she says she doesn't want to get married. So far, three suitors have come for her, and she has rejected them all."

"Three! When? Why has no one told me anything?"

"I know, son," Marjan sighed, "she didn't want to make a big deal out of it, but this lady's brother is the perfect man. Agrin has to get married and have a family one day, she can't stay alone for the rest of her life."

"I don't know what to say, mother ..."

"Are you okay, son? Your face has turned pale," Marjan said.

"Yeah, I'm fine ... I just wasn't expecting this." Mevan looked away, deep in thought.

"Son ... son ... are you sure you're okay?"

"Oh yeah ... sorry, mother. I need to go for a walk, then we will talk about this, okay?"

"Okay." Marjan watched Mevan walk away.

She was left wondering what was wrong for what seemed like ages before Mevan returned. "Oh, son, you are back. What took you so long?"

"I'm sorry, mother — can we speak in confidence?" Mevan said, looking unsettled. "I need to tell you something."

"Okay, son."

Mevan closed the door and sat next to her.

"Tell me what is going on, son," she said. "You seem nervous."

"Well, I don't know how to say this," Mevan began.

Marjan looked him in the eyes. "I am like your mother and, as a mother, I love you more than anything, so you can tell me whatever is on your mind, darling."

"It's Agrin ... I love her so much. I didn't want to say anything, because if she doesn't love me and finds out how I feel about her, it would be so uncomfortable for her since we live in the same house – and I don't want that." Mevan paused to gather his thoughts. "But, uh ... now I'm afraid that if she accepts one of her suitors, I will lose her forever."

"What can I say, my son? She might. She is a beautiful, kind and brilliant woman. But if you want my opinion, I say that you better talk to her and see how she feels."

Mevan shook his head and said, "But I know she's not ready for it. She still sits looking at her photo album for hours. I don't want to make her feel uncomfortable around me."

"Son, in that case, I'm sure she will be fine. She knows what a good gentleman you are. To be honest, the girls and I knew that you had feelings for her, and I can see how comfortable and happy she is around you. When the time is right, you tell her how you feel and I'm sure something good will come out of this."

"Okay, mother, I will talk to her."

One afternoon, Mevan was watching Agrin in the backyard through his bedroom window. She was sitting under the big tree while Marjan was combing her beautiful hair. Mevan decided that now was the time to speak with Agrin and stepped out of his room into the yard.

Marjan looked over at Mevan and said to him, "Hello, son, did you have a good nap?"

"Yes, I did, thank you, mother."

"Come, I'm almost done with Agrin's hair, then we can have some tea."

"Thank you, mother, but I wanted to talk to Agrin."

Marjan knew what was going on. She stood up and said, "Okay, I'm going to make the tea and leave you both to talk."

"No, mother, I want you to stay," Mevan said.

"What do you want to say?" Agrin asked. "Is there some news about my mother?"

"No, no, it's not about that," Mevan said, then paused for a moment. "Agrin, we have known each other for more than two years now. I have wanted to tell you something for a long time, but I was waiting for the right time." He lowered his head and continued, "After Henan's death, I could never believe that one day I would be able to love and want a family again. But since then I have grown to love you so much that I would like to spend the rest of my life with you. I thought that those dreams had been buried with Henan ... but every time I look in your beautiful eyes, I tell myself that I might have a chance to have it all again."

"I don't know what to say," Agrin replied. "I wasn't expecting this."

Marjan said, "Agrin, I know you said you don't want to get married again, but, sweetheart, you can't stay alone your whole life. You are young with a long life ahead of you."

Agrin was silent and put her head down.

"Agrin, tell me the truth," Mevan said, "whatever is inside your heart. If you don't like me and you don't want me, please say it. I promise you I will understand, and I won't mention it again."

"It's not that ... I do like you, but I'm not ready and I don't know if I ever will be."

"I know ..." Mevan said, "and I didn't want to bring it up anytime soon, but seeing this suitor who came for you, I was afraid to lose you one day. I wanted you to at least know how I feel about you."

"Agrin, I have known both of you for quite some time now," Marjan said, "and let me tell you that you are a good match, and you know Mevan will make you happy. I know that you can start a beautiful life together."

"I do want you to be in my life, Mevan, but I'm not ready right now."

"That is okay with me, as long as I know that I won't lose you, I am willing to wait as long as you need." He took a necklace from his pocket. "Here, last time you gave this back to me over my son's grave. I made this for Henan, and now I want you to wear it. That is all I want you to do, then take your time. I promise if it takes my whole life, I will wait."

Agrin accepted the necklace, with tears in her eyes.

"You made the right decision, my daughter," Marjan said. "Mevan is a good man and I am sure he will make you happy. Now, aren't you going to wear the necklace?"

Agrin didn't say anything.

"That is okay," Mevan said, "there is no pressure — wear it when you are ready."

Marjan stood up, went to Mevan and kissed him on the head. "Congratulations, son, I pray for you and Agrin to have a sweet life."

Mevan kissed her hand with respect. "Thank you, mother." He then went to Agrin.

Agrin stood, then Mevan hugged her and kissed her forehead, looking into her eyes. "Okay, darling, I will leave you and mother alone. I'm going for a walk," Mevan said, as he left the yard.

Marjan congratulated Agrin. "Sweetheart, you won't regret this, he is a real man. Look how he made us like a family and how good he is at taking care of us all. This man can give you a good life with beautiful kids. Did you see what a hopeful smile you put on his face? You did well, darling."

Agrin didn't say anything and smiled falsely.

From then on, Agrin withdrew into herself and spent time alone more often. She treated Mevan differently and avoided him when she could.

One day at work, while Galavij and Ronak were setting up the lunch, Mevan asked, "Where is Agrin? Why hasn't she come yet?"

"She is on the other side," said Ronak. "I'll call her to come."

"Don't you call, Ronak," Mevan said. "I'll see if I can get her attention. Why isn't she working close to us any more?"

Mevan walked towards her and called out, "Agrin! It's lunchtime, let's go. Galavij and Ronak are waiting for us."

"I'm not hungry," Agrin called back.

Mevan walked up to her. "Okay, at least come and rest. You can't stay out in this heat. Let me carry the basket for you."

"No, I can take it myself," Agrin said. "You go, I will come after I fill my basket."

"Then let me help you and we can go together."

"No, you go. I'm coming, I said."

"Agrin ... is everything okay? You have been acting strangely these last few days. Have I done anything wrong?"

"No, it's not you, it's something I have to take my time with."

"What is it?" Mevan asked.

"I don't want to talk about it. Let's just leave the basket and go. Ronak and Galavij are waiting."

Mevan took her hand. "Well, tell me what is bothering you?"

"I don't know yet. I will, but not now," she said.

The four of them sat together and started eating and talking. But Agrin played with her food, deep in thought and didn't contribute to their conversation.

"Okay, Agrin, you have changed," Mevan said. "You have been staying away from me and ignoring me since I proposed to you. I love you so much, but I would never force you to be with me, if you don't want to."

"He is right, my sister," Ronak said, "you have changed. You are not like yourself any more."

"Agrin, I sense that you have changed your mind ..." Mevan said, in a deep voice.

Agrin dropped her head and said nothing.

Mevan knew that his instinct was right and went quiet.

Galavij looked at Mevan's sad face. She felt bad for him and said, "Agrin, tell us what the real reason is. I know you love Mevan."

"Yes, I do like him. It's not Mevan, it's me," Agrin said. "Just give me some more time to sort out my feelings ..."

"Then say something," Mevan insisted, raising his voice. "If you don't trust me or are not comfortable telling me what —"

"I said I will, but not now," Agrin snapped. "Let me deal with it myself. I'll let you know if I need your advice, Mevan. Until then, please ..."

"Okay, whatever you say."

"Thank you," Agrin said.

"I guess I raised my voice again," Mevan said, looking at them.

"Yeah ... you do have a bit of a temper at times," Agrin said, as a smile crept across her face.

"Do I ...?" Mevan asked.

"Yeah, and I would have to deal with that for the rest of my life," Agrin joked.

"I'm so relieved to hear that from you," Mevan said, smiling.

*

A few days later, Mevan came home one afternoon and heard Agrin talking to someone in the backyard. She called out, "Will you come down here for one second and try it. Come here, let us be friends, you beautiful thing. See ... I brought you food and water ... Ahhh, it's useless. Back home it wasn't this hard to make a friend, but maybe you don't understand plain Kurdish ... Anyway, you'll regret it, I'm telling you. Maybe not for being my friend, but for the food. Yes, you will, because I will take this food and eat it myself. Yep, you're a lost cause ..."

"Hello, Agrin," Mevan said.

"Oh God ... when did you come back?" Agrin said, startled.

"Sorry, I didn't mean to scare you. Who are you talking to?" Mevan looked around the yard.

"Nobody ... myself."

Mevan looked up into the tree and pointed. "Is that a parrot?"

"Yes, isn't it beautiful?"

"Were you talking to a parrot?"

Agrin was embarrassed. "No, I was not."

"Okay, where are the others?"

"They took the kids to the park, and Mother Marjan is having her nap and I wanted to stay home to ..."

"I know ... to make a new friend," Mevan said, laughing and pointing at the parrot.

"Will you stop!" Agrin exclaimed, then smiled.

"Okay, girl ... who has a temper now?" Mevan joked. "Come here and have a seat. I've got you something." Mevan handed her a small bag.

"What is it?"

"Find out, look for yourself."

Agrin opened the little bag, then smiled. "Oh, a scarf ... and it's so beautiful."

"Are you sure? Because your face says otherwise."

"No, no, I definitely do like it, but I have so many," Agrin said. "You should give it to Kany."

"I got something for her as well."

"Oh, okay then, I'll take it."

"Agrin, can we be serious for a moment and talk this out. I know I told you I would wait for you as long as you need. Still, aside from that, I want you to allow me to care for you, be around you, show you my love and make you happy — I need that. So please tell me why you are avoiding my love and care ..."

"It's ... I think it's not fair to you, telling you what I'm struggling with. That is why I try to get over it myself, because I don't want to hurt you."

"But I want to know. I'm sure it won't hurt as much as seeing you like this and not knowing what I can do about it. My thoughts about why are you doing this are killing me."

"What thoughts?" Agrin asked, a little alarmed.

"I don't know ... I notice you keeping yourself away from me, and it makes me wonder in a thousand ways how I might lose you."

"Since you proposed, a terrible feeling started growing inside my heart, a sense of guilt that I am betraying my husband and daughter and leaving them behind. And that I'm being selfish by going after my life, seeking happiness, without them. I'm still living with them every day, every second. I want them to be in my life and in my heart. I can't and don't want to ever forget about Delovan and I don't think it's fair to you."

"Agrin, I would never want or expect you to forget about them. I want you to keep them in your heart and your life forever, as I will keep Henan and Agid in my heart ..." Mevan put his hand on his heart. "Let me give you something," he said, then reached for his necklace and held it out to Agrin which he had hold a ring in it, "This is yours."

"What is it?"

"Well it's ... mother Marjan told me that you sold your marriage ring for Agid's needs. But I found the man you sold it to and re-purchased it."

Agrin was shocked. "You bought it back?"

"Yes, now give me your hand." Mevan put the ring back on her finger.

Agrin was momentarily speechless.

Mevan grinned. "And if, one day, you accept my love, then my ring will go next to it."

"I thought I would never see this again," Agrin said, staring at her ring.

"I should have given it back to you a long time ago, but I wanted to wait for the right moment. Now stop your tears falling like this and smile, my sweet darling. I believe in love, and that true love will never die. And I see this in your heart for Delovan, and I have nothing but respect for it in my heart."

Agrin hugged him. "Thank you, Mevan, for understanding me."

19

A month passed. One night, after dinner, as everyone was sitting together having tea, Mevan's phone rang. He looked at the screen. "It's from the man who is looking for our family!" he cried.

The others gasped.

"Hello?" Mevan said, as put his phone on speaker.

"Hello, brother Mevan, I have good news. There is a photo of a young girl on the market and I'm sure she is one of those who you sent me a picture of. I'll send the picture, so you can take a look to make sure."

"Okay, I'm waiting," Mevan said. The photo arrived with a ping. Mevan opened the message.

Kany went and sat next to him. When she saw the photo, she shouted in excitement, "Uncle, it's Narin! It's Narin's photo!"

Mevan nodded at her, then said into his phone, "Yes, brother, she is my sister. Where is she now?"

"She will be on the market in two days. The price that they are asking for her is below the picture. If you can sort out the money, then we can buy her."

"I will do it as soon as possible," Mevan said.

"Brother, make sure the money is ready, otherwise someone else might come to buy her."

"Okay, I will, don't worry. Please don't lose her," Mevan said, then hung up the phone. He looked at his sister's photo several times and stayed silent.

Galavij came over to see the photo. "Oh God, look at her ... poor Narin."

Ronak asked, "Brother, how much money do they want for her?"

"It's a lot, and I don't know exactly how much we have," Mevan said.

"So, let me look at our savings to find out," Marjan said.

"I know roughly what we have saved and it's still not enough," Mevan said.

Agrin went to her room and came out with a small bag. She sat next to Mevan. "Here, this is my jewellery. With this, I think we would have enough."

"Thank you, thank you, Agrin, and all of you ..." Mevan said, breathing deeply.

"Don't say anything more, brother, we just hope it's enough to bring her back," Ronak said.

"Okay, thank you," Mevan said. "Tomorrow I will see how much I can sell this for."

The next night Mevan returned late.

"Welcome home, son," Marjan said. "Do we have enough money now?"

"Yes, mother. I sold Agrin's jewellery, and it was enough." Mevan sat down. "I went with Diyar to talk to an official to help us to find out the right way to do this." His phone started ringing. "Hello?" Mevan said.

"Did you get the money?" the man said.

"Yes, I've got the money. I will send it to you. When are you going to get my sister?"

"Tomorrow around 10 or 11 am here, I'm going to see her and negotiate to buy her, then I'll let you know what we are going to do after that. Don't worry, I'll call you if anything comes up."

The next day, around the time that the man had said, everyone was sitting and waiting for the phone to ring.

Finally, Mevan's phone buzzed. "Hello, what happened?" Mevan asked. "Did you get her?"

"No, I'm on my way to the market. I checked her profile and saw that they put her price up again," the man said.

"Brother, please, this is not the time to play for more money. I promise you, that is all I have."

"Do you think that I would use you in this situation? I put my life and my family in danger to rescue your sister." The man hung up the phone.

Mevan immediately regretted his words and called the man back several times, but he didn't answer.

After ten minutes, Mevan tried again. This time the man picked up, but Agrin could see how stressed Mevan was, and quickly said, "Give me the phone, let me talk."

Mevan gave her the phone without saying a word.

"Hello?" Agrin said. "Please don't hang up. Mevan didn't mean to sound harsh, he is just so worried about his sister. Do you have any money yourself to add to ours? We will pay you back."

"No, sister, I used all the cash I had last month to pay for a ten-year-old girl who I returned to her family." Something interrupted the man. "Hang on, sister."

Agrin heard some voices in the background.

Suddenly, the man called out, "Hey, hey, don't go there! I was waiting for her before you. Stay in the line, brother. We might not see it, but God will." The man didn't hang up the phone and kept speaking.

"Put the phone on speaker," Mevan whispered to Agrin.

Agrin pressed the button and they listened to the men arguing.

A deep voice barked, "Are you a customer or not?"

"Yes, I am, but it's still too expensive. Let's negotiate a good deal, so that we will both be happy."

"No, brother, I won't sell this one cheap. She is gorgeous. Look at her blue eyes, her hair – I paid a lot for her."

"But look at her face, her whole body is injured. I will have to take her to a doctor and it will cost me a lot."

"No, no, brother!" the salesman said. "I didn't beat her that badly, I assure you. None of her bones are broken, and I haven't damaged her body. Take off her dress and see for yourself."

Mevan couldn't bury the painful anger he was feeling. He started pacing around the room. Agrin kept listening to the men's voices as they haggled.

"Okay, but that tells me that she is not an obedient slave. She must be a bit of a handful."

"Okay, brother, if you don't want to buy her, don't waste my time," the salesman snapped.

With that, the phone was disconnected.

Agrin called the man back, but he didn't answer. Mevan headed for the back door.

"Where are you going, son?" Marjan asked.

"I need some fresh air," Mevan said, storming out.

"Agrin, go after him," Marjan said. "Maybe you can help him. Poor man – I'm afraid of something happening to him."

Kany was standing beside the window. "He is outside sitting under the tree."

"It's better to leave him alone for a while," Agrin said.

After a short time, Agrin went out and sat next to Mevan. "Don't you want to come inside?" Agrin said. "Everyone is worried about you."

"Did he call back?" Mevan asked.

"No, not yet. Here, have some water." She tried to give him a glass.

"No, I'm good. Why hasn't he called back yet? What if we have lost her again?"

"We will get her back, we are so close, and we know where she is."

"If he can't get Narin, I will go back after her," Mevan said. "There is a chance for us to save her, now that I know which city she is in."

"Agrin, Mevan, hurry!" Ronak shouted from the window. "The man is calling back – quick!"

Agrin and Mevan ran back into the house and Agrin answered the phone. "Hello, what happened? Why didn't you answer your phone?"

"Good news, sister, Narin is here with me," the man said. "I'm taking her home."

"Oh, thank God!" Agrin sat down with eyes full of tears but a smile on her face.

"Where is my brother Mevan?" the man asked.

"I'm here, brother, I'm listening to you. I owe you my life," Mevan said. "Sorry I misjudged you. How is she now?"

"I know, brother, hear me out. When I was negotiating, she

started to vomit so badly that he agreed to sell her for a lot less money. I got her, and while carrying her to my car, Narin started hitting herself, wanting to die. I tried to convince her to listen and stop struggling. She said, 'On one condition, I will listen to you, that you swear to your God, if you get tired of me, you will kill me. I never want to see this market again.' My brother, only an evil coward could take advantage of her situation. I will use some of the money left to take care of her and send the rest back to you with her."

"You are a good man, my friend. As I told you, I owe you my life. How is she now? Can I talk to her?" Mevan asked.

"I tried to explain to her that I was saving her. Still, she started vomiting again and passed out. Now she is unconscious. I'm on my way to the clinic to make sure there is nothing seriously wrong with her."

"At least video-call me so I can see her," Mevan pleaded.

"I know you are worried, brother, but trust me, it's better not to see her in this condition, and I'm sure she wouldn't want her brother to see her like this. After I take her to a doctor, I will take her to my house, then I will call you back to talk to her."

"How are you going to take her out of the city safely?" Mevan asked.

"It's not my first time, brother. She will stay with my family, and my mother and my wife will take care of her until I find a safe way to get her out. Don't you worry about it. She is like my sister, and I won't let anything bad happen to her again."

"Okay, brother, I trust you," Mevan said.

"Now I'm at the clinic. I will call you when we get home," he said, then hung up.

Marjan came over and hugged Mevan. "Congratulations, son, to you and all of us. She is in a safe place now."

"I'm so happy, Uncle," Kany said. "I cant wait to see her again. I miss her so much."

"I know, sweetheart, we are going to see her soon," Mevan said. "Don't cry any more – she is safe and being taken care of."

Everyone was so happy and hugged Mevan and each other.

Galavij said, "I'm going to set the table. You haven't eaten anything since the man called."

"You all eat, I'm going to talk to Diyar and tell him what happened," Mevan said.

"But you haven't eaten anything, son," Marjan said.

"I can't eat now. I'll be back soon," Mevan replied. Mevan was walking out the front gate, but stopped when Agrin called him. "Yes, what's happened?" he said.

"Nothing, I got you this bite to eat on your way," Agrin said, handing him some food.

"Thank you, darling. I will call you if anything comes up," Mevan said.

Mevan returned home around midnight. When he closed the front gate behind him, a small voice called out, "Is that you, Mevan?" Ronak came to the front door.

"Yes, but why are you still awake?" Mevan said. "I called Agrin to say that I was going to be late."

"Yes, she told us," Ronak said. "The kids are sleeping and Galavij has just gone to put her son back to sleep."

Mevan and Ronak walked into the living room, where Marjan and Agrin were waiting for him. "Come, son, don't stand over there,"

Marjan said, "come and sit with us."

"Have you received a call from the man yet?" Agrin asked.

"He sent me a message that he would call, but he hasn't yet," Mevan said.

"Let me warm some food for you, son," Marjan said.

"I'm not hungry, thank you, but I'll have a tea."

They waited for a couple of hours, then Mevan took his phone and called his contact. "Hello, brother, how is my sister?"

"Ah … she is good. I asked her to talk to you, but she still doesn't believe me and keeps crying," the man said.

"Can you give her the phone now, please?" Mevan asked.

"She is hiding behind my mother, running away from the phone, brother," the man said.

"Okay, put the phone on speaker."

"Okay, she can hear you now," the man said.

"Narin … sister … talk to me, I miss you so much, my beautiful sister, Narin … Narin … don't you want to talk to your brother? My beautiful Narin, please say something, so I can hear your voice …"

"Hello, Mevan …" came Narin's voice through the phone, melting Mevan's heart.

"Hello, my beautiful baby sister."

"Mevan, I thought they killed you, too. I thought I would never see you again," Narin cried. "Where are you now? I'm so scared."

"You are safe now, I promise you, nobody will hurt you again. Tomorrow I will be on my way to get you."

It was a long, tearful conversation and, in the end, they both said goodbye with immense hope.

Early the next morning, after breakfast, Mevan said to the family,

"I will go with Diyar to find out how I can go back for my sister."

He returned two hours later.

Agrin asked, "What happened? When are you going?"

"They said I can't go, but I told them everything they wanted to know and gave them all the information they needed. They said that they would coordinate everything and try to bring her here."

20

A week had passed since Narin had been found, and now she was on a flight to Melbourne. Everyone was so happy and ready to give her a warm welcome. Kany was especially full of excitement and joy, and she had bought a nice present for her Aunt Narin. Mevan had organised a minibus for them to pick up Narin. He called the family to join him and they drove to the airport.

Inside the international terminal, they met with a group of officials and a translator to welcome Narin. Everyone was friendly and they talked at length to help pass the time for what seemed like hours.

Finally, Narin emerged from behind the walls of customs and immigration. Her slow and hesitant steps showed her uneasiness. She was apprehensive, but, when she saw Mevan, she stopped and a smile began to form.

Mevan hurried forward and hugged her. "Narin! My dear, dear sister, thank God!"

Narin hugged him back. "I still can't believe it's you, Mevan, I can't trust my eyes. What if this is another dream? What if I wake up to my nightmares again?" Narin began crying.

"Hey, hey ... darling sister, they are all gone, I'm here now. I'll never let anything bad happen to you again, okay?" Mevan said tearfully. "Now let's take you home." Mevan took Narin's hand and led her over to Agrin, Kany and the others, who welcomed her with open arms.

When they arrived home, everyone was so happy to finally have Narin with them.

Marjan said, "My daughter, you have come a long way, you must be tired. Go take a bath and wear something comfortable. Rest a little until we make dinner."

"Let me take you to my room," Mevan said. "It also has a bathroom and you will be more comfortable there."

"Wait, let me get some clothes," Agrin said. She brought Narin a bag of things she might need.

Narin said, "Thank you, everyone. Agrin, will you come with me, too?"

"Sure, let's go," Agrin said.

Agrin prepared the bathroom, and Mevan prepared his own bed for Narin. When all was ready for Narin, Mevan said, "Okay, I'm going back inside to help the others, if you need anything, call me." He closed the door to his room and went back inside the house.

"The bath is ready," Agrin said, facing Narin.

"Okay, thank you, Agrin," Narin said.

"I will wait outside, so you will be more comfortable," Agrin said.

"No, please stay, I need you to help me take off my dress, I can't do it myself," Narin said.

As Agrin was helping take off Narin's dress, she saw that most parts of Narin's body were burned and scarred. Bruises were still visible on her shoulders and back. "Oh, my God, what have they done to you?" Agrin asked.

"I've suffered a lot, my sister, and the most horrible part are the memories, the horrible memories of those days, which will stay with me forever like these scars."

"I'm so sorry, Narin, for what you have been through," Agrin said tearfully.

"Well, that was the price I paid for living in this world. I wasn't one of the lucky ones," Narin said bitterly.

"Now you are in a safe place, and we are all here for you. I'm here for you with all my heart. You will get through this pain, I promise you, my sister," Agrin said, wiping Narin's tears. "Let me take you to the bathroom and help you."

After the bath, Agrin said, "Now you sit here and I will help you to get dressed as well."

"Thank you for everything, Agrin, you are so kind and sweet."

Agrin smiled at Narin. "Don't mention it."

Narin said, "Kany told me over the phone that you sold all your jewellery for me, and how you helped my brother and took care of my nephew Agid, and how you have been like a mother to her."

Agrin did not reply as she began combing Narin's hair.

Narin continued, "It's only been a few hours since I met you, but you have been like a big sister to me as well. You have a good heart, Agrin."

There was a knock at the door. "Can I come in?" Mevan asked.

"Yes, the door is open," Agrin said.

"How are you doing, sweetheart, are you feeling better?" Mevan said, hugging Narin.

"Yes, I am, thank you," Narin said.

"Okay, Narin, your hair is done," Agrin said, "and I will put this towel on your shoulders until your hair is dry."

Mevan noticed tears in Narin's eyes. "Why are you crying, has something upset you?"

"Oh, no, no," Narin said, "I'm all right. It's just that having Agrin comb my hair reminded me so much of our mother and I miss her so much."

Mevan hugged her. "I know, my sweet sister, I know ..."

"Is there anything you need?" Agrin asked.

"No, but I'm so tired now." Without saying anything more, Narin put her head on Agrin's lap and closed her eyes.

Agrin whispered, "Mevan, put that small blanket on her so she won't catch a cold after her bath."

"Okay."

From behind the door, Kany asked, "Can I come in?"

"Yes, darling." Mevan opened the door.

"Oh ...! I see Aunt Narin is sleeping," Kany said. "She must have been tired." Kany sat next to Agrin, then lay down and put her head on Agrin's lap as well.

"Kany, sweetheart," Mevan said, "Agrin will get tired like that. Here, I'll get a pillow for you."

"No, Uncle, I like it like this. Aunt Agrin smells like my mother," Kany said, and held Agrin's hand, kissed it, then put it on her eyes.

"She is right," Narin said, under her breath.

"That's okay, I don't mind," Agrin said warmly.

Agrin was a source of peace and comfort for everyone around her, especially for Mevan, who was now looking at her with deep emotion. Agrin said to him, "You lay down on this pillow and try to have a nap, too, until dinner time. It was a long day for you as well, and you still have a lot to do."

"No, sweetheart, I'm okay," Mevan whispered, holding Agrin's hand. "I'll go and help Mother Marjan and the others."

A few days passed and Narin began to settle in. But one night, when everyone was asleep, Narin was having a nightmare that made her cry out through the darkness. Agrin rushed to her and said, "Narin, Narin, wake up …!" Agrin shook Narin and she woke up.

"Oh god, what a terrifying nightmare!" Narin said, breathing heavily, with tears in her eyes. "I hate sleeping … hate it."

"Let me get you some water," Agrin said.

"No, no, I'm okay, thank you for waking me up," Narin said, feeling her belly and taking a deep breath. "Can we go out and get some fresh air, please?"

"Sure, sweetheart, let's go and sit under the tree, but quietly, so we don't wake the others."

Outside, under the tree in the backyard, Agrin organised a place for Narin to sit. "Come, have a seat, Narin, and tell me what that nightmare was about."

But Narin was silent and withdrew into her thoughts.

"It's okay if you don't want to talk about it," Agrin said. "Let us relax for a few minutes and then go back to bed."

"I do want to talk," Narin said, "but I don't know how you will react and feel about me after I tell you."

"What do you mean?"

"Just give me a few more days, then I will tell you," Narin said.

"Okay, anytime you are ready, I'm here for you."

Mevan's voice came through the dark, "Hello! What are you two doing out there in the middle of the night? Is everything okay?"

Mevan walked over to them.

"Yes, I needed some fresh air, Brother," Narin said. "Sorry to wake you up."

"That's okay. Do you want me to stay with you?" Mevan asked.

"Yes, if you want to," Agrin said.

"No, no, brother, you go back to bed," Narin said. "We were about to go as well. I'm wearing Agrin's jacket – it's chilly."

"Then I'll go, and see you in the morning," Mevan said, as he left.

Agrin said, "Narin, can I ask you something?"

"Yes, what is it?"

"I kind of feel that you are trying to avoid your brother," Agrin said. "I mean, he loves you so much and is doing all he can to build a relationship like you had before, which was beautiful, Kany told me. Is there something that we don't know about?"

"He is my most favourite person in the world," Narin said. "I love him more than anything in this world."

"Then why have you been so cold to him?"

"I'm afraid of losing him again." Narin stopped talking when she saw Mevan coming back across the yard towards them.

"What happened, Mevan?" Agrin asked.

"Nothing – I got you my jacket. Here, wear it," Mevan said, handing his jacket to Agrin.

"That is much better, thank you," Agrin said, putting on the jacket.

"No problem, I'm off to bed," Mevan said, as he left.

"He does love you very much, Agrin," Narin said, watching Mevan walking away.

Agrin smiled and looked at him, too.

Narin said, "He is an amazing man – strong, thoughtful, and caring. I promise you, you'll never regret being with him."

"I know, but I'm not ready yet," Agrin said. "Do you want to tell me why you are afraid of losing him?"

"I don't know how to say it. I'm scared to death about this. What if, after hearing it, you don't want me any more?"

"Hey, hey, calm down," Agrin said, holding Narin's hand. "Say it and I promise you I'll be beside you, no matter what."

"I'm ... I'm ..." Narin mumbled under her breath.

"You're what?"

"I'm pregnant," Narin said, looking into Agrin's eyes.

"You're pregnant? Who by? How long?" Agrin whispered, horrified.

"It's from the last man who sold me. I found out before I left. I asked them not to say anything to my brother until I found the right time ..."

Agrin paused for a moment, then said, "I don't know what to say; I never expected this. Now, what do you want to do?"

"I want to keep it, I want to be a mother. Please, Agrin, you promised me that you would help me. I'm begging you ... don't leave me alone."

"What are you talking about? Of course, I'll help you. We will all help you to find a way out. Now let me think."

"Okay, whatever you say, I'll follow your advice," Narin said.

"I don't know exactly what to do yet, but let's talk to Mother Marjan tomorrow and leave Mevan out of this for the moment," Agrin said. "Let's go to bed now and tomorrow, after work, we will tell her."

The next afternoon Narin was waiting for Agrin, Mevan and the others at the gate. "Hello, welcome back home," Narin said.

"Hello, sweetheart, why are you waiting here?" Mevan asked.

"No reason, brother," Narin replied. "Can I come to work with you tomorrow as well?"

"You can, but it might be better for you to wait a couple of weeks, because you need some time to get better," Mevan said. "Here, take this bag — it's black grapes, your favourite."

"Thank you, brother," Narin said, then waited for him to walk away with Galavij and Ronak, while Agrin remained behind.

"So, what did you do today?" Agrin asked.

"Not much," Narin said. "I was so nervous all day that I couldn't eat anything."

"Let's go call Mother Marjan and tell her," Agrin said. They walked into the house. "Mother, can you come to my room for a second?" Agrin said.

"Yes, my daughter, I'm coming, but let me first make the tea ready for Mevan."

"No, mother, he went to his room to have a shower," Agrin said.

Marjan went into Agrin's room and sat down with Narin. "Okay, now tell me what you want to say."

"Well, mother ..." Narin began, then stopped.

"What, my daughter, have you got bad news?" Marjan asked.

"I'm pregnant, mother," Narin said.

"What? How? When?"

"It's from the man who sold me last time," Narin said, with tears falling.

"Oh God, oh God, this nightmare will follow us to our graves! It will never end ..." Marjan cried, as she started hitting herself on her lap.

"Calm down, mother, please," Agrin said. "Mevan might hear us."

Galavij and Ronak came running into Agrin's room.

Galavij asked, "What? What is this noise about?"

"What happened, mother?" Ronak asked.

After Agrin explained the situation to them, Galavij sat next to Narin and said, "Now what are you going to do? Oh, my God, if Mevan finds out, he will kill himself."

"Stop, Galavij," Agrin said, "don't make it worse – look at Narin! We have to find a way to ask for help."

"If I were you," Ronak said, "the second I found out that I had their disgusting blood growing in my body, I would have an abortion."

"But I want to keep it – it's my baby, too," Narin said.

"Don't cry, my daughter, let's keep things quiet and have dinner," Marjan said. "After the kids go to bed, we will tell Mevan."

"Tonight! But I'm so scared, mother ..." Narin said.

"We all are, my daughter, but we will find a way together," Marjan said. "Now go and wash your face – he might come now."

After dinner, Mevan was sitting down with Kany and listening to her reading her storybook. "And that was how the story finished, Uncle Mevan," Kany said, closing her book. "For tomorrow night, I have picked an excellent book to read over the coming week."

"Bravo, my beautiful daughter, I'm so proud of you," Mevan said. "You learned this new language fast, and thank you for reading it for me. Now it's late, and you should go to sleep. Nalan is waiting for you – she looks sleepy." Mevan kissed both girls good night.

"Now, where is Narin? I haven't seen her since dinner," Mevan said.

"I'm here, brother, in the kitchen," Narin called out.

"Why don't you come here and sit next to me? I missed you, sister."

Narin came out of the kitchen but sat behind Agrin and Marjan.

"Is everything okay?" Mevan asked.

"Son, we need to tell you something," Marjan said.

"Yes ...?"

"How to say this?" Marjan began. "God, help me, hmmm ... son ... Narin ... Narin is pregnant."

Mevan raised his head. "What? Pregnant?"

"Yes, my son, she is," Marjan said.

Mevan turned to Narin. "Are you?"

Narin lowered her head and didn't respond.

Mevan shouted, unaware of how his temper was flaring, "Narin, I asked, are you pregnant?"

"Yes," Narin said, nodding tearfully.

Mevan's face flushed with anger. He stood in front of Narin with Agrin and Galavij holding his arms to restrain him.

"Who has done this? Who's the father? Narin, answer me ... I asked you ... who has done this to you?"

Narin stepped back in fear and hid behind Marjan.

"It's from the last coward that held Narin captive," Ronak answered, with apprehension.

Mevan was shocked, breathing heavily.

Marjan said, "Calm down, son, we will come up with a solution."

Mevan, with red eyes, full of tears, trembling with anger, glared at Narin and stormed out of the house. Marjan ran after him but came back after a few minutes.

"Where did he go, mother?" Narin asked, crying loudly.

"He went away so fast I couldn't catch up with him," Marjan said, closing the door.

"Now, what will happen?" Ronak asked.

"For now, it's better to wait and see what he decides," Agrin said, watching out the window.

A few hours passed before they heard the sound of the gate. "Let me see," Ronak said, looking out the window. "It's Mevan, it's Mevan."

"Narin, you stand behind the girls and, whatever he says, don't say anything," Marjan told her. "Let us talk to him."

Mevan stood by the door with a pale face, looking down. "Early tomorrow morning, we will go to a doctor, and you will have an abortion."

Narin came out from behind Ronak when she heard Mevan's words, and said, "But, brother ..."

Mevan interrupted and shouted, "Narin, I said tomorrow we will go to a doctor and get rid of it. I swear to God, sister, if you say otherwise, I will sit in the yard and wait until morning, do you understand?"

"No, I want to keep it. I *will* keep my baby," Narin said, raising her voice.

"What baby? Do you hear yourself? Do you hear what you are saying to me?" Mevan yelled, rushing towards her.

Marjan, Galavij and Ronak tried to stop him from getting closer, and Narin ran behind Agrin, crying.

Mevan growled, "Do you want to keep *their* child? Do you have feelings for their blood? Our land is still covered red with the blood of our people, thousands of babies, men and women have been

beheaded by them, and you want to raise their child? How dare you
... how dare you look into my eyes and say that!"

"It is not their child, the baby is mine, not anybody else's but
mine!" Narin shouted tearfully. "Please, brother, I want to keep
my baby."

"Do you want to kill me, Narin, ha, do you ...? Answer ... come
on ... because you are killing me, sister."

"No, no, please hear me out, brother ..." Narin said, crying.

"Hear you for what, huh? Put this in your head: there is no way
— do you hear me? — no way for me to accept the blood of those evil
killers into my family." Mevan tried to reach past Agrin to grab
Narin.

"No, no ... back off, Mevan!" Agrin yelled. "Do not touch her!"
Agrin pushed him back. "You can't think straight now. Before you
make any trouble, which I promise that you will regret for the rest
of your life, get out of here ... now." Agrin held his arm and forced
him to walk away.

Mevan stopped for a few seconds, looking into Agrin's eyes, then
shut the door behind him.

Ronak, who had been silent up until that moment, said, "My
sister, put yourself in his place. The child is from the enemy aggres-
sors who cowardly took everything from him. What do you expect
from the poor man?"

Narin sat on the ground, crying helplessly. "I know, but I can't
lose another baby. It's so painful, my heart can't bury another one
this time. This is the fourth time I have been pregnant."

"What ...? Fourth time!" Agrin exclaimed.

"When they attacked our village, they gathered my father and brothers and killed everyone. I saw it from behind the bus window. They also killed my mother, shooting her in the chest, then took me with them, and hassling me so much that I surrendered to their demands. The first time I found out that I was pregnant, I tried everything to lose it, and I did. The hate and disgust I felt made it impossible even to imagine having their baby. After the miscarriage, they took me to a doctor because of heavy bleeding, and they found out that it was on purpose. I was beaten so severely that I lost consciousness. The following day, they put me up for sale. I was in the market for a few days until an older man bought me and took me to his home. I was working all the time. He forced me to worship his God, and he would punish me if I made any mistakes. Soon, I got pregnant but had another miscarriage after three months because of a nasty infection in my weakened body. He sold me, too, and many more times after that, I have been sold. Each time was worse than the last. Until I got pregnant again. I went through a difficult pregnancy, but I made it to eight months. One day I heard the news of the defeat of ISIS and the killing of many of their soldiers. One of the deaths was my owner's wife's brother. The wife and her mother started beating me, swearing at me out of anger. I stayed in the cold hallway that night, then, the next day, they threw me in their dark and dirty basement. I stayed there for a few days with little or no food, and a horrible pain started in my back. I kept asking and begging for help, but no one came to me."

Narin took a deep breath, then continued, "Eventually, the wife came to the basement's window, sat down and looked through the glass. She yelled at me, 'Stop shouting for help! No one will help you. I hate hearing your voice. I lost my brother because of your infidels.

He was trying to save you from hell, and yet you killed him. You don't deserve to be saved, you don't deserve the great religion of God. As soon as my husband comes back, he has to sell you ...' But I begged her, 'No, please wait, I'm in a lot of pain. There is something wrong with the baby ...' All she said was, 'So what?' I dragged myself to the window, then said, 'It's your husband's baby, at least tell him ...' But she shouted back, 'What? Are you crazy? You are a slave. He hasn't married you ... your kid will be a slave like you. He will sell it. He doesn't care for it because he doesn't care for you.' The wife left me alone in the basement. At midnight, my baby was born. After I discovered my baby was dead, I backed away from her, terrified. I was alone and scared to death. I looked at her body, saw her face in the moonlight ... she was so beautiful. I picked her up and cleaned her with my scarf, and hugged her cold little body for hours. The following day, my owner came down, opened the door and saw me. He had a big fight with his wife and his mother-in-law, accusing them of causing him a financial loss, saying he would lose a lot of money by selling me like this. He took the baby away from me by force. It was so painful ..." Narin couldn't carry on more and dissolved into tears.

"My poor sister," Ronak cried out, hugging her.

"You will never go through that pain again, I promise you," Agrin said, hugging Narin.

"Yes, my daughter, it's not fair to ask you to get rid of your baby now that we understand your whole story," Marjan said. "We will find some way to keep it."

"Tomorrow we will go and talk to the authorities and ask them for help," Agrin said.

The next day, Marjan prepared breakfast for Mevan and took it to his room. "Open the door, son. I brought you breakfast. Let's talk."

Agrin came up behind Marjan. "Maybe he didn't come back last night, let me see." Agrin stepped around her and looked through the window. "He is not in his room."

"Let's ask our neighbour Barwar," Marjan said anxiously. "Maybe he knows where Mevan has gone or can help us find him."

Agrin went next door and invited Barwar to their house. As soon as Barwar and Agrin walked into the living room, Marjan asked, "Barwar, my son, we don't know where Mevan is. Do you know?"

"Do not worry, mother. He is on the farm where he was working last week. We crossed paths last night as he was leaving. He looked distraught and told me he was going to stay at the farm for a while."

"Thank you, at least we now know where he is," Marjan said.

"What has happened, aunt? Why are you all looking so upset?" Barwar asked.

"Okay, son, come and have a seat. It's about our daughter Narin," Marjan said.

"What about her?" Barwar said, looking at Narin.

"She is pregnant with the last man who had her," Marjan said. "We told Mevan last night and, as you saw, the news really upset him."

"What can I say, aunt? It doesn't seem that we can ever get away from those horrible days. They follow us and keep causing more pain. Unfortunately, most of the girls and women we succeeded in returning were pregnant or had children with those monsters."

"Now, what we should do?" Agrin said.

"You know, in our culture, it is tough to accept a child out of marriage, and this is a type of disgrace among most families. They say that every time the mothers see those kids, they remember the torment and torture they were put through by their fathers."

Narin's tears started falling as she listened to Barwar's words.

"But there are a few things that we can do. I'll look into it and see what our options are. I'll let you know." Barwar looked directly at Narin. "And you, Narin, my beautiful sister, please don't cry. I know Mevan and I'm sure he will never leave his sister alone. Give him some time, okay?"

"Okay, brother Barwar, thank you," Narin said.

"Until Mevan comes back home, whatever you need, let me know. Take care, I'll see you again soon," Barwar said, then left.

Three days went by, then late one afternoon, Nalan ran inside saying, "Mother, mother, Uncle Mevan has come back – he is outside!"

Agrin thanked Nalan, then turned to Narin. "Don't you come out, Narin. Marjan and I will go."

Marjan and Agrin walked out into the front yard. Mevan nodded to both of them, but did not say hello. Marjan broke the ice and said, "Hello, son! Where have you been? We were so worried about you. Come, let's go inside and rest."

"No, thank you," Mevan said, and went straight to his room, shutting the door behind him.

Agrin spotted Narin watching them from behind a curtain in the front room. Narin was devastated.

Agrin rushed back inside, then said, "See, he came back and he is calmer now. Please let's go to the kitchen and eat something, Narin. You are not alone now, you have a baby."

"I can't, Agrin, didn't you see how miserable he was — all because of me. I'm stuck so badly and I don't know what to do!" Narin burst into tears and ran to her room.

Agrin went to the kitchen and put some food on a tray.

Marjan was in the kitchen and asked, "What are you going to do, my daughter? Is the food for Mevan?"

"Yes, I'm going to talk to him," Agrin said, carrying the tray out.

"Okay, but be careful and talk wisely. He's mad and needs help. Don't get angry like last time. It's not a good idea to make an angry man more furious."

"Okay, mother, don't worry," Agrin said, and she went into the backyard. She stood in front of Mevan's door and knocked. There was no answer, so she opened the door halfway. "Can I come in?" she asked.

"Yes, come in," Mevan said, sitting on the floor, deep in thought.

Agrin didn't quite know Mevan's state of mind, so without saying anything else, she sat next to him and waited silently.

After a while, Mevan asked, "Did you convince her?"

"No."

"So, she still wants to keep it?"

"Yes, she does," Agrin said.

"Why aren't you talking her out of this? Why don't you make her understand, remind her what kind of monster's baby she wants to keep."

"I can't tell her to kill her baby. I'm not even sure I could do it if I were ..."

"Hush ... Agrin, hush, I warn you to watch your words ..." Mevan held her arm.

"I know, I swear to God, I feel your pain, and I understand your hate, but she is in a difficult situation, too," Agrin said. "Okay, look at it this way: they killed her parents and brothers, sold her, harassed her, beat her, and her whole body is covered in wounds and bruises that you can barely imagine. If someone should hate that child, no one could hate it more than Narin."

"Then why the hell is she fighting me over this?" Mevan asked.

"Because she can't take it any more. She has been pregnant three times so far, and every time she has lost her child in agony. She can't do it again, it's too hard for her."

"I can't do it, either, Agrin. Every time I see that child, every-thing will come back to me ... This child belongs to the man who destroyed whatever I had."

"But what about Narin? Why don't you see things her way? It's Narin who is giving life to the child, raising it, naming it. The child will not get anything from its father, who will never see or even know about him. The child will be like Narin, smell like her, talk like her, and behave like her ... If they told you that your sister had been killed or died and this child was the only thing that was left of her, would you still not want it?"

Mevan turned away to hide his tears.

She held his hands and continued, "Narin does not want you to accept the baby; no one expects this from you. She wants you to know that yesterday we went for help and told our story to the welfare officials. If you can't accept her with the baby, because you feel tormented, they will take Narin away and give her a place to stay so that she can live her life with her baby."

Mevan looked at her but said nothing.

"She is waiting for your decision. If you say you want her to go, then she will go with the officials tomorrow." Agrin pushed the tray of food towards him. "Come now, eat something, you haven't eaten anything."

"I'm not hungry," Mevan said.

"Narin asked me to give you a message, which is: 'I haven't asked anything from you until now. If you want to do as you promised me, now is the time that I need you.'"

"Narin said that?" Mevan asked.

"Yes, last night. Now here, start eating. Don't say you're not hungry. You have to."

Mevan was silent, deep in thought.

Agrin put some food in his hand. "You have to eat. Poor Narin hasn't eaten anything. She says she can't eat, seeing her brother like this." She picked up a glass of water and gave it to Mevan.

Mevan took the glass and drained it, then finally started eating without saying anything.

"Okay, I better go and talk to her," Agrin said, getting up to leave.

"Stay," Mevan said.

"Do you need anything?" Agrin said.

"No, stay with me," Mevan pleaded. Agrin sat back next to him. Mevan held out a piece of food to Agrin. "You have some, too. I don't like eating alone."

They started eating together.

After they had finished the food, Mevan said, "Thank you, Agrin."

"Do you want to come and have tea with the others?" Agrin asked.

"No, I want to rest," Mevan said, lying down on the pillow and closing his eyes.

Agrin took the blanket off his bed and put it over him, kissed him on his head, picked up the tray, then closed the door after her.

The following day, everyone was busy helping to make breakfast. Mevan came in and sat at the table. "Morning," he said, without looking at Narin.

Narin wasn't worried. She was relieved and happy just to see him come to the table. She went over to Marjan and hugged her.

Marjan whispered in her ear, "I told you, your brother has a big heart, my daughter. However, you have to respect him and not push him. Let him have the time he needs. Until then, try not to be around him." Marjan then took Mevan's tea to him.

"Thank you, mother," Mevan said.

After breakfast, Mevan got ready for work. Then he called out to the others, "We've got to leave soon. I'll be waiting out the front." Mevan turned to Marjan. "Mother, I haven't shopped for the house in a few days. Let me know what we need and I'll get it on the way home."

"We have everything but some medicine that the doctor prescribed for Narin."

"Okay, whatever she needs. Tell Kany to message me the list," Mevan said, then went out the front.

Before Agrin left her room, she hugged Narin and said, "He will never let you be by yourself, so you can stop being so worried. Be happy and take care of yourself — I'll see you tonight." Agrin left with Ronak and Galavij.

21

A few weeks passed. Late one afternoon, Agrin was sitting in the living room with Narin and Marjan. "Narin, the weather is perfect today," Agrin said. "Do you want to go for a walk?"

"Thank you, I'd like that," Narin said.

Agrin stood up. "Mother ... we will go to the park for a walk."

"Yes, my daughter, please take Narin for some fresh air and a walk," Marjan said. "She hasn't been out in two days. It's not good for her and the baby."

"That sounds good," Narin said, getting ready. "I didn't want to ask because I thought it's not fair to ask you to walk with me after a long day at work."

On the way, they noticed a car coming towards them. "Agrin, isn't that Mevan's car coming our way?"

"Let me see ... Oh, yes, it is. He must have seen us coming this way."

Mevan stopped the car at the kerb beside them. "Where are you going?" he asked, winding the window down.

"We are going to the park," Agrin replied.

"Do you want me to take you there?" Mevan asked.

"No, thank you, Mevan," Agrin said. "Narin should have her walk every day."

"Okay then, I'll go home," Mevan said. "Don't be late. If you need a ride home, then call me and I'll come for you."

Agrin and Narin thanked him, then Mevan drove away.

Narin said to Agrin, "He wouldn't even look at me."

Agrin held Narin's hand and said, "Try to understand how hard he's fighting his anger. He loves you and will love your baby, too. He just needs time."

"I know, but I miss his attention so much. When he is hugging me, I remember my father and I feel like I'm in the safest place. To see him not even looking at me is so hard."

"That day is not so far away. Even today, after your doctor's visit, he asked if everything was okay with you and your baby."

"Are you for real?" Narin said, smiling. "He asked about my baby, too?"

"Yes, and I'll help him to get over this."

"You know what, Agrin? I'm so happy for him that he has you. I see how much he loves you."

Agrin smiled. "Narin, can I ask you a question?"

"Yes, what is it?"

"What was the promise that Mevan gave you? When I mentioned it, his response was puzzling."

"You know, to Mevan, I was so different from the others when I was a child. Mevan was already a married man. He is our oldest brother, but they didn't have any children and, because of that, most of the time I was living with Mevan and Henan. They loved and cared for me like their child they wished to have. The time passed for me with happiness and love from all my family, as I was the youngest. Until I was seventeen years old, when I fell in love with a boy named Jouvan. We were cute and romantic teenagers in love until the rest of the family found out. That is when they realised Jouvan was a different religion from us. They forbade me to continue our relationship and asked me to end it. They were so scared of me seeing Jouvan that they wouldn't let me be alone. I tried so many ways to get in contact with him, but I couldn't. A few months later, I was depressed and ill because I thought he had forgotten me. Until one day, Mevan, who was worried about my health, took me to see a doctor. While we were waiting at the clinic, Jouvan came in and sat down. It turned out that one of his friends had seen me going into the clinic and tipped off Jouvan. It was difficult, but we found a way to talk for a few minutes. I missed him so much. We hugged each other, then he gave me a beautiful bracelet and said 'Take this as a sign of my love. I swear to God, I will never leave you.' And he asked me to give him the same promise. From that day on, even though I knew I might never see Jouvan again, I was happy that he was still in love with me and our love was still alive. I started laughing and talking – once again, life had meaning."

"Did you ever see him again?" Agrin asked.

"A few months passed," Narin sighed, "and he managed to send a message to me. We were both tired of living apart and he asked me to run away with him. At first, I was terrified and rejected the idea, it was too frightening for me. I tried not to think about him and, over time my love of life and independence grew without him."

"Was that the end of the relationship?" Agrin asked.

"For a while I thought it was, but eventually I felt like my life didn't mean anything. I left the house one day, without telling anyone, to see Jouvan. However, Mevan saw me and asked where I was going. I lied and made up a story so he wouldn't be suspicious, but I wasn't sure he believed me, so I didn't risk going to see Jouvan. Instead, I waited until the right time came. I got a message through to Jouvan and he agreed to meet me one night. When everyone was asleep, I climbed out the window and headed to where we were supposed to meet. But when I was nearly there, I saw Mevan standing in the middle of the road. I was so shocked and scared that I couldn't move. I thought that this was the end of my life and he would kill me. But instead of fighting and punishing me, he grabbed my arm and said, 'Let's go home.' I said, 'Brother, please don't be mad.' He growled at me, 'Don't say anything. Walk before I lose control. Come on.'"

"So, it was over between you and Jouvan?" Agrin asked.

"I was sure that I would never see Jouvan again. So, as Mevan was leading me back home that night, I started to plead with him for one last chance. I begged Mevan with all my being, and said, 'Please, brother, for the love of God, I love him very much. I can't take this separation from him any more, either kill me or let me go with him.' He wasn't impressed, and said, 'Narin, believe me, these feelings will pass sooner than you think. Listen to me, if you go with him, then it is over, you will never see us, you will be rejected by our family forever. My baby sister, you know our culture and religion, you know our people better than me, if you go, there is no way you can come back — you will lose us forever.' I cried and he started shedding tears as well. It was the first time I had seen him cry, and he said, 'It's not just us, you know Jouvan's family also doesn't want you because their beliefs are so different from ours. How would you two face the hardships of life without us beside you? Please, for your brother, get over this, and let's go home.'"

Agrin said, "Something tells me you still didn't give up on Jouvan."

"Yes, I was still determined to see Jouvan. Moments later I heard the sound of Jouvan's car coming up behind us, then it stopped. I turned to see two shadowy figures in the car. My heart was pounding. Mevan shushed me and took out his gun. I was so scared, I didn't know what he was thinking. He held my hands and said, 'You know how much I love you, and I could never hurt you, but, I swear to God, if you go with them, either I will kill him or myself. If you listen to me and stay, I promise that I will do whatever you say, and I promise you I'll never let anything or anyone upset you.' I knew in my heart that Mevan would never shoot Jouvan, but I didn't know who was with Jouvan and what might happen. So even though I wanted to go to Jouvan with all my heart, I didn't. Then we began walking away up a hill. After a few minutes, I asked Mevan for one final favour."

"What was that?" Agrin asked.

"I said I wouldn't go with Jouvan, but begged Mevan to let me see him one last time. Reluctantly, Mevan agreed. By now, we were standing high above the road and so we walked to the edge of a cliff to look down on the road. I could see Jouvan was standing in front of his car. He was still waiting for me, looking into the night. His friend leaned out the window of the car, and I could hear him say, 'Let's go, she won't be coming now. We have to leave, it's dangerous.' It was the last time I saw Jouvan. Seeing him leave was the most painful thing I have seen to this day. I cried so hard, but Mevan wiped my tears and hugged me, saying, 'I saw what you did for your brother and, in time, you will know it was for your own good. So, I promise you, from now on, I owe you, my beautiful sister. Whatever you ask, I'll never say no, and I will always be beside you.' From that night on, he was always by my side, like an angel taking care of me. I'm so thankful for him."

After Narin finished her story, Agrin sat with her on a bench at the park. They looked at the park's beautiful lake with two lovely swans swimming along with their babies.

"Agrin, there is something that scares me a lot," Narin said.

"What is it? Tell me," Agrin said.

"How I am going to raise my baby? She can't become one of us because our religion doesn't accept a child whose parents have a different faith. I don't know what to tell her and which religion I should raise her under."

"When we came here, it was the first time I realised how big the world is and how limited my life had been. She may not be one of us, but she will be a beautiful Kurdish girl and a valuable part of this world. She will be a beautiful colour among all these colours."

"I hope you are right," Narin said.

"Think of all the people who came to our aid. They were from all around the world, they all had different beliefs and cultures, and yet they still helped us here. They don't care about where we come from or our differences. They are full of respect and as happy as they can be. Maybe she would have a hard time in our country, but she will have no problem here."

"Yes, I suppose that is true," Narin said. "But what about her religion? She can't live without belief."

Agrin held her hand and said, "What do you want? What do you want your child to believe and what rules do you want her to live by?"

Narin touched her belly and answered, "Well, not much, I don't like complicated stuff. I want my child to be free and kind and to see and respect everyone as they are. And not to hurt herself or anyone. I want her to always laugh, to be happy, to value herself and not let anybody, even me, choose her future. And so much more …" Narin laughed.

"My sweet sister, if you teach her all that you have just said and raise her well, then this would be the most beautiful religion that she could have." Agrin smiled and added, "You will be a fantastic mum."

Narin looked back at the lake with a beautiful smile on her face. "God, here is so peaceful."

There were some fast footsteps behind their bench. It was Mevan coming towards them. He called out, "It's getting dark, Agrin. I told you not to be late."

"Sorry, we were so busy talking that we forgot about the time," Agrin said.

Mevan said, "That's okay, but let's go home. Mother is worried about you."

Narin and Agrin went with Mevan and he drove them home.

22

The next afternoon, Mevan, Agrin, Ronak and Galavij arrived home after work. Marjan welcomed them all, then pulled out a seat at the table for Mevan. "Welcome back, son," Marjan said, "come and have a seat. I'll get you some tea while the girls put the food on the table. Come on, girls, hurry now, my son is hungry."

"Thank you, mother," Mevan said.

As Narin was putting food on the table, she said, "Mother, you love Mevan so much, just like our own mother – she adored him."

Marjan nodded. "I have to, my daughter. If it wasn't for Mevan, I couldn't have survived for so long without hearing from my son and his father. Whenever Mevan calls me mother, I hear my son's voice, and now I see Mevan as my son. And I love all of you as my children."

"Yes, that is true," Ronak said, smiling. "But, when it comes to our brother Mevan, your attention is all on him."

"Now, now, girls ..." Marjan said, "don't get jealous of the way I treat him. He is the man of our house, the head of the family. My daughters, we should all take care of him." Marjan kissed Mevan on his head.

Mevan smiled and kissed her hand with respect.

When they were all sitting around the table, Kany said, "Uncle, there is going to be a big party held for the Kurdish community very soon, and everybody will come. My teacher told us at school."

"Yes, I heard that, too," Agrin said. "My friend said that it's planned for us."

"Can we go, please, Uncle Mevan?" Kany asked.

"Which day is it?" Mevan asked.

"It's in two days," Kany replied.

"Two days! Let me look into it, then I will let you know," Mevan said.

"Can we go, please, uncle? I do want to go," Nalan said.

"Oh, look everyone, my beautiful daughter Nalan wants to go to the party!" Mevan said. "Okay, okay, I'll ask you some questions and if you answer them right, we'll go. What do you say, Baba?"

Nalan smiled. "Okay."

"Are you going to wear one of your beautiful dresses?"

"Yes, the white one."

"Very good — right answer."

"Are you going to dance?"

Nalan laughed. "Yes."

"Well, in that case," Mevan said, "we have no choice — we all have to go to see my daughter dance."

Nalan jumped in his arms and kissed him. "Thank you, uncle!"

A day before the celebration, Agrin, with a big bag in her hand, knocked on the door of Mevan's room. "Mevan, it's me — Agrin. Can I come in?"

"Yes," Mevan said, and opened the door.

Agrin sat on the side of his bed.

"Welcome, sweetheart," Mevan said, "and thank you for cleaning my room and for these beautiful flowers." He pointed to a pot of flowers on his bedside table.

"Narin told me those are your favourite flowers, and you love their smell," Agrin said, touching the flowers. "So, I planted some in this pot, and that way you can have them in your room all the time. They look nice next to your bed."

"Yes, I do love these flowers," Mevan said, smelling them, then looking back at Agrin. "So did you want to tell me something?" Mevan sat next to her.

"Yes," Agrin said. "You always buy us everything we need, but, so far, you haven't bought anything for yourself."

"Don't worry about me. I'm fine."

"We are all so grateful for you, Mevan."

"And I am so grateful for all of you. I can't be thankful enough to have a nice, big family like you around me. And I'm so grateful for you, Agrin – to have you in my life, my beautiful love." Mevan stopped for a few seconds, looking at Agrin. "Now finish your words," he said.

"You don't have any clothes for tomorrow's party, so I got you some clothes." She reached for the bag that she brought with her and took out two Kurdish outfits. "These are Delovan's clothes. My parents gave him this brown one for our wedding. This dark blue one was a gift from his father and mother when our daughter was born, and he became a father. Your height and size is almost the same as his, but, if you try it on and it doesn't fit, then I'll fix it tonight."

"But these are so special to you," Mevan said.

"Yes, that's why I want you to have them."

"Thank you, Agrin, that means a lot to me."

"Also, here are two shirts that Ronak bought you. I also have a pair of shoes that Mother Marjan and Galavij asked me to give you." Agrin took a pair of shoes from the bag and put them on the bed. "First, try the brown suit with the black shirt. I'll stay outside. Call me when you're done."

Mevan put on the clothes and called Agrin.

Agrin came back into his room. When she saw Mevan in Delovan's clothes, she remembered her husband and her eyes filled with tears. She adjusted parts of his clothes and said, "They fit you perfectly, Mevan."

"Thank you, Agrin, it's a very meaningful gift, and I appreciate it."

"You are welcome."

Mevan held her hands and looked in her eyes. "Agrin, is it okay for me to hug you?"

Agrin nodded. "Yes."

Mevan smiled and hugged her. He gently touched Agrin's hair and put a wisp behind her ear. "If only I could find a way to show you how much I love you …" he whispered into her ear, then kissed her on the cheeks.

Agrin raised her head, putting her hand on Mevan's heart and said, "I already know. I can feel it every time I look into your eyes. I am a fortunate woman to have you …" She put her head back on his chest, and took a long, calming breath that brought a beautiful, peaceful smile to her face.

Mevan hugged her back again. "I love you," he said.

Agrin raised her head and smiled. "I better go now because last night Narin told Mother Marjan about your favourite bread, and so she is planning to bake it and she needs my help." Agrin gently eased herself out of Mevan's arms.

"Okay, my love." Mevan kissed her again and let her go.

The next day, Mevan and Mother Marjan were waiting in the front yard to leave for the party. Agrin led the girls out the front door to join them.

Marjan turned to them and said, "You are all looking so beautiful."

When Mevan saw Agrin coming towards him in her stunning green dress, with a beautiful smile on her face and sparkling black eyes full of hope, he couldn't hide the happiness he felt. But he soon came to his senses when he realised the others were watching him. Quickly, he said, "Okay, let's go. Some of you can come in my car and some can go in my friend's car, which is waiting for us on the street."

At the community hall, they mingled with the many families who had come to celebrate the Kurdish community. After chatting with familiar and new faces, they all sat down at tables that had been laid out across the floor in front of the stage. Several officials welcomed the families as they took their seats. Soon, one of the officials went up on the stage, switched on the microphone, then greeted them in a few words of Kurdish that he had learned.

The official began his speech in English, but he paused regularly so a translator could convey his words in Kurdish. "The Kurdish people, indeed the world, have suffered a great calamity. ISIS tried to steal the soul of the Kurds by spilling the blood of their innocents. Thousands were murdered in the name of ISIS's religion. Many houses and prosperous lives were destroyed. Many people were displaced and made homeless. Many were enslaved and trafficked in unthinkable ways. This tragedy will forever remain in our memories and in the history of the world. We know the Yazidi people have suffered the most casualties. Many of you have told me what you witnessed during the horrific massacres that aimed to wipe out the Yazidi people. In this country, we stand with you, we want to help you come to terms with the suffering you have endured, we want to help you start new lives and build hope for a bright future, and we want to help you celebrate your beautiful and valuable ceremonies and rituals that can be traced back across thousands of years of history. I ask you to open a fresh page in your history, by making a happy and prosperous life together in Australia."

At this point, the families at their tables could hold back no longer and burst into applause.

When the clapping subsided, the official continued, "Tonight we look forward to experiencing your rich culture with you. We understand traditional Kurdish dancing is symbolic of the beauty, unity and hope with which to restart and reconnect with life again. In the words of a new friend who wrote down these words about what to expect tonight: 'We hold each other's hands and tap on Mother Earth's chest, so that she knows her children will rise again and make their lives more prosperous than before.'"

Another round of applause erupted. The official nodded appreciatively and smiled. "Thank you. To finish, I would just like to remind you that you are not alone. We, all the people of the world, are with you and by your side. We are all in this together and will strive to make sure such a tragedy never happens again."

The room burst into applause again, then the official thanked everyone for coming and sat down.

The curtains on the stage opened as a Kurdish band began to play a happy traditional song. Out strode a famous Kurdish singer who took up her position at a microphone in front of the band, then launched into a beautiful melody.

Around the tables, people were looking at each other, wondering who would be the first to stand up and dance. No one wanted to start.

So, several people, who were employees, despite not knowing the traditional dances, went onto the dance floor in front of the stage, and began dancing to encourage others to join in.

Mevan looked around at his people and felt heartbroken to witness them like this. In times past, they would have all joined in the dancing without hesitation. However, the trauma they had all suffered had restrained them from expressing their culture. Mevan took a deep breath and walked to the dance floor and started a traditional dance.

After he began, a few of his friends joined in. Then Ronak, Galavij and Kany. The band launched into another song and gradually people started to hold hands. Mevan caught Narin's eye. She was standing next to Marjan and looking back at him. Mevan went over to Narin, then led her back to the dance floor.

Marjan turned to Agrin, who was still in her seat. "Agrin, my daughter, you go, too."

Agrin looked at everyone dancing, at their feet tapping on the ground. She looked at their hands that were now tied together. She looked at their faces that were drowning in memories – some staring at the floor, perhaps thinking of early, happy days dancing with loved ones who would never return. She looked at their eyes, some dripping tears, perhaps in disbelief that they could still enjoy dancing again. She looked at how thankful they appeared to be once again, together and holding hands. She looked at Mevan, who was inviting her to join in the dancing.

Agrin walked towards the circle on the dance floor. She took off her scarf on her way to Mevan, and she held it in her hand. Her long hair fell about her shoulders.

Mevan caught sight of Agrin coming towards him and saw his necklace on her neck. He smiled, then went forward to greet her.

Agrin held his hand and led the dance, waving her scarf in the air, tears in her eyes, a smile on her face.

People danced in a big circle of happiness. Around them were their children. They were holding hands and learning the traditional dances from their parents with a mixture of excitement, sweet laughter and occasional shyness.

Beauty appeared on that part of the earth on that night, as colourful souls of Mother Earth started to raise their heads once again with hope.

www.ingramcontent.com/pod-product-compliance
Lightning Source LLC
Chambersburg PA
CBHW031117020426
42333CB00012B/112